Financial Management in the Voluntary Sector

The accounting and financial management of voluntary organizations poses as many difficulties and challenges as that of major profit-seeking organizations, if not more so given the absence of the profit motive upon which much traditional accounting and financial practice and theory has been developed.

This book explores the unique environmental, managerial and philosophical aspects of voluntary organizations as well as the technical specialist characteristics of financial accounting, auditing and taxation that make their roles so different.

Financial Management in the Voluntary Sector introduces and describes the main applications of accounting and finance as they apply to the role of a financial manager. Using real life case studies and examining the debates presented by other writers in the field, this book helps the reader to make critical judgements and contributes to an understanding of the distinctiveness of voluntary sector accounting and financial management.

Paul Palmer has published widely on, and worked extensively in, the field of charity finance. He is currently Head of the Centre for Charity and Trust Research at South Bank University, where he is also Charity Courses Director.

Adrian Randall is an independent charities management consultant, and a nationally recognized expert on charity financial management. At present, he is also Visiting Professor at South Bank University. He has gained broad experience of the sector through a variety of roles, and is currently a member of several groups and committees in the charity field.

Routledge Studies in the Management of Voluntary
and Non-Profit Organizations
Edited by Stephen P. Osborne
Aston Business School, UK

The Management of Non-Governmental Development Organizations
An introduction
David Lewis

Financial Management in the Voluntary Sector
New challenges
Paul Palmer and Adrian Randall

Strategic Management for Nonprofit Organizations
Roger Courtney

Also available in the Management of Voluntary and Non-Profit Organizations series from Routledge Research:

Financial Management in the Voluntary Sector

New challenges

Paul Palmer and Adrian Randall

London and New York

First published 2002 by Routledge
11 New Fetter Lane, London EC4P 4EE

Simultaneously published in the USA and Canada
by Routledge
29 West 35th Street, New York, NY 10001

Routledge is an imprint of the Taylor & Francis Group

© 2002 Paul Palmer and Adrian Randall

Typeset in Garamond by Wearset, Boldon, Tyne and Wear
Printed and bound in Great Britain by Biddles Ltd, Guildford and King's
Lynn

British Library Cataloguing in Publication Data
A catalogue record for this book is available from the British Library

Library of Congress Cataloging in Publication Data
Palmer, Paul, 1955–
    Financial management in the voluntary sector : new challenges / Paul
Palmer and Adrian Randall.
        p. cm.
    Includes bibliographical references.
    1. Nonprofit organizations–Accounting. 2. Nonprofit organizations–
Finance. 3. Nonprofit organizations–Accounting–Case studies.
    4. Nonprofit organizations–Finance–Case studies. I. Randall, Adrian,
1944– II. Title.

    HF5686.N56 P355 2001
    658.15–dc21   2001034792

ISBN 0-415-22159-5 (hbk)
ISBN 0-415-22160-9 (pbk)

To James – the red engine – and Christopher – who has yet to discover the pleasures of steam

Contents

The authors

Paul Palmer BA Hons PhD FCIS FIIA
Paul Palmer is Professor of Charity Finance at South Bank University, London. He is Head of the Charities Research Centre and Director of Charity Courses. Prior to joining the University in 1989, he worked in the charity sector for ten years in finance and administration. He is a trustee of the Royal Society of Health and of the Friends of Southwark Cathedral and a member of the Finance Committee of Sargeant Cancer Care for Children. He also serves as the independent member on the Institute of Charity Fundraising Managers Accreditation panel.

An author of numerous articles on aspects of charity finance and management, he co-edited *Voluntary Matters* and jointly authored *Rethinking Charity Trusteeship*.

Adrian J. L. Randall FCA BSc(Econ)
Adrian Randall, now an independent Charities Management Consultant, was until February 2000 a partner in BDO Stoy Hayward which merged with Moores Rowland in 1999. He joined Moores Rowland as Director of the Charities Group in 1994 from the Cancer Research Campaign, where he had been Director of Finance and Administration from 1987. Adrian is Visiting Professor in Charity Finance at South Bank University.

He is a member of the Charity Commission Charity Accounting Review Committee that produced the Revised Charities SORP in 2000 and Chairman of the Institute of Chartered Accountants in England and Wales Charity Accounts Working Party, Deputy Chairman of SOS Children's Villages UK, a trustee of the Child Accident Prevention Trust, of the Dancers' Career Development and Training For Life, and a member of the Audit Committee of SCOPE.

Adrian was co-founder and the first Chairman of the Charity Finance Directors' Group, Chairman of the Charities Tax Reform Group and first Chairman of the European Charities Committee on VAT.

He is co-author of *Charity Taxation: A Definitive Guide* and *Preparing Charity Accounts*, and author of *The ICSA Guide to Charity Accounting*.

Preface

This book has three aims:

- to advance the understanding of financial management in not-for-profit organizations;
- to contribute to the wider debate of what is different about non-profit organizations;
- to facilitate discussion countering the view that charity accounting is simple and that financially managing a charity is not of the same complexity as found in commercial organizations.

The need for such a book grew out of the dissatisfaction we have with the current literature on non-profit accounting. While there are many good accounting texts written for practitioners working in the charity sector, most are purely descriptive in that they are 'technical literature' texts. While useful, they do not place financial activity and the role of the finance manager within the wider external environment in which voluntary organizations have to operate.

This book provides technical instruction with illustrative examples and exercises but it is also analytical, critical and thematic. Voluntary sector accounting and finance is examined within a perspective that goes beyond description. For example, our discussion on reserves goes beyond calculation and financial prudence to consider the issue within the context of the organization, and accountability. This book is written for finance directors, general managers and students who will already be conversant with a general understanding of accounting and finance as taught on most Business School courses and in professional accounting examinations. While the book will introduce and provide a description of the main applications of accounting and finance applicable to the role of financial manager, it will quickly move into application and understanding, using examples from our own work in this field. However, we will also draw upon and lead the reader to follow debates from other writers. It is our intention that such an approach will both inform the reader in making their own critical judgements and contribute to the understanding of the distinctiveness of voluntary sector accounting and financial management.

It has been our intention in writing this book to provide a foundation for charity accounting and financial management; to progress from these being seen as a relatively unsophisticated backwater. It is also to recognize that the accounting and finance of voluntary organizations pose as many difficulties and challenges as those for major for-profit corporations. Indeed, we would make a bold statement to the effect that the financial management of voluntary organizations is in fact more complex, given the absence of the profit motive upon which much traditional accounting, finance practice and theory has been developed. In addition, the role of the charity finance director contains components that make the job more complex than their private sector counterpart. We would suggest that much of this complexity does not exist within the finance function internally but in the external environment within which charities operate. The finance director who believes that their job begins and ends with the accounts is rapidly becoming a figure of the past. Voluntary organizations in the next century face both opportunities and considerable threats. As the private sector retailer Marks & Spencer found in the late 1990s, being a venerable retailer with a glorious past of quality service provides no guarantee of continuing success. Large charitable institutions of a century or even a half-century in existence (for example the RNIB; Bruce 1994) will have to continually update and reinvent themselves if they are to survive. The finance director in such organizations will need to be a proactive person who understands the external environment in which the organization operates, while internally addressing the needs of the myriad of stakeholders within the charity. As we argue in this book, the lack of equity shareholders – the final and ultimate decision maker in a commercial organization – makes the task harder rather than easier. Charities have 'external customers', some of whom may not have economic power as commercially defined customers, which have been traditionally and historically defined by charities as beneficiaries. However, charities also have customers who do have resource power, and who are increasingly becoming more demanding. Government, government agencies and organizations, such as the Community Fund, are setting down as a condition of their funding, issues of accountability and governance. As recent and authoritative statistics on the funding of the sector confirm (NCVO 2000), traditional charity income as defined by donations has been stagnating in the 1990s. Selling Goods and Services defined by the Office for National Statistics as

> Sales means income from the provision of specific goods or services provided to the customer under contract, or through direct payment by the client or beneficiary. Usually there is an identifiable price per item of goods or unit of work done applicable to all customers (subject to discounts). The nature of such sales will depend upon the sort of work which your organisation is doing, for example, patient care or residence fees, sales of goods made in sheltered workshops and hire of rooms for meetings.
>
> (Palmer *et al.* 1999, p. 122)

now accounts for a third of the sector's income (NCVO 2000).

The modern charity finance director needs to be both a commercial and a financial director. They could be accounting for a shop chain of some 850 outlets with an income of £57 million (Phelan 2000), but in addition to their accounting skills they also require other skills that their accountancy training would not have prepared them for. The finance director who also operates in a non-profit environment does so without the certainty of taxation revenues, which their public sector counterpart enjoys. The charity finance director has no shareholders, with no normal commercial accounting ratios to benchmark performance, for example return on capital employed, and reports to a 'Board of Directors' who are known as trustees. They have 'Bosses' who are not allowed to be paid for their time, appointed for a variety of reasons, of which commercial knowledge and the understanding of accounting and finance are not the primary reason for appointment or indeed their motivation for doing the 'job' (Harrow and Palmer 1998).

It is these unique environmental, managerial and philosophical aspects of voluntary organizations, as well as the technical specialist characteristics of financial accounting, auditing and taxation, that make the role different. In this book we explore them in detail and illustrate them in the real environment.

A final word on the text. Within the book there are illustrated examples, and at the end of some chapters, exercises with recommended answers. For tutors, students and practitioners seeking more exercises, we would recommend *The Good Financial Management Training Guide* written by Paul Palmer and published by NCVO. This booklet has numerous governance and computational exercises in accounting and tax.

Paul Palmer and Adrian Randall

To access web pages for this series please go to:
www.routledge.com/textbooks/fmvs

Acknowledgements

We thank Graham Smith at the Charity Commission and the Members of the Charity Accounting Review Committee (1999/2000). We also thank the Charity Commission for permission to use the SORP examples, and Fiona Young, a former student and colleague, for her assistance on the SORP exercise. We thank all our colleagues and students at South Bank, who over the past ten years have taught us more than we could ever teach them, especially Norbert Lieckfeldt, Alan Read, Glyn Farrow, Richard Roberts, Tim Clifford, Beverley Glover, Philip Mould and Martyn Craddock.

A book of this kind inevitably needs administrative support and we are very grateful to Tristan Deighton, Cristy Meadows, Rosalind Palmer and Jenny Randall for their considerable effort in helping us to produce this book.

The authors and publishers would like to thank the Controller of Her Majesty's Stationery Office for granting permission to reproduce the material appearing in Appendix 1 of this work.

Every effort has been made to contact copyright holders for their permission to reprint material in this book. The publishers would be grateful to hear from any copyright holder who is not acknowledged here and will undertake to rectify any errors or omissions in future editions of this book.

1 Voluntary sector environment – definitions, history

Introduction

The sponsored chartered accountancy publication *Financial Reporting by Charities* (Bird and Morgan-Jones 1981) can arguably be cited as the authoritative beginning of the modern era for charity accounting practices. As Professor Gambling and his colleagues state:

> [it] . . . was the first systematic study of the charitable sector by accountants, certainly in recent years.
>
> (Gambling *et al.* 1990, p. 8)

We would not disagree with this pronouncement. Prior to this first modern major research study into charity accounting there had been a number of charity accountant practitioners who had published on issues pertaining to the specialist nature of charity accounts. Most notable are Manley (1977, 1979), Fenton (1980) and Sams (1978). In the United States, thirty years before the Bird research, there was the defining work of Vatter (1947). Vatter's published doctoral thesis had laid out the principles of fund accounting upon which modern charity accounting and the SORP is now based. Bird's work, however, ranks as important for three reasons. It is the first milestone in the development of modern charity accounting in the United Kingdom as it leads directly to the first Charity Statement of Recommended Practice (SORP). Second, the work is in the finest tradition of academic research in being critical of the subject matter it looked at. Third, a follow-up study (Bird 1986) was based upon empirical research, which has enabled the study to be replicated and tested to see if the findings are still applicable (Williams and Palmer 1998). What is particularly interesting is the timing of the report. In the introduction to their 1981 discussion paper the authors state:

> the whole area of private non-profit organisations seems to have been neglected by accounting researchers by comparison with business.
>
> (Bird and Morgan-Jones 1981)

The early 1980s can be seen as one of the defining periods in the history of the charity sector. In 1978 a report by Lord Wolfenden on the future of the voluntary sector described the following historical periods for charity:

- Paternalism to 1834
- Voluntary expansionism 1834–1905
- Emergence of Statutory Services 1905–1945
- Welfare State 1945–

The Wolfenden report's mission was

> to review the role and functions of voluntary organisations in the UK over the next twenty-five years.
>
> (Wolfenden 1978, p. 9)

Wolfenden was published at the beginning of dramatic change, which was to see the end of the consensus of British political parties to the Welfare State that had been established since the end of the Second World War. The election in 1979 of a radical Conservative Government and its subsequent policies of privatization were fuelled by an economic theory that rejected State intervention and placed market forces as the determinant of survival. There was an emphasis on the individual taking responsibility for their life thereby leading to lower taxation and a limiting role for the State. The 1979 Conservative Government saw the voluntary sector as enhancing this role and therefore increased funding to the voluntary sector. At the end of the 1980s the Charities Aid Foundation (CAF) estimated that central government funding had increased in real terms by 90 per cent over the decade (CAF 1989, p. 5).

The Conservative Government of 1979–1997 also began to radically change the whole philosophical thrust of welfare delivery that had been developing since the end of the last century – giving responsibility for welfare back to the individual, for example, on State old-age pensions and compulsory social insurance which the Liberal Government had introduced at the beginning of the twentieth century. Instead, people were encouraged to 'contract out' of the State scheme and take up private personal pensions. No longer was the provision of personal welfare services to be delivered primarily by local government. Instead, the role of government both central and local was to be a resource provider in partnership with both existing voluntary organizations and the private sector. New and revised government organizations were also formed to be both resource agencies and service deliverers. For example, a revamped Housing Corporation in the early years of the government began to initially fund housing associations to provide the majority of new public homes for rent. It later encouraged associations to take up private finance to build homes. At the local level the Health Service was reorganized to allow GP fund-holding, health trusts were created and schools could 'opt out' from local government control.

The revolution of these changes has created what has been referred to as a 'mixed economy of care', in which the barriers between the providers are blurred. It has also meant that there are major issues in both social policy and micro management to be considered. As Professor Knapp and colleagues state:

> The voluntary sector sits in an increasingly complex mixed economy. The variety of producers grows, the funding sources multiply, and different regulatory styles proliferate. Although it is still possible to distinguish four basic production or supply varieties – public, voluntary (non-profit), private (for-profit) and informal – the margins between them are blurred. Some behave in a manner fully consistent with the maximisation of either profits or managers' salaries, and a growing number of public agencies are developing direct labour organisations and all the trappings – but without the benefits – of a commercial enterprise.
>
> (Knapp *et al.* 1990, p. 184)

Before discussing the current government and policy it would be useful to devote some space to what is meant by or how we define the voluntary sector and a short history of its origins and principal developments. If a charity finance director is to fully contribute to their organization they should know how their sector has developed.

The issue of definition

The definition of 'Charity', in 2000, relates to the estimated 200,000 charities registered respectively with the Charity Commission in England and Wales, the Scottish Claims Branch of the Inland Revenue and in Northern Ireland. This definition, however, fails to encompass the estimated 300,000 voluntary bodies in this country, which, while not being registered charities, are viewed as belonging to the 'Charity Family'. Moreover, these non-registered charities can equally enjoy the tax exemptions of registered charities; for example, the 10,000 Industrial and Provident Societies which are 'exempt charities' under the 1993 Charities Act. As former Deputy Charity Commissioner and Barrister Francesca Quint explains:

> The word 'charity' has a general meaning in ordinary speech and a special meaning in English law.
>
> (Quint 1994, p. 1)

In our book we are primarily interested in registered charities, in part due to the accounting regulations which prescribes statutory practices they must follow, but also because the top 10,000 charities account for approximately 90 per cent of the sector's income (NCVO 1998). However, we use this terminology as a generic interchangeable term with voluntary organization, which we will define by reviewing the definitions of the sector that have been debated. The first question to answer is: why does a definition matter?

Without a clear definition how do you attempt any form of quantitative analysis, for example, as a percentage of the economy, and thereby how important is it or how does a government determine an appropriate regulatory regime? At an organizational level without a context and statistics how can you plan? How can you evaluate the organization's performance against others?

The lack of a clear definition has engendered an active debate (Perri 6 1991) on the need for and attempts to formulate a definition to encompass activities and organizations that do not fall into the categories of profit-making or government organizations. Indeed, Salamon and Anheier (1994) have argued that the absence of a precise and conceptual definition is a principal reason for the relative deficiency of academic studies and a distinct body of literature on this sector of activity. The lack of a definition is not an exclusively UK problem. The European Commission in 1987 established a working party to attempt to provide a legal personality based on the French concept of the 'economie sociale', which refers to associations, co-operatives, mutual and other voluntary organizations. However, by 1991 the working party, recognizing the difficulties involved, instead produced three separate statutes governing respectively co-operatives, mutuals and associations. The lack of a precise definition has also applied to the United States where the economist Burton Weisbrod argues:

> The wide diversity in the non-profit sector is both what makes it difficult to formulate consistent and appropriate public policy and an effective existing public policy.
>
> (Weisbrod 1988, p. 162)

The legal definition

From the English perspective the debate in Charity Law can be said to begin in 1601 with the 'Preamble' to the Elizabethan Statute of Charitable Uses. The 1601 preamble provided a series of headings, which were classified as charitable activity. The tradition of defining charity law in this way, it has been argued by charity law academic and Charity Commissioner Jean Warburton, is due to the influence of Chancery lawyers, who belong to the 'black letter law tradition', which is

> concerned with the exposition of the law rather than detailed consideration of its effect beyond the actual imposition of duties and obligations on institutions and individuals.
>
> (Warburton 1993, p. 5)

Warburton argues that it was not until 1979, with Chesterman's *Charities, Trusts and Social Welfare*, that a lawyer effected a different approach. In his book Chesterman places the 1601 Act in a historical context reviewing the law against the political and economic crisis of the Tudor period. The absence of lawyers questioning the definition as opposed to the interpretation of charity is probably the reason why Quint can state:

> There is no exhaustive list of charitable purposes, and no strict legal definition of charity, but charitable purposes have been classified as:
>
> - the relief of poverty;
> - the advancement of education;
> - the advancement of religion; and
> - other purposes beneficial to the community.
>
> Every charitable purpose will come within one (or more) of these four categories, but not every purpose which is within these categories is necessarily charitable. Deciding whether a given purpose is charitable depends on legal precedent and analogy from legal precedent. Sometimes, a purpose, which was not regarded as charitable in the past, will be accepted as charitable as times change. An example of this is the promotion of racial harmony, which was accepted as a charitable purpose only during the 1980s. The opposite can also occur.
>
> (Quint 1994, p. 1)

The opposite occurs in the case of gun clubs, which were encouraged and founded at the time of the Boer Wars towards the end of the nineteenth century, when riflemanship was found to be lacking and the defence of the realm was considered to be at risk. Following the Gulf War, the reality of amateur riflemen still being needed to defend the national interest was questioned and gun clubs were no longer considered charitable. The tragic events at Dunblane perhaps also contributed to the decision.

The four headings quoted by Quint derive from the Pemsel case of 1891 and the judgement by Lord MacNaghten. The MacNaghten judgement in the tradition of Common Law was in turn based on an earlier judgement by the then Master of the Rolls, Sir Samuel Romilly, in 1804.

The MacNaghten judgement is still in force and represents for the Charity Commissioners the litmus test as to whether they will register a new charity. A government committee in 1952 (Nathan) and a review of charity law in 1976 chaired by Lord Goodman both wished to retain the MacNaghten judgement in a statutory definition of charity, but this recommendation was rejected. The 1992 Charities Act did not attempt a new definition as the government White Paper *Charities: A framework for the future* explained:

In considering the question of charitable status the government have taken note of the deliberations of the Nathan and Goodman Committees, both of which went into the subject in some depth. They have also taken into account the views expressed more recently at seminars, which have been held by the Home Secretary and the Charity Commission. These seminars were designed to test opinion in the legal and charitable worlds and were attended by, amongst others, Chancery judges.

The view of the legal experts and of others who were present on these occasions was not, as might be expected, unanimous on all points, but was quite clearly against any substantive change in the present law. The Government incline to agree with this view . . .

(Home Office 1988, p. 5)

Most recently, the National Council for Voluntary Organizations (NCVO) has again begun a programme of work reviewing the law on charitable status (NCVO 1998). It has set up a research programme which will examine the foundations of charity law by an examination of the intellectual case for a special status for certain types of organization or activity. In particular, the following questions were posed:

- How is charitable service distinct from public service and what role does altruism play in modern charity?
- How would we define 'genuinely charitable purposes' and how do they relate to public benefit considerations?
- Should advancement of religion continue to be a charitable purpose?
- Are politics and charity inevitably opposed?
- What is the role of the Charity Commission and does it have appropriate powers and duties?

Alternative definitions

In the absence of a statutory definition for charitable activity, alternative definitions of 'charitable activity' have arisen, which also have the advantage of encompassing the whole sphere of economic activity that is not in either the private or the public area. Academics attempting to define the sector have adopted one of three distinct approaches (Kazi *et al.* 1992):

1   The residual, or negative, approach explicitly defines the sector of terms of what it is not.
2   The categorical approach, based on particular principles, attempts to define the sector in terms of organizations that meet particular criteria, in essence a quasi-legal approach.
3   The aggregational approach enumerates the sector in terms of accepted sub-categories, using various consensual or implicit criteria.

Chronologically, in post-1945 academia, the starting point is that provided by Lord Beveridge in 1948 in his book *Voluntary Action*:

> The term 'Voluntary Action' as used here means private action, that is to say action not under the directions of any authority wielding the power of the State.
>
> (Beveridge 1948, p. 8)

The problem of the use of the word 'voluntary' is that it fails to recognize that many voluntary organizations employ paid staff. The Nathan Committee, in the introduction to their report, borrowed heavily on Beveridge's definition in describing the rationale for their appointment:

> The essence of voluntary action is that it is not directed or controlled by the State and that in the main it is financed by private, in contradistinction to public, funds. It embodies the sense of responsibility of private persons towards the welfare of their fellows; it is the meeting by private enterprise of a public need.
>
> (Nathan 1952, p. 1)

The consensus to the Beveridge term voluntary action was beginning to be challenged in the late 1950s. Madeline Rooff's definition instead using the term 'voluntary organizations' (Rooff 1957, p. xiii). Perri 6 (1991) suggests that the change was in part due to the shift in the nature of government relations to voluntary organizations with an increase in grant aid.

The term 'non-profit' has also acquired a degree of currency in attempts to define voluntary organizations. This has primarily derived from American economists (Hansmann 1980; Weisbrod 1988; Steinberg and Gray 1993) and has become the wholesale definition in the United States. Weisbrod defines the term non-profit as

> restrictions on what an organisation may do with any surplus (profit) it generates.
>
> (Weisbrod 1988, p. 1)

This concept of 'non-distribution constraint', that is that any surplus or profit generated cannot be distributed to those in control of the organization leading to the adoption of the term 'non-profit', has not, however, become widespread in the United Kingdom. In part this may be because of the different national traditions that have conceptualized the respective UK and US voluntary sectors, the most obvious difference being the creation of a Welfare State in the UK after the Second World War, which determined relations with the voluntary sector. Recognizing these cultural differences, not just in the UK but throughout the world, there has been a concerted attempt in the United States to widen out the definition by adding additional characteristics, notably by Salamon and Anheier for the John Hopkins Comparative Non-profit Sector International Study. The definition for this study of the voluntary sector in twenty-six countries around the world encompasses not only non-profit distributing but also concepts of independence and voluntarism.

Termed the Structural/Operational Definition, it comprises five key features:

1 Formal – institutionalized to some extent, for example legal incorporation, or if not, having regular meetings or rules of procedure.
2 Private – institutionally separate from government, fundamentally private institutions in basic structure.
3 Non-profit distributing – not returning profits generated to their owners or directors, whereby the profits are ploughed back into the organization.
4 Self-governing – equipped to control their own activities.
5 Voluntary – involving some degree of meaningful voluntary participation. The presence of some voluntary input, even if only a voluntary board of directors, suffices to qualify an organization as in some sense 'voluntary'.

As Salamon and Anheier clarify:

> Needless to say, the five conditions identified in this structure/ operational definition will vary in degrees, and some organisations may qualify more easily on one criterion than another. To be considered part of the non-profit sector under this definition, however, an organisation must make a reasonable showing on all five of these criteria.
>
> (Salamon and Anheier 1993, p. 184)

Different cultural traditions can perhaps also explain the usage of the term 'non-statutory' that has also been suggested in the United Kingdom. The usage of 'non-statutory' as a definition can probably be attributed to the post-1945 development of the Welfare State, supported by a political philosophy developed in the late nineteenth century and dominant by the 1970s that welfare services should ideally be provided by statutory authorities (Webb and Wistow 1987). In this philosophy, the role of the voluntary sector is to pioneer developments until, as a 'natural process', the State takes over. The 1960 Charity Commissioners Report illustrated this view:

> After the post-war social legislation the traditional objects of charity were largely overtaken by the statutory services, new and old, which now provides for the welfare of the individual from the cradle to the grave; and the basic question confronting the committee was what remained for charities to do. The answer, in broad terms, was that while

charity should not withdraw from a field where it is performing a useful service, its peculiar function is to pioneer . . .

(Charity Commission 1960, p. 5)

Thirty years later, after the market reforms of the Thatcher government, the Charity Commission was describing a somewhat different role:

As a major part of the voluntary sector. Charities are now recognised as essential contributors to the well-being of our society, meeting needs which neither the State nor the commercial sector can fully address.

(Charity Commission 1991, p. 1)

The Wolfenden Committee was critical of the term non-statutory as it was a negative definition, which attempted to describe the relationship between statutory and voluntary agencies in a rigid manner (Wolfenden 1978, p. 11). It also failed to recognize that the boundaries of that relationship are continually moving.

The term 'third sector' has been adopted in recent years and promoted by economists, who have rejected the view that economies have only two sectors. The origin of the term has been chronicled:

The term 'third sector' was first used by several US scholars (Etzioni 1973; Levitt 1973; Nielsen 1979) and the influential Filer Commission (1975) and is now increasingly applied by European Researchers (Douglas 1983; Reese 1987; Reese et al. 1989; Reichard 1988; Ronge 1988). The term has both normative and strategic roots. For Etzioni (1973) the term 'third sector' suggested elements of the then widely discussed convergence thesis. 'Third Sector' was intended to express an alternative to the disadvantages associated with both profit maximisation and bureaucracy by combining the flexibility and efficiency of markets with the equity and predictability of public bureaucracy.

(Anheier and Seibel 1990)

A criticism of the use of the term 'third sector' derives from the conceptual assumption that there are distinctive divisions in the economy and thereby in the characteristics of organizations between the sectors. Vinten (1993) suggests that distinctive sectors emerged with the evolution of industrial society. The public sector provided an infrastructure of utilities and services for the benefit of industry and commerce, which paid taxes, the voluntary sector filling the gaps between the two. Each sector, having very different roles, developed independently of each separate characteristic and practice. Notably in the public versus private sector, the emphasis is on the role of the 'professional' over organizational and managerial authority (Flynn 1993).

Are there distinct sectors?

The antithesis to the view of different sectors is that the public, private and voluntary sectors are now conceptually indistinct and have become blurred. As Leat comments:

> there is an increasing convergence of non-profit and for-profit organisations. The reasons for this apparent convergence are complex. On the non-profit side, convergence is related to the growth of contracting, to new resource dependencies and to institutional isomorphism. On the for-profit side, convergence may stem from growing disenchantment with existing management practices and a new emphasis on quality and other less tangible values both inside and 'outside' the organization.
>
> (Leat 1993, pp. 49–50)

Leat still believes that despite these convergence arguments there remain differences between the sectors. She suggests that the key differences in the visibility of for-profit and non-profit organizations may lie at the level of theory rather than practice, and that what is needed is a radically different approach focusing on similarities and differences between organizations within and between sectors. For example, within the non-profit sector the constituent subcategories function with little or no commonality. Leat asks what the following have in common:

- statutory bodies and quangos
- foundations and grant-making trusts
- service-providing non-profits
- fund-raising non-profits
- trade associations and societies
- sports, social, community associations and clubs.

Instead Leat suggests:

> it might be more fruitful to compare management needs and tasks in for-profit and non-profit organizations with intangible goals and/or a preponderance of professionals/knowledge workers requiring high degrees of autonomy; or the problems of managing non-profit and for-profit organisations with strong traditions of egalitarianism might be considered.
>
> (Leat 1993, p. 50)

Billis (1993) has developed a series of arguments from a British perspective against convergence. He first argues that the British voluntary sector was not invented, a feature of the US convergence thesis. The 'deep roots' of the British voluntary sector can draw on a 'variety of organizational forms stretching back to medieval times' (p. 245). While government has encouraged the growth of intermediate organizations, so the sector has itself developed such organizations. Billis claims that there is an illusion of a unified sector with common views; the reality, however, 'is substantially different'. The problem, he claims, is using the word 'sector' to describe a homogeneous group of organizations. Clearly, the voluntary sector is not homogeneous, but the same can be applied to the respective private and public sectors, which have diversity and competition in them. Billis, however, rejects abandoning the notion of sectors as concepts, believing the metaphor still has utility.

Billis poses and answers three questions for the concept of a sector.

1　What does the voluntary sector do? Traditionally this has focused on its unique role of identifying and pioneering new responses to need. Others have focused on the process of democracy and sensitivity to need, while economic arguments have focused on cost effectiveness and, more recently, as part of the government initiative to bring competition to welfare services.
2　Why does the sector exist? Negative theories, primarily from US economists, have tried to explain the sector. Billis in turn questions that the failure has been in economic theory itself. For the UK, he argues, the terminology does not apply as such negative definitions have never been used.
3　What is the fundamental nature – the essence – of the social phenomenon under consideration? While legal definitions have been used, Billis prefers to cite the substantial literature that describes its distinctive features and attributes; for example, the absence of precise market value, voluntarism, distinct resources and service systems, special constituency, legal status and distinctive social character.

Billis believes the phenomena of sector blurring can be explained as the size of different sectors can vary in size and significance in different countries and at different times as a result of political, economic, cultural and societal forces. In addition, there may well be crowded zones according to such conditions, as the following diagram demonstrates:

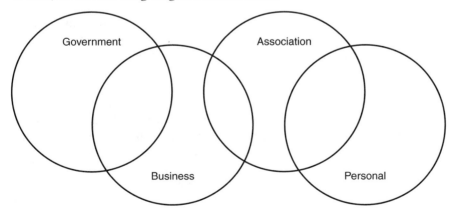

The future avenue for research, Billis suggests, is to define for the core of each sector its membership and parentage. In addition, this should lead on to questions of who can ultimately close the organization down or sell it off.

The term 'social economy' has been developed to define economic activity that encompasses not only 'social service' but also not-for-profit organizations like co-operatives, trade unions and associations. The term originates from the French 'economie sociale'. This expression provides a conceptual definition of what should be in the third sector and also has the merit of not incorporating 'voluntary'. It is meritorious equally, because it does not define, as Professor Charles Handy has described:

> There is in fact a sense in which the voluntary sector is defined negatively – by what it is not, rather than by what it is. It is not profit seeking, it is not government run, it is not owned by anyone.
>
> (Handy 1988, p. 10)

Paton (1993) describes the 'social economy' in a six-sector model based upon the provision of goods and services they offer to society:

The corporate sector	*The public sector*
Large mutual societies[a]	Large non-statutory agencies. Small State care units[b]
SMALL- AND MEDIUM-SIZED ENTERPRISES	THE SOCIAL ECONOMY (value-based organizations)
Independent schools and care providers[c]	Informal mutual aid networks[d]
THE SUBMERGED ECONOMY	THE NATURAL ECONOMY

Notes
a For example, building societies, retail co-ops, the Automobile Association.
b For example, large housing associations, Barnardos, local authority family centres, a cottage hospital.
c For example, charitable public schools, nursing homes (private but professionally run).
d For example, baby-sitting circles, mothers and toddlers clubs.

One approach to definition not attempted to date would be one embracing a critical theory perspective based on 'dialectic method'. American accounting academic Cheryl Lehman on the nature of accounting and the accounting profession has described critical theory as follows:

> By theorising about accounting practice in a social and political vacuum, controversies involving stakeholders, managers, pension holders, employers, consumers, the State and others have been misapprehended, silenced, or given anomalous meaning. To balance the debate and to devise policies that are worthy of the profession's public mandate, we must move beyond posturing about 'objectivity' and 'efficiency' and examine the social genesis of accounting ... our claim is a

more dynamic, interactive, socially constructed view of the subject, one that we call dialectic.

(Lehman 1992, pp. 1, 3)

One aspect a critical theoretical perspective would adopt would be an analysis of power and independence of voluntary sector agencies to State policy. We believe such an appraisal would be beneficial for the charity finance director in practice. As a starting point a charity would appraise their portfolio of income sources in terms of the independence of the funding stream. For example, charitable donations from the public would imply a degree of independence from government. But are donations also subject to the perception of the charity by the public? Oxfam, for example, was 'attacked' by the *Sun* newspaper in the early 1990s over its political activity. What effect did such an attack have on its public donations or shops' income? Are all charities so affected? Certainly bad publicity can lead to major problems for commercial organizations, as Gerald Ratner found after his infamous 'prawn sandwich' speech. Following the publicity of fraud on the Salvation Army, however, this charitable organization found that donations during Salvation Army week actually increased as many 'gave more, to help make up your loss' – a loss that became non-existent following successful pursuit of the fraudsters. Perhaps the most interesting example, and one that defies the application of commercial financial logic, was the case in the early 1990s of the overseas aid charity War on Want. War on Want had been subject to a critical Charity Commission enquiry, which was widely publicized. Instead of this meaning the end for War on Want the exact opposite happened. New volunteers came forward to energize the organization and it received compensation from its former auditors (Jack 1993). We cannot imagine a similar situation for a commercial organization.

To conclude our discussion on the definition debate, it is our contention that there will never be a definitive end. We believe the voluntary sector role has been and is determined by its relationship with the State. The voluntary sector does not exist in a vacuum, but neither does it have to be a passive player in determining what that relationship has to be. Within this context it is perhaps appropriate to return to the 1940s when the modern debate began and record the observation by one of Beveridge's colleagues who wrote on the definition of charity:

Definition is a perpetual state of growth.

(Bourdillon 1945, p. 8)

It also means that a historical analysis of the voluntary sector and its relationship with the State needs to be undertaken if we are to understand the current role of the voluntary sector.

Religious influences

One contribution to defining the sector we have not discussed has been that
provided by religion. This is not to deny the importance of religion in
today's charity sector both numerically and financially. Its importance was
recognized by government who singled out religion for discussion in the
1989 White Paper on Charities (Home Office 1989). Religion also features
in the NCVO review of charity law as a distinct question. Nor are reli-
giously motivated definitions all historic, as former Jesuit, now fund-raiser,
Redmond Mullin proves with his definition:

> an agency, which exists solely to make an adequate and relevant
> response to need within the community.
>
> (Mullin 1995, p. 18)

The contribution from religious scholars, however, perhaps reflecting the
more secular nature of our society, is relatively minor today and religion's
real importance is historic as recognized by the government White Paper:

> the very concept of charity is essentially religious in origin.
>
> (Home Office 1989)

The charity law debate in the House of Commons in 1960, opened by the
then Home Secretary R. A. Butler, gives a very clear picture of the decline of
the Church:

> In the Middle Ages the Church laid stress on giving by the rich for the
> benefit of the poor as a Christian duty and means of salvation. Indeed
> the Church undertook to distribute benefits on behalf of those who
> could not do so in person because they had left this world for
> another. . . . In Tudor times the State took over from the Church the
> enforcement of the founder's intentions.
>
> (Butler 1960, pp. 409, 410)

A more forthright announcement was made in the 1992 Charity Act debate
by Lord Houghton describing the origin of what he termed the 'Charity
Industry':

> It began with Henry VIII when he dissolved the monasteries . . . the
> relief of the poor moved from churches to the charities and that is the
> origin of our charitable movement.
>
> (Houghton 1992, p. 371)

Tigar (1977) describes the seizure of the monasteries by the Tudor mon-
archy as being a response to the serious financial problem in the kingdom

following the collapse of the wool trade. A commission had been established which had estimated the value of Church property to be a third of the total wealth of the kingdom. The commission also listed scandals and maladministration, which provided a context that the Church was failing to meet the needs of the poor and led to the call for the seizure of such property. The assumption was made that schools, hospitals and other charitable institutions would continue under royal auspices, while land would be let at reasonable rents. Some voices, notably Thomas Moore, were sceptical of what would happen but were brushed aside. Their fears, as Tigar (1977, p. 208) records, were, however, realized as the property was disposed of to the King's supporters, which accelerated the breaking up of the old feudal system:

> The breaking up of the medieval village commune emancipated the serf, but it also destroyed the very basis of his security: in freeing him from his attachment to the soil it created the conditions under which he could be driven off the soil altogether. The creation of a free peasantry implies the development of an economy based on simple commodity production, and this in turn implies the creation of a new kind of landowner, whose power was not based on the multitude of his dependants but on the amount of cash profit he could extract from his estates.
>
> (Morton 1969, p. 47)

The dissolution of the monasteries left a vacuum in the provision of relief to the poor. A problem, which a Protestant monarch still unsure of the security of her position had to answer in a secular way. The respective passing of the Poor Law and the definition of charity by the State were the answer: the point at which Ware (1989) argues charity effectively became an agent of the State and Lord Houghton's 'industry' begins.

As Benedict Nightingale forthrightly asserts:

> The Tudor monarchs well aware that poverty and vagabondage could create civil disorder encouraged charity in order to buy off trouble. The merchants and gentry were made to understand what was expected of them, in church as well as outside. From about 1540 there was a 'drum-fire of exhortation' in contemporary sermons: formal reminder became fierce injunction, social irresponsibility was denounced, and men were urged to shame Rome by showing how generous a reformed Church could be. The good opinion of his peers, enduring good works and (of course) treasure in heaven was promised to the rich merchants who gave well.
>
> (Nightingale 1973, p. 107)

The State and charity

The establishment of 'modern charity' was primarily due to the positive action by the State (Jordan 1958, pp. 98–108). In the absence of any conceivable alternative, after the dissolution of the Catholic Church, the State encouraged charity to meet a crisis which had arisen, a crisis precipitated by the change from a feudal economic system to an emerging capitalist State. However, the Tudors had not left it entirely to charity. As Beveridge (1948) noted, the 1601 Statutes of Elizabeth were co-ordinated with the Poor Law, specific relief for soldiers and mariners and the statute of charity uses, all being part of the same programme. Statutory assistance was afforded to the destitute by the State with charity having to meet a greater variety of purposes and needs through voluntary funds. A binary system for social welfare was developed, partly as insurance against social unrest but also because charity was seen as a vehicle for opportunity. For example, promoting education through charitable schools, Eton School was founded for bright 'poor' scholars. The respective relationship between State and charity from the onset was established as the State providing the absolute minimum, with charity intended as the principal agent of delivery. This was to be the pattern of delivery until the advent of the twentieth century.

The role of the respective relationship of State to charity is of course part of a much wider philosophical debate of the role of the State to the individual. A debate that is not unique to Britain, as Young articulates:

> Since de Tocqueville's time, the vitality of the American democracy and economy has been seen to lie in the diversity of its economic and political system, owing in part to the ability of citizens to organize themselves on a private, voluntary basis.
>
> (Young 1983, p. 14)

The very nature of the charitable sector is therefore inextricably linked to how much of a role should the State play. As Rooff (1957) articulates for voluntary organizations in the nineteenth century they were faced with two conflicting forces. The then dominant political theory of 'laissez-faire' which supported the 'natural inclination' to let people get on with their own affairs and the 'stress of circumstance' which called for spontaneous activity on those in need.

A minimalist role for the State with an emphasis of charity action was articulated by Thomas Malthus (Owen 1965) who argued that poverty would only be abolished if the State used its power as a last resort and a disciplinary measure. The hatred of many socialists for charity, particularly in the twentieth century – for example Aneurin Bevan, the first minister of the National Health Service (Foot 1972) – was moulded by these debates and their consequences:

The working class movement has ... in particular painful memories of the abuse of the spirit of charity.

(Cole 1945, p. 131)

The debate, beginning with 'laissez-faire' minimalists against Liberals and ending with the emergence of a socialist philosophy, committed to State intervention and universal services. Nor are these debates historic. In the mid-1970s it was raised again by 'right reformists' led politically by Margaret Thatcher and 'left reformists' led politically by Tony Benn and it continues with the 'Third Way' agenda and the proposals by the Chancellor of the Exchequer Gordon Brown on the role of volunteering (Brown 2001). The late-nineteenth century combatants were the 'Fabian' socialists led by Sidney and Beatrice Webb against the Charity Organization Society (COS). The COS represented the minimalist role of the State but promoted an efficient network of services to be provided by charities. The Webbs, on the other side, proposed a universal welfare of services funded and provided by the State, with a supportive role for the charity sector.

The Nathan Committee (1952) observed that the nineteenth century was the last great attempt to establish a universal system of welfare based on charities. The failure of charity was apparent by the beginning of the twentieth century to resolve the considerable social problems and major poverty identified in surveys by Booth and Rowntree. An alliance between liberals, those socialists who were not Marxists and conservatives who wished to see radical reform emerged:

Many from Dickens to Bagehot, from Spencer to the Webbs, were sceptical about charity and the charitable, for their different reasons. On the one hand, there was wasteful management by well-meaning do-gooders; and hence the need for a Charity Organisation Society. On the other, the Charity Organisation Society itself became synonymous with much that was grudging, callous, dogmatic and reactionary. Its support was wide; but it may perhaps be seen as the protestant capitalist's compromise with a conscience that told him that, alas, charity could not be rejected with impunity. It was charity made businesslike; the businessman's attempts to impose middle-class ethics on the working class, and make its members as industrious and thrifty as he. The emergent socialists, in turn, mistrusted both this utilitarian, quasi-scientific approach and its sentimental opponents, the 'softhearted' people', in Canon Barnett's words, by whose generosity 'a state of things to make one's heart bleed is perpetuated'. Charity delayed social progress; it was the expression of an unjust society, an attempt to conceal its real nature. Beatrice Webb thought it 'twice cursed, it curseth him that gives and him that takes'; Shaw declared that 'he who gives money he has not earned is generous with other people's labour'; and even Wilde argued in his under-rated 'Soul of Man Under Socialism' that it was 'immoral to use private property to alleviate the horrible evils that result from the institution of private property'.

(Nightingale 1973, p. 111)

The early part of the twentieth century saw the emergence of services provided directly by central government, for example social insurance, and through local government, i.e. council housing, but also an uneasy and unclear relationship with the government (Beveridge 1948). Finance in particular caused confusion. Before 1914 government payments to voluntary organizations were almost non-existent. However, there were some notable exceptions; for example, the Royal National Lifeboat Institution used to receive a grant from the government in the mid-nineteenth century. The inter-war years, however, saw payments to voluntary organizations for providing certain services. Trustees, believing in old independent philanthropy, were suspicious of these new forms of income deriving from the State (Rooff 1957), and there were tensions in staff and volunteering. Emerging professions, such as social work, fitted uneasily, with much of the profession in the voluntary welfare agencies interacting with local enhanced officers for health who had taken on much wider roles, for example in child care. Professionalism versus amateurism emerged as another conflicting force, with perhaps the voluntary agencies all unfairly being 'tarnished' with the same brush of the latter and seen as being outdated and reactionary. As the NSPCC demonstrated, however, much of this criticism was fairly placed, with its campaign against the provision of child places at work for working women (Wrong 1945).

The emergence of statutory services and particularly the formation of the Welfare State were seen as being historically inevitable. The prevailing view until the 1980s was that there was a 'natural order' of events for welfare services to be provided by statutory organizations. This perspective was given theoretical legitimization by what is referred to as 'functionalism'. Functionalists view the development of welfare services, from primitive societies to industrial societies, as a form of scientific development – the decline of religious organizations, the proliferation of voluntary organizations and then to meet the increasing needs of advanced societies the involvement of the State.

An alternative to the functionalist perspective is to appraise the relationship as being far more complex, driven in part by a clear political agenda to change society with opportunities and unexpected events. Beveridge, the architect of the Welfare State, had argued for a major role for the voluntary sector, particularly for the use of friendly societies and national insurance. The decision for a statutory service Welfare State was based on a political philosophy, which was distrustful of the voluntary sector. There is no 'scientific' rationale for why the State should have become a financier and deliverer of welfare services. The stimulus to the State taking the major role can be seen as a result of the effects of modern wars and the impact on a civilian population. The importance of war as a catalyst for direct intervention by the State in welfare has been chronicled in the US. Pollack (1994) notes that the US State involvement in welfare programmes did not originate in the twentieth century but much earlier. One quarter of the US government budget expenditure between 1880 and 1910 was devoted to civil war veterans and their dependents. The importance of war as a stimulus to State action was evidenced at the beginning of the twentieth century in the United Kingdom. The Boer War call for volunteers had discovered massive problems in the health of the nation, which threatened the defence of the realm. The sacrifice of the population in the Second World War, when Britain stood alone, cannot be underestimated. The advent of rationing, the conscription of women and their involvement in munitions manufacturing, food production, and so on, led to British society becoming more egalitarian. Social interaction between classes, and comradeship during adversity, led to the spirit that we must not return to the pre-war problems. Acknowledging the importance of the Second World War, the historian Eric Hobsbawm (1969) offers a further dimension to the universal acceptance of a Welfare State:

> By the middle 1930s 'laissez-faire' was therefore dead even as an ideal, except for the usual financial journalists, spokesmen for small business, and the economists ... Two economic policies therefore faced each other, both equally remote from John Stuart Mill. On the one hand there was socialism, based essentially on the aspirations of the working class movement, but gradually strengthened by the experience of the USSR, which impressed even non-socialist observers by its apparent immunity to the great slump. It contained little by way of precise policy except the ancient demand for the nationalisation of the means of production, distribution and exchange and the slogan of planning which the Soviet five-year plans made extremely fashionable. On the other hand there were those – mainly economists who came from liberalism (like J. A. Hobson) or who still remained liberals (like Keynes and Beveridge) – who wished to save the essentials of a capitalist system, but realized that this could now be done only within the framework of a strong and systematically interventionist State; or even through a 'mixed economy'. In practice the difference between these two trends was sometimes hard to discern, especially as some Keynesians abandoned the liberalism of their inspirer for socialism, and as the Labour Party tended to adopt the Keynesian policies as its own, in preference to the more traditional socialist slogans. Still, broadly speaking, the socialists favoured their proposals because they were for social equality and justice, the non-socialists theirs, because they were for the efficiency of the British economy and against social disruption. Both agreed that only systematic State action (whatever its nature) could get rid of and avoid slumps and mass unemployment.
>
> (Hobsbawm 1969, pp. 244–245)

The emergence of welfare services run by the State as opposed to voluntary agencies was therefore not part of some inevitable scientific process. A different policy (Brenton 1985) could have emerged such as financing and regulating voluntary organizations to deliver services. This alternative policy did not emerge and instead charities as service providers were viewed as being unimportant and it was assumed that they would wither away. Most were ignored by the new public services that were more concerned with resourcing their own services (Brenton 1985; Webb and Wistow 1987). It was also the belief of many of the voluntary agencies of the time that they no longer had a place or role (Murray 1969). To survive, charities it seemed would have to develop a new approach to justify themselves and their continuing existence. As the Charity Commission Annual Report of 1960 commented, much of the traditional objects of charity were largely overtaken by the statutory services. Instead its role should be to pioneer, or where it still had a substantial role to play, then this should be one of partnership with statutory authorities.

The perspective of the pioneering role of the voluntary sector, which as Knapp and his colleagues (1990) have highlighted has 'become legendary', we would suggest is a relatively new phenomenon. The voluntary sector prior to the twentieth century was naturally pioneering, given the 'laissez-faire' attitude of the State. Just how naturally innovative the voluntary sector is when it is not the only service provider is questionable (Phillips 2000). In many cases, Knapp argues, public authorities that wanted an 'arms-length' relationship to innovate, encouraged much of the innovation accorded to the voluntary sector in the twentieth century, e.g. drug services. After the innovation stage, the 'natural order' would be for the State to take over. Indeed, many campaigning voluntary organizations saw this as their reason for existence as the following excerpt from the Family Planning Association's 1988 Annual Report illustrates:

> Five distinct phases can be seen in the nearly sixty years of the Family Planning Association's Life. In our first decade, up to World War Two, we were bravely pioneering the availability of birth control with a small staff paid to travel around the country gathering local groups to start clinics. After the war, in the 1945–55 decade, we were building up the organisation to gain recognition for services by then described as family planning. In 1955 the late great Ian Macleod, when Minister of Health, gave us that recognition and started the third phase: there followed twelve years of entrenchment and steady growth in the numbers of clinics, training, clinical trials and information work. The fourth phase began in 1967, the year of Edwin Brooks MP NHS (Family Planning) Act (as well as David Steel's Abortion Act). The Brooks Act set the scene for a seven year phase of wildlife growth as hundreds of new FPA clinics were established through an agency scheme offered to local authorities by the then head of the FPA, Casper Brook. In the same

years we were launching the parliamentary campaign for full integration of family planning into the NHS, which was victorious in 1973.

(Family Planning Association 1988, p. 4)

As late as 1987, seminars organized by the NCVO and the Royal Institute for Public Administration (RIPA) on the voluntary sector still focused on the question:

> Once a voluntary organisation has demonstrated new ways of providing service, should it not be trying to ensure that the State takes on this responsibility?
>
> (Taylor 1988, p. 5)

Many charities continued to be the major service providers and did not advocate for their role to be taken over; for example, services to the blind and deaf in which the statutory services did not take a leading role (Rooff 1957). Barnardo's and other child-care charities continued to run homes for children as an alternative to places by statutory services, as the Younghusband Report on the social workers identified there was a considerable residue of voluntary agency activity, some of which was part financed by local authorities. Nor were the post-war years a stagnant period in voluntary sector development. Many now major charities were formed to meet problems both overseas (Oxfam and War on Want were founded in the late 1940s) and at home as the 'gaps' in the provision of universal welfare services became apparent (Spastics Society – now SCOPE – in the mid-1950s, Shelter and the Child Poverty Action Group in the 1960s). As Crossman, the Labour Secretary of State for Social Services in the late 1960s, observed:

> One of the things I learned as a Minister was the staggering extent of voluntary activity in our Welfare State.
>
> (Brenton 1985, p. 21)

The post-war period in reality to 1979 did not therefore see the withering of charity on the vine of the Welfare State with the exception of the Charity Hospitals, which had been incorporated into the National Health Service on its creation. That there was a perception both politically and by professionals and academics that the voluntary sector was becoming irrelevant during this period is, however, clear. In part this perception can be seen as relating to, on the political agenda, the desire by politicians, particularly Labour ones, to be seen to have nothing to do with charities and the past, but as Beach (1994) argues, such rhetoric should be treated with caution:

> Much of our understanding of Labour's attitude to voluntarism during the formative years of the Welfare State is shaped by the image, built up by Richard Crossman amongst others, of Labour's hostility to 'the

do-good volunteer'. The volunteer was portrayed as amateurish, indeed, the opposite of the professionals and trained administrators who it was envisaged would staff the socialist Welfare State. Voluntarism essentially meant Philanthropy which itself was narrowly interpreted as, in Crossman's words, an 'odious expression of social oligarchy and church bourgeois attitudes'. 'We detested voluntary hospitals maintained by flag days', he says, 'We despised Boy Scouts and Girl Guides'. These words spoken to an audience by a lecturer looking for an impact, were phrased more for effect than for posterity, yet this retrospective interpretation of Crossman's has, nevertheless, assumed a certain credence and authority. Its black and white rhetoric too often has been taken at face value and perhaps we have been misled.

(Beach 1994, pp. 4–5)

Following the Second World War in which the State had assumed responsibility for all aspects of life including how to plant and cook potatoes, there was a belief that 'government' knew best. In particular there was considerable faith in the technique of planning and the benefit of large-scale organization, which were seen as providing the solution to resolving Britain's problems. A Statest approach, as we have seen, had always been part of British social policy as opposed to that found in the United States (Orloff and Skocpol 1984). Welfare professionals and academics, themselves in the newly emerging disciplines such as social work and social policy, wished to distant themselves from the past and viewed voluntary organizations as unscientific and amateur (Murray 1969; Brown 1977; Byrne 1981; Webb and Wistow 1987).

The relationship between the State and the voluntary sector during these years leading to Wolfenden was never clear as later observation studies illustrated (Hatch and Mocroft 1983). By the time of the Wolfenden Report in 1978 there was emerging a consensus that the voluntary and statutory services should be working in partnership. The Labour Government of 1974–1979 was beset with a host of economic problems, Sterling, for example, lost 23 per cent of its international value in the twelve months to October 1976 and had to borrow from the International Monetary Fund (Lloyd 1986). The government, faced with the need to cut public expenditure, saw the voluntary sector as perhaps offering a 'better buy', as David Ennals the then Secretary of State for Health and Social Security stated (Brenton 1985), a suggestion that became official government policy as the following Department of Health and Social Security statement in 1976 illustrates:

support for voluntary effort and encouragement of self help schemes may represent better value for money than directly provided services.

(Vinten 1989, p. 11)

The Conservative Government 1979–1997

The election in 1979 of a radical Conservative Government was fuelled by an ideology that rejected State intervention and placed market forces as the determinant of survival. Emphasis was placed on the individual taking responsibility for their life with a limiting role for the State. The Conservative Government saw the voluntary sector as enhancing this role and funding by Central Government in the 1980s increased by 90 per cent in real terms (Charities Aid Foundation 1989, p. 5). Part of this philosophy was to also curb the power of local authorities, the principal providers of personal welfare services. The impact of these changes cannot be underestimated as the case of public housing illustrates. Forest and Murie (1988) estimated that the sale of council houses was financially the most important in the privatization programme, raising more money than any privatized former nationalized industry.

It was therefore surprising that in 1988 the new Community Care Act continued to provide a role for local government (Deakin 1994). It was certainly against the political ideology of the government as evidenced by the Adam Smith Institute who saw no role for local government. Pirie and Butler (1989) instead envisioned welfare services moving beyond the State, with a role, though not explained, for the charitable sector to an expanded private sector:

> Government can, by providing very modest encouragement to the private sector, help it grow with that rising demand. It can, by means of incentives to personal saving and personal provision, make it easier for most people to provide for their own care needs in retirement.
>
> (Pirie and Butler 1989, p. 32)

Local government was to move from being primarily a service deliverer to a resource provider, which was termed the contract culture (Deakin 1993). In this system a 'market of care' is created, which is intended to provide a degree of choice for the consumer. The contract for care issued by a local authority can be to either a non-profit or a profit-making organization. The implementation of the contract culture in the early 1990s and its importance as an income source to voluntary organizations (by 1996 income from contracts was larger than from traditional grant sources; NCVO 1996) caused considerable debate, with some questioning whether the voluntary sector would lose its specific identity (Burt 1992; Deakin 1993, 1994; Leat 1993; Gutch 1992; Harris 1993). The attributed characteristics of voluntary organizations as flexible, innovative and advocacy it was suggested would be placed at risk as voluntary organizations would have to adopt a business-orientated approach to win contracts. A more conservative approach would be adopted as voluntary organizations would be reluctant to upset funders. Constraints on funding and the dictation of the funds by statutory authorities would lead to services becoming less innovatory. The Left think-tank Demos (1994) believed at this time that there was now a 'Crisis in Charity Finance', citing the stagnation in giving by the general public and businesses. A Home Office sponsored report *Voluntary Action* (Knight 1993) further caused concern by questioning the tax concessions to the sector, the effectiveness of voluntary management boards and whether many voluntary organizations should retain such description or charitable status. The talk was of crisis in the sector and its ability to cope with the new demands of the post-Thatcher era (Billis and Harris 1992) and it provided the opportunity for the NCVO to establish a Commission on the Future of the Voluntary Sector (Deakin 1995). A separate commission for Scotland chaired by Arnold Kemp also came into existence.

Both Commissions' reports followed an extensive period of evidence gathering by verbal and written submissions ranging from the context of the sector and an extensive discussion of its role in a democratic society to making specific recommendations on issues covering the relationship with central and local government, the role of intermediary bodies, business relationships, resources, Europe, volunteering, legal and fiscal matters and governance of the sector. As the Deakin report observed:

> Fundamental issues are arising around what the respective roles, rights and responsibilities of the State, the market voluntary bodies and ordinary citizens should be (p. 1) ... The sector's influence rests principally on the values that it is taken to exemplify. From de Tocqueville's famous study of American democracy in the early nineteenth century onwards, independent voluntary associations have been portrayed as the backbone of civil society and their presence as the essential precondition for the health of democracy (p. 15) ... there is a fundamental reconsideration now taking place in most western democratic countries of the role of the State, the health of civil society and about the rights and responsibilities of their citizens ... this rethinking has fundamental implications for the future of voluntary action.
>
> (Deakin 1995, p. 17)

Underpinning the Commission's report were six basic principles:

1   Public policy must recognize the unique qualities of the sector and provide the right context for it to flourish.
2   Successful partnership is partnership negotiated between equals.
3   The role of users is crucial to the sector's future.
4   Voluntary bodies must be free to be advocates even where they are also partners.
5   The voluntary sector must learn to manage professionals but not allow professionalism to dominate its agenda.
6   Diversity of funding sources is one of the best guarantees of continuing independence.

One of the key recommendations was the relationship with government and that:

> a concordat [be] drawn up between representatives of government and the sector, laying down basic principles for future relations. As part of this process, each government department should make their funding requirements and policy priorities for the sector explicit.
>
> (Deakin 1995, pp. 3–4)

Government welcomed the report officially but the concordat in particular was rejected:

> However, the term 'concordat' seems to imply a more rigid relationship than is appropriate, given the diverse and dynamic nature of voluntary organisations.
>
> (Bottomley 1996, p. vii)

New Labour

An alternative response was offered by the Labour Party, then in opposition, who welcomed the recommendation. Alun Michael had been charged by Tony Blair, shortly after assuming the leadership of the Labour Party, on continuing his work on the role of the voluntary sector. Michael (Kendall 2000) had consulted widely in the mid-1990s and in April 1997 issued a policy document entitled *Building the Future Together*, the key conclusion of the document being that a concordat was needed as a basis for future partnership between government and the voluntary sector. *Building the Future Together* emphasized the invaluable contribution to society made by voluntary organizations and noted that the aims and objectives of the government and voluntary organizations were often the same. The aim of the proposed concordant was to develop a framework that recognized the complementary functions and shared values of the voluntary sector and government and so enable a mutually beneficial partnership to develop. The Wolfenden Report of twenty years earlier had made these bold words to describe its mission:

> to review the role and functions of voluntary organisations in the UK over the next twenty-five years.
>
> (Wolfenden 1978, p. 9)

This agenda was soon to be dramatically changed, with the election of a Conservative government.

The election in 1997 of a Labour government committed to the economic expenditure plans of the previous government did not see a massive injection of money into existing public services or the re-nationalization of former public utilities such as the railways. The timidity of Labour's first few years was in contrast to its relationship with the voluntary sector. Within the first budget a charity tax review was announced and in November 1998 a 'Compact' was published with an introduction by the Prime Minister:

> This compact between Government and the voluntary and community sector provides a framework, which will help guide our relationship at every level. It recognises that Government and sector fulfil complementary roles in the development and delivery of public policy and services, and that the Government has a role in promoting voluntary and community activity in all areas of our national life.
>
> The work of voluntary and community organisations is central to the Government's mission to make this the Giving Age. They enable individuals to contribute to the development of their communities. By so doing they promote citizenship, help to re-establish a sense of community and make a crucial contribution to our shared aim of a just and inclusive society. The Compact will strengthen the relationship between Government and the voluntary sector and is a document of both practical and symbolic importance.
>
> (Blair 1998)

The Compact outlines and establishes a series of principles, which should govern the relationship between the government and the voluntary sector. The word 'shared' is used with vision and principles and the document makes an impressive presentation of working in partnership and respecting the independence of the sector.

The Commission on the Future of the Voluntary Sector 'big idea' was now part of government policy but has its critics (Whelan 1999) who have suggested that the sector is sacrificing its independence by both receiving government funds and becoming an 'agent of the State'. Other commentators (Kendall 2000) noted that the tax concessions to the sector were in part compensation to the abolition of Advance Corporation Tax estimated to have cost charities some £350 million.

Two contrasting views emerge on the relationship of the Labour Government with the voluntary sector. The first advocates that the voluntary sector has 'come of age' and has led to the position of the voluntary sector at the heart of public policy. The alternative view is that 'spin' of New Labour has prevailed and rather like a 'piece of paper' of sixty years ago it will prove to be damaging and of little real value (Lee 2001). At the time of writing we currently have no reliable research as to how the Compact at the local level is working in practice. At one level the Local Government Association (2000) has issued guidelines on how to develop a successful compact; at another, grass roots voluntary organizations complain that nothing has changed (Community Accounts Conference 2000).

Conclusion

We are of the opinion that the voluntary sector financial manager has to be aware of the public policy context in which the voluntary sector operates. Understanding policy and the implication for funding and accountability is vitally important in being able to contribute to planning and forecasting. Independence from the State as advocated by Whelan (1999) is more complex than simply not taking government funding. Voluntary organizations with a portfolio of different income sources in contracts can exercise a degree of independence of action that many a supposedly 'independent' charity with no government funds but instead subject to the 'mood of the public' would envy. All sources of funding have associated problems and issues as, for example, the British Heart Foundation discovered in its partnership with food manufacturers Nestlé and 'bite-sized' Shredded Wheat which it withdrew from after a Sheffield court could not support the claims made. Even the endowed trust is not immune as the Baring Foundation unfortunately discovered.

We began this chapter with a description of the Wolfenden report and its four phases. While the Welfare State phase is still ongoing we stated that we believed the reforms of the Conservative Government in the 1980s would be a major milestone in the history of the sector. We believe it can be seen as the beginning of a new phase, which we have called *The Period of Exchange*. We believe this reflects the nature of the sector as a marketplace not just for the exchange of goods and services but also of ideas as, for example, the current debate on civil society and the third way illustrates (O'Connell 2001). We return to this theme and its consequences for financial management in the voluntary sector at the end of this book.

2   Management issues

Governance

Interest in governance was provoked in the late 1980s by a series of scandals in public companies (Maxwell, BCCI, Pollypeck) and in the public sector following public alarm about MPs' extraparliamentary incomes ('cash for questions') and the ease with which ministers moved from Whitehall to lucrative jobs in the City. The Cadbury Committee issued the first major report for the corporate sector in 1992. The report defined governance as

The system by which organisations are directed and controlled.

Initially, the focus on governance was on the control issue but subsequently, through the work of successor committees in the private sector (Greenbury, Hampel and Turnbull), and in the public sector the 'Nolan' committee, the concept of governance has been extended to include the broad-based formulation of policy and the development of strategy as the starting points of good corporate governance. The Commission on the Future of the Voluntary Sector established a subgroup, 'Performance and Governance', which in turn led to Joseph Rowntree's sponsored report, *Towards Voluntary Sector Codes of Practice* (Ashby 1997, p. 5), which stated:

As a voluntary organisation, which seeks to be effective and accountable, we will be clear and open about our work and conscious of our social responsibilities. In particular, we will:

- state our purpose clearly and keep it relevant to current conditions
- be explicit about the needs that we intend to meet and how this will be achieved
- manage and target resources effectively and do what we say we will do to evaluate the effectiveness of our work, tackle poor performance and respond to complaints fairly and promptly
- agree and set out for all those to whom we are accountable how we will fulfil these responsibilities

- be clear about the standards to which we will work
- be open about arrangements for involving users
- have a systematic and open process for making appointments to our governing body
- set out the role and responsibilities of members of our governing body
- have clear arrangements for involving, training, supporting and managing volunteers
- ensure that our policies and practices do not discriminate unfairly or lead to other forms of unfair treatment
- recruit staff openly, remunerate them fairly and be a good employer.

The Charity Commission and charity trusteeship

Of the estimated 500,000 voluntary organizations, just over 180,000 in England and Wales are registered charities and come under the supervision of the Charity Commission, which was established in 1853. The Charity Commission is a government department that since 1960 has been within the authority of the Home Secretary (except for a short period when it was part of the National Heritage Department). However, uniquely, the senior civil servants of the commission – the Charity Commissioners – when making decisions, do so independent of government ministers. Prior to 1960 the Charity Commissioners reported to parliament through a designated senior MP. The Commission and its predecessors have had an interesting history (Owen 1965; Palmer 1999); however, it is a relatively small department with a budget of £22 million (Charity Commission Annual Report 1999/2000). However, this budget is to grow quite dramatically by 20 per cent over the next two years (Stoker 2001). The Charity Commission is only responsible for registered charities in England and Wales. Different arrangements apply to Scotland and Northern Ireland where the Inland Revenue is the registering body. The Charity Commission is also not responsible for Excepted and Exempt Charities which are organizations that are too small, i.e. incomes under £1,000 and no permanent endowment, or are exempt organizations which come under other regulatory authorities, for example The Registrar of Friendly Societies.

While by number of organizations the Charity Commission is a minority regulator, the registered charities with a combined gross income of more than £24 billion are financially more significant. In public perception as well, it is the registered charities which are in the public eye and enjoy significant tax concessions estimated at a cost to the exchequer of over £1 billion (Randall and Williams 1996).

The Commission has a statutory duty to register organizations which are charitable (within the decisions of the court), and is able to change a charity's existing purposes which are no longer suitable and effective to new ones which are similar in character. Thus it is both responsible for registration of organizations and in part for determining what is charitable (though its decisions can be challenged in the courts), and for supervising such bodies once it has registered them. The Charity Commission also has a promotional role in encouraging the effective use of charitable resources by giving advice for which it may not charge.

The very nature of charity activity as a voluntary act, involving people with passionate beliefs perhaps, makes the Charity Commission's role as regulator harder than any other. People driven by cause and belief and not by profit are less amenable to being told what to do. The Charity Commission does not have the power to administer charities and may not normally interfere with the trustees' exercise of those duties. When the Charity Commission uses its extensive powers to intervene in a charity, which can include freezing bank accounts, removing trustees and appointing new trustees or a receiver manager (discussed in Chapter 6), it inevitably causes controversy. Such cases, however, are very rare and the Charity Commission to date has generally been a regulator, which prefers to work with the existing charity trustees rather than to remove them if a charity has a problem.

Within this philosophy, the focus of the Charity Commission in recent years has been on improving the performance of charity trustees through advice and annual reporting. Section 97 of the Charities Act 1993 defines trustees as 'the people responsible under the governing document for controlling the management and administration of the charity, regardless of what they are called'. Only an adult (i.e. over 18 years old) of sound mind may be a trustee and certain persons are disqualified from being trustees. These include people with criminal convictions for dishonesty, undischarged bankrupts, disqualified company directors and anyone removed from the trusteeship of a charity by the court or Charity Commission on grounds of misconduct or mismanagement of a charity. Charity trusteeship, particularly following the Charities Acts of 1992 and 1993, has become a demanding role with responsibilities and potentially unlimited liability for the charities' financial debts if the trusteeship has not been discharged properly, for example breach of trust (Charity Commission 1996).

The duties and standards of conduct of a trustee can be summarized as

1   Management of the charity including a duty to ensure accounts are properly kept and that the right amounts are paid for the right purposes. Trustees should meet regularly enough to ensure they retain control over the running of the organization.
2   Duty to protect assets and ensure the charity's property is under their proper control.
3   They must not profit from their role as trustees which is a voluntary unpaid office, trustees may be paid reasonable out-of-pocket expenses but unless the governing document allows or the Charity Commission gives approval may not receive remuneration.

4   Must act in the best interests of the charity and must not allow their own personal interests to conflict with their duties as a trustee.

5   The Charity Commission publishes over sixty advice leaflets for charity trustees ranging from general advice to specialist issues including contracts, trading and campaigning activities. Charity trustees must complete an annual return to the Charity Commission. The annual return requires information and disclosure to the effect that the trustees are active and are effectively managing the charity. The recent change in the SORP to improve on the reporting aspect has been another step in this direction (see Chapters 5 and 6).

Except in the smallest of charities, the trustees will also employ paid staff. The relationship between paid staff and trustees is crucial to the success of an organization. A seemingly simple question of who is responsible for authorizing an element of expenditure can sometimes be fraught with difficulties and can lead to internal strife, which only damages the organization. The Association of Chief Executives of Voluntary Organizations has published a model code of conduct for trustees, which also covers the relationship between the trustees and senior staff.

Charity organizations and governance

Good governance is important for the voluntary sector for maintaining the confidence and financial support of the public. Mayo (1999, p. 5) states: 'Trust in charities is at an all time low'. A MORI poll for the Charity Commission (1998) found 74 per cent of the general public surveyed agreeing with the statement 'there needs to be tighter control over the laws governing charity affairs'. In the same survey 41 per cent disagreed with the statement 'When I give money to charity I feel confident that most will go to the cause'. One response to these problems is the exhortation that voluntary organizations should be clear and open about their work and conscious of their social responsibilities.

Various codes of good practice have been written which ask voluntary organizations to demonstrate:

- Effectiveness: showing clarity of purpose, being explicit about the needs to be met and ways in which resources are managed.
- Accountability: evaluating effectiveness and performance, dealing with complaints fairly and communicating to all stakeholders how responsibilities will be fulfilled.
- Standards: having clear operating standards.
- User involvement: making arrangements to involve users of services.
- Governance: having a systematic and open process for making appointments to the governing body, setting out the roles and responsibilities of members.

- Volunteers: having clear arrangements for involving, training, support-ing and managing volunteers.
- Equality and fairness: ensuring that policies and practices do not dis-criminate unfairly.
- Staff management: recruiting staff openly, remunerating them fairly and being a good employer.

Governance for registered charities is markedly different from the principles underpinning the Cadbury Report and much of the writing in the corporate sector on governance. Cadbury placed considerable emphasis on the role of non-executive directors who would be of sufficient number and calibre that they would question and when appropriate challenge the decision of the executive directors. Charities are different because of the estimated 750,000 unpaid charity trustees (NCVO 2000). In charities all the trustees are non-executive directors, should have no pecuniary interest and are part-time. There are limitations on the extent to which they can delegate their powers to senior paid staff and they are legally accountable for the finances of the charity, which for breach of trust can mean unlimited personal liability.

Research on charity trusteeship (NCVO 1992a, 1995) found a confusing picture with many charity trustees unaware of their responsibilities or that they were charity trustees in the first place. The 1992 Charities Act, while not increasing trustee responsibilities, prompted a greater awareness for trustees of their responsibilities. Subsequently, there has been a plethora of Good Practice Guides from the various voluntary sector umbrella bodies, the Charity Commission and writers advising charity trustees of 'how best' to carry out their duties. One excellent prescriptive model was developed by a charity executive Andrew Hind (1995) who developed a five-point model which is still highly relevant today and provides a useful checklist for char-ities to appraise themselves:

1   Functioning effectively at trustee level

    i   Are there procedures for nomination, re-election and retirement?
    ii   Succession planning
    iii   Appropriate subcommittee structures
    iv   Trustee job descriptions
    v   Trustee induction and training
    vi   Board self-assessment

2   Planning strategically

    i   Clarity about vision and mission
    ii   Environmental analysis
    iii   Sources of competitive advantage
    iv   Benchmarking
    v   Formulating strategies and key tasks
    vi   Establishing a financial plan

3   Defining the boundaries of management authority

    i   Financial policy framework
    ii   Performance evaluation process
    iii Demonstrating effectiveness externally
    iv   Assessment of risk

4   Managing the charity's activities productively

    i   Clarifying trustee–management interface
    ii   Relationships within management team
    iii Managing growth
    iv   Establishing an appropriate culture
    v   Human resource management
    vi   Utilizing volunteers

5   Understanding the charity's external environment

    i   Charity Commission annual reports
    ii   Charity Commission inquiries
    iii Umbrella groups

The NCVO's 'Going for Gold' initiative on trustee training and organizations such as the Directory of Social Change run regular inexpensive trustee training and development sessions on management best practices. The Charity Commission inquiries highlight annually a few examples of charity trustees failing in their duties but when measured against over 750,000 individuals spread over less than 200,000 organizations these are rare cases. Despite this seeming lack of a problem and abundance of training and advice, there is still a degree of anxiety over trusteeship and whether trustees are up to the job (Harrow and Palmer 1998).

In particular, questions have been raised over whether the Charity Commission's legal framework and focus on 'maximalist role of active engagement' is appropriate for unpaid trustees. Recent consultation on whether trustees should be paid by the Charity Commission saw the consensus being maintained but there is now strong evidence that recruiting trustees who are not white and over fifty is becoming increasingly problematic. Whether payment is an answer seems to reduce the debate to a technical level. In our opinion, much wider questions need to be asked and researched first. There is, for example, a lack of enquiry and understanding on fundamental questions such as why people undertake trusteeship and what trustees' predominant attitudes towards their trusteeship. The focus of work to date has been on trusteeship as a corporate activity as opposed to taking an individualistic perspective.

The role of the charity secretary

Some voluntary organizations are also incorporated as companies and therefore are required under company law to appoint a secretary. Voluntary organizations and charities which are not registered companies also usually appoint a member of staff or a volunteer on the management committee to be the organization's secretary. The principal duties of the charity secretary do not differ from those of a company secretary and embrace responsibility for

- Meetings
- Maintaining key statutory registers
- Filling statutory returns
- Ensuring the safe-keeping and conduct of company seals
- Annual reports and accounts publication and distribution.

In addition, the charity secretary will usually also have responsibility for legal matters and insurance.

The debates in corporate governance, particularly Cadbury, placed great emphasis on the role of the company secretary. Such a focus has not occurred in the debates on voluntary sector governance; however, the Institute of Chartered Secretaries and Administrators (ICSA) supports a Charity Secretary's Group and actively promotes the recognition of the role similar to the company secretary. The ICSA assisted the Charity Commission (1999a) in producing guidance on 'Charities and Meetings'.

The financial management role of the Management Committee

With the absence of profit and shareholders the financial management role of a voluntary organization management committee is different from a commercial organization's Board of Directors' priorities. In a public-listed company this should be the aim of maximizing shareholder value but for voluntary boards we suggest their financial priorities are

- Accountability. Most voluntary organizations are financially accountable to a far greater number of stakeholders because they are funded by a combination of tax concessions and money from the general public, local government and charitable trusts.
- Value. The goal of maximizing shareholder value is not relevant to voluntary organizations. The whole management committee must demonstrate value for money and effectiveness, which we discuss in Chapter 8.

The three main functions of the board are financial monitoring, financial procedures and financial management. The *Good Financial Management Guide*

(Bashir 1999) identifies the key points relating to the role of the board in each of these key functions.

Financial monitoring

The financial monitoring carried out by boards is often typified by:

a   The comparing of budgets of income and expenditure with actual results;
b   The consideration of projected sources and levels of income and expenditure.

But its effectiveness can be limited by:

- The need to report to funders
- The lack of any value added, instead seen as a compliance function
- Information which is too detailed and conforming to accounting regulations
- Totally reactive responses conditioned by when information is presented.

Ideally financial monitoring should be characterized by:

- The use of key financial ratio analysis (which can, for example, highlight financial stability).
- The inclusion of financial performance information against predetermined financial policies (for example, income reserves).
- A committee that is adequately empowered in its role by proper induction, an understanding of financial structures and its relationship with management.
- The provision of information that is understandable, timely and accurate.

Financial procedures

Procedures are designed to ensure the propriety and efficiency of the organization's activities. The board should ensure that there are proper policies and procedures governing:

- Trustees' financial responsibilities
- Controls on expenditure
- Controls on the financial assets
- Budgetary control
- Controls on human resources
- Controls on physical assets
- Controls on income generation.

A review of the accounting systems and related internal controls should be undertaken by the internal or external auditor who should report weaknesses to the management committee at the conclusion of their audit.

Financial management

Financial management is more than just ensuring there is sufficient cash and keeping to budget. Financial management according to the Chartered Institute of Management Accountants (CIMA) involves (Wise 1998):

- Setting financial objectives
- Planning and acquiring funds
- Ensuring funds are being effectively managed
- Management and financial accounting
- Formulating strategy
- Planning and controlling activities
- Decision taking
- Optimizing use of resources
- Disclosure to others external to the organization
- Disclosure to employees
- Safeguarding assets.

There needs to be clear procedures that ensure that the management board has the skills to ensure effective financial management takes place. Where staff are involved the individual responsibilities should be clear to avoid 'stepping on each others' toes'. The role of the honorary treasurer or a chair of a finance committee is often crucial in discussions with key financial external advisors – investment managers, auditors, etc. Other board members must however recognize that they hold a joint responsibility and must not assume that the honorary treasurer will do everything.

Internal auditing

How do boards ensure they are achieving these aims? Research on financial information received by voluntary boards (Vincent *et al.* 1998; Harrow *et al.* 1999) found that while boards received information, particularly financial information such as budgetary control reports, they had no way of independently appraising the quality of such information. Equally, reports on the organization's performance were not subject to any independent verification. Ensuring accountability and getting best value in local authorities has focused on the role of auditors and particularly internal auditors. Concern over governance previously discussed in the private sector has equally focused on an expanded role for internal audit and a focus on internal control processes that directors should ensure are in place (Turnbull 1999). The Institute of Internal Auditors (IIA) define internal auditing as:

Internal auditing is an independent appraisal function established within an organization to examine and evaluate its activities as a service to the organization.

There are a number of key words in this definition and it will assist our understanding if we examine them more closely.

- Internal – makes it clear that auditors employed within the organization undertake the work, as opposed to external auditors who are not. Therefore, attitudes and organization knowledge are going to be very different.
- Auditing – is defined in the Concise Oxford Dictionary as 'an official examination of accounts; searching examination'. This definition neatly encompasses the particular role of the external auditor but in addition the use of 'searching examination' covers other activities than reviewing accounting records – internal auditing while including aspects of accounting has a wider role.
- Independent – this concept is vital to all auditors but particularly to internal auditors who need to have a sufficient degree of independence to make the role acceptable to auditees and of value to the organization. Internal auditors should be independent of the activities they audit – if an internal auditor has advised and participated in setting up a new computer system they should not then audit it.
- Established within an organization – this signifies that internal auditing must be formally acknowledged as part of the structure of the organization.
- Appraisal, examine and evaluate – mean approximately the same, that is the internal auditor is not only required to make a searching examination to ascertain the facts but also to evaluate performance in terms of the value and quality. This requires the internal auditor to exercise judgement, which implies a degree of experience and wisdom.
- Its activities – note the breadth of appraisal implied – in essence internal auditing should only be limited by the ability of the internal auditors to carry out an effective appraisal.
- Service to the organization – it is the responsibility of internal auditing to make a contribution to the organization.

Internal auditing, therefore, requires employees to conduct searching examinations with an independent attitude and to make judgements based on their findings. To be effective the function must be officially recognized and be given appropriate status to enable it to make a contribution to the organization's goals and objectives by giving service to management and the board. Internal auditing is very different from external auditing which is concerned with the verification of financial statements and is conducted within a statutory framework. Unlike public authorities, charities, even the largest, are not statutorily required to have an internal audit function. Research into those charities that do have internal auditors (Billis and Harris 1987; Palmer 1992, 1996) found that only a few of the largest charities did, and most of these were singleton functions located primarily in the finance department. An active group of charity internal auditors meets under the auspices of the Charity Finance Director's Group (CFDG) and the Institute of Internal Auditors and practitioner publications (Hassell 1999) have started to raise the profile, but internal audit is still relatively underdeveloped in the voluntary sector compared to the public and corporate sectors.

A boost to internal audit in charities may come from two very different sources and their focus on risk – the Turnbull report (1999) which states that

> A company's system of internal control has a key role in the management of risks that are significant to the fulfilment of its business objectives

and the Charity Commission which in the new SORP (discussed in Chapter 3) now requires the trustees in their annual report to provide

> confirmation that major risks facing the charity have been identified and steps taken to mitigate them.

Responding to Turnbull, the Institute of Internal Auditors in the UK revised its 1995 professional briefing note on *Control Self-Assessment and Internal Audit* to *Control and Risk Self-Assessment (CRSA)* (IIA.UK 1999) and defined CRSA as

> a systematic and participative technique used to identify, classify, assess, measure and evaluate risks and controls.
>
> (IIA.UK 1999, p. 7)

Key elements to CRSA are to help management:

1   Assist in discovering root causes of problems
2   Establish management's responsibility for risk management and control
3   Contribute to risk management
4   Assist people within the organization to a better understanding of the purpose and effectiveness of risks and controls
5   Improve the quality and quantity of information
6   Improve communication and motivation
7   Link risk to objectives and strategies.

Control and risk assessment cannot be viewed in isolation and can only work if they enjoy the support of top management and the commitment of the whole organization. They must also be seen as part of the governance process which in turn requires the organization to be clear of its missions and aims.

The planning process

Defining the mission

Voluntary organizations should be clear as to why they exist and how they will fulfil their mission. This may seem obvious but many voluntary organizations become confused between why they exist and how they plan to fulfil their mission. Meeting a financial goal is not the mission of a voluntary organization but is essential if it is to fulfil its mission. For example, the ambitious campaign by the NSPCC on child abuse – the mission is to eradicate cruelty to children – requires £200 million to achieve. Aspirations and financial resources are related and it is the task of managers to co-ordinate the two. A voluntary organization mission and its financial goals are complimentary to each other, not in competition.

Planning

Planning can be defined as the establishment of objectives and the formulation, evaluation and selection of the policies, strategies, tactics and action required to achieve these objectives. Planning comprises long-term strategic planning and short-term operations planning, which is usually for up to one year. Voluntary organizations need to plan effectively but often do not, because in many voluntary organizations, the demands of the moment leave little time for strategic analysis.

Planning really happens in three stages as detailed below.

DECIDING GENERAL GOALS

These are usually long-term aims to pursue and tend to be set at top levels. Using the WWF–UK strategic development plan this would be: 'To seek to slow down, and eventually to reverse, the destruction of species and habitats throughout the world'.

SETTING OBJECTIVES

Within the context of general goals, objectives are set as clear steps on the way to achieving the goals. They are statements of specific measurable results to be achieved in a given time. For example, WWF–Scotland has the opportunity through the Scottish Parliament to advocate its community-based participatory approach to conservation. For its core costs WWF–Scotland will continue to seek funds as part of WWF–UK but for its programme expenditure this will be increasingly sourced from within Scotland.

Although objectives are set within the context of the goals set at the top, they also depend on information from the bottom up, to ensure they are feasible.

ACTION PLANS

These are detailed plans of how the goals and objectives are to be achieved, using information from those who will carry out the task. In respect of the objective of WWF–Scotland sourcing project finance from Scotland it may intend on research and education to:

> XYZ pieces of research in progress, 70 per cent of which are funded from Scottish sources;
> XYZ publish research reports this year, with 60 per cent of costs funded from Scottish sources.

Understanding the strategic position

To answer the question 'What is, or will be, our strategic position?' requires the organization to understand the external environment in which the organization operates and the internal structures of the organization. This has four aspects:

1   Environmental analysis (external appraisal) is the scanning of the organization environment for factors relevant to the organization's current and future activities. To assist this process the NCVO has developed a 'Third Sector Foresight' project which seeks to understand these external factors and how they impact on the sector.
2   Position audit examines the current state of the entity in respect of resources, both financial and organizational, e.g. the qualities of the management committee.
3   Organizational appraisal (or SWOT analysis) is a critical assessment of the Strengths, Weaknesses, Opportunities and Threats in relation to the internal and environmental factors affecting an entity in order to establish its position prior to the preparation of a long-term plan.
4   Gap analysis arises from a projection of current activities into the future to identify if there is a difference between the organization's objectives and the results from the continuation of current activities.

Undertaking this assessment helps to identify the strategic choices open to the organization, for example to grow or to stay the same size or even reduce in size; issues of current and future service provision, geography and policy. To assist this process the following tools can be used (from Bashir 1999, p. 36):

- Management audit. This sets out to assess the effectiveness of the trustee board, management team and organizational structure in achieving charitable objectives. It will therefore be looking at leadership, culture and structure to identify existing and potential weaknesses and recommend ways to rectify them.
- Ratio analysis. Key ratios – such as liquidity, fundraising performance, cost ratios and trading profitability (for trading groups) – can, when analysed over time and compared with those of other voluntary organizations offering comparable services, provide a valuable indication of trends and highlight key relationships.
- Contribution analysis. This identifies the absolute or percentage amounts that a particular programme contributes to the general overheads (after deducting direct programme costs from any earned or unearned income for that programme). The aim is to ensure that each programme makes a contribution to these overheads.

Evaluation

Once choices are identified they need to be evaluated as it is unlikely that all options will be feasible within available resources. Each option should be examined on its merits as to whether it:

- increases strengths
- strengthens existing weaknesses
- is it suitable to the organization's existing position
- is it acceptable to stakeholders.

In addition in testing their feasibility the following questions need to be asked:

- Is the leadership suitable?
- Is the culture capable?
- Is the organizational structure appropriate?
- Are the functional policies appropriate?
- Are the resources available?
- Is this strategy an improvement on not changing at all?
- Are there procedures for implementation and monitoring?

Each chosen strategy needs to satisfy all these points. If it fails on any, the organization must assess whether remedial action is possible.

Preparing day-to-day plans

Once the strategic goals have been identified they must be translated into day-to-day activities. For example, a cancer charity aiming to reduce the incidence of smoking might set an objective to reduce smoking in women attending antenatal clinics by 25 per cent within the next six months. To achieve this objective the following action plans have been formulated:

- a pamphlet explaining the dangers
- a counselling session
- a chance to attend an anti-smoking course.

The pamphlet may be further broken down as follows:

- Identify major issues, medical and otherwise, of which expectant mothers need to be aware.
- Identify main contributors to pamphlet.
- Prepare draft, check accuracy of content and design.
- Conduct a limited testing with a readers/users panel.
- Print.
- Market and promote pack to expectant mothers attending the clinics.

The persons responsible for each of these tasks, and the time allocated, should be identified, so as to provide a basis for performance appraisal.

Planning within a quality framework

A quality framework makes possible a rigorous and consistent approach to quality throughout an organization. The Quality Standards Task Group developed an excellence model, which can be applied to any organization and is based on the following premise:

> Customer satisfaction, people satisfaction and impact on society are achieved through leadership driving policy and strategy, people management, resources and process leading ultimately to excellence in business results.

The proposed quality principles for voluntary organizations state that such organizations:

- Strive for continuous improvement in all they do.
- Use recognized standards or models as a means to continuous improvements and not as an end.
- Agree requirements with stakeholders and endeavour to meet or exceed these first time and every time.
- Promote equality of opportunity through their internal and external conduct.
- Are accountable to stakeholders.
- Add value to their end users and beneficiaries.

Programme and organizational resource assessment

Mission-orientated goals and financial goals are interdependent. Any changes that give a new strategic direction to charitable programmes will also mean an adjustment to the financial resources devoted to that programme. For example:

> A voluntary organisation providing counselling services decides to increase the number of its qualified counsellors. The education department, which runs the training course, responds by planning to increase its intake by 20 per cent next year. In planning this expansion there will be implications for changes in the number of tutors, teaching rooms, equipment, administration, etc., which will need to be costed. In addition to these changes, the budget for the training department must include an allowance for the likely changes in the price of relevant items during the budget period: salaries, etc.

Often a voluntary organization is faced with a situation where the committee has to prioritize options as it does not have sufficient resources. In drawing up a list of possible solutions the link between mission and financial resources should be explicit and criteria rating each solution as viable or unacceptable can be used. For example, the Royal Society for the Promotion of Health, in reviewing its Annual Lecture, notes that it constantly makes a loss and considers the option of increasing income by seeking sponsorship. Its mission is to promote health awareness and therefore to accept sponsorship from a tobacco company would not be acceptable no matter how attractive the financial offer.

Voluntary organization management committees also need to consistently consider their organization's financial stability, which considers the stability of sources of finance and impact on reserve levels, etc. This is referred to as 'organizational resource analysis'. The following case study illustrates this process.

Case study

'Friends' had been established in the early 1980s as an alternative to what had been seen as the hostile attitude of health professionals to people with HIV/AIDS. The organization's funding came from a series of small active Friends groups and large donations from wealthy individuals.

By the late 1980s Friends had developed the following profile:

- A political campaign that had raised the organization's profile but had necessitated the setting up of a separate non-charitable subsidiary upon the insistence of the Charity Commission.
- The organization's income was just over £1 million a year and it owned its own freehold London premises which had been donated to it.

- The management style was characterized by a succession of young charismatic directors who went on to larger charities or political careers.
- While Friends had originally been a campaign against discrimination, it now focused on the issue of support.

In the early 1990s Friends was successful in obtaining a large grant from central government of some £8 million pounds spread over three years to establish an education campaign, advice centres and accommodation projects.

The number of staff of Friends increased dramatically. The organization had no official pay scales and no human resource function as it relied primarily on volunteers. The new staff, who joined the organization in the early 1990s, were professional social workers, many from local and health authorities. Major differences began to emerge on employment conditions. The staff began to demand professional salaries and conditions of service. They also wanted to move to modern offices and talked of Friends being in the first division of charities.

A culture of tension and conflict began to develop between the volunteers and the new paid professionals. In 1995 the director resigned. The issue of the successor became a major contest between the two groups. The 'professional' group wanted to see the post advertised with a salary similar to a Director of Social Services in a local authority. The volunteers wished to see a charismatic entertainer with HIV appointed instead.

The decision focused on the managing board of trustees. This was a group of twenty-one individuals who were elected every year. Whilst presented as democratic, reality was different. The elections were never contested, with local branches nominating an individual when a vacancy occurred.

The professional group rallied friends to join the charity. They also lobbied business and media supporters, arguing that the charity was old-fashioned and not business oriented. The traditional group were caught by surprise and were too late to stop a new group of trustees being elected.

Advertisements were placed but the eventual appointment was the head of the Campaigns Unit who had previously worked for a large advertising agency. The organization went into overdrive with the latest IT equipment being purchased, a human resources director appointed and a new business plan that forecast income rising at 10 per cent above inflation for the next five years.

The following year saw the professional group supporters lose places on the trustee board as the traditional group was better organized. Disputes over membership lists and eligibility led to court injunctions. Trustee meetings were acrimonious, with all decisions being debated on personality grounds. Despite this conflict, the organization continued to grow, with the business plan being outperformed in income terms. Although income from groups and donations for the political campaign declined, the government increased its grant as services increased.

During this period the finance director left the organization and the honorary treasurer, a personal friend of the director from a leading merchant bank, became more involved. The new finance director also came from the City where they had been involved in corporate finance and take-overs financed by short-term loans. They proposed a more aggressive strategy of purchasing freehold shop-fronts with flats above that a butchery firm was selling, rather than the current policy of leasing space in local authority libraries and special projects with housing associations.

Purchasing and equipping the properties was capital expenditure explained the honorary treasurer to his fellow trustees: 'We are swapping assets and acquiring new ones that will provide a firm bedrock in the long term. We will also be independent of the housing associations and the local authorities that charge us for the privilege.' Financing the deal involved a combination of reducing the large cash reserves of the organization to an overdraft with a series of short-term loans secured on the freehold assets and serviced by the grant income. The property transactions were completed a few days before the election in 1997. Asked if a new government would have any effect, the director remarked that 'as an independent organization with substantial assets why should it and if it did it would campaign against them.'

Three years later the organization was in crisis, unable to pay its loans. The central government grant initiative had been replaced by a series of local government contracts most of which had been awarded to other organizations. Many were voluntary organizations who in partnership with housing associations were able to use their joint finance to supply a service cheaper than that of Friends. The Charity Commission had also informed the charity that it was investigating a complaint that funds had been used for political purposes. Most of the shop premises were closed and unsold due to the crisis in high-street retailing.

Questions

1   Compile a checklist of factors that had contributed to the organization's downfall.
2   What could Friends have done differently?

Analysis of case study

- Reasons for becoming a trustee had little to do with the primary purpose of the charity. The political conflict meant that the trustee board exercised little or no control and had no rational debates on the future of the organization.
- The big increase in income was for social care not for political campaigns. Had Friends kept proper financial records between the two organizations? Did it charge the political organization rent for its office space and other services?

- The organization had gone from being an independent charity with a diversity of income to being dependent on government grants. The trustees had not taken a strategic view of how the organization was changing. The organization was now operating within a public policy arena and was no longer independent.
- The organization had lost its way as a voluntary organization both in relation to its core mission and in its understanding of finance and risk. In its aim to be in the 'first division' it stopped sharing risk with other voluntary organizations. Voluntary organizations do not have commercial objectives. The organization was seen as aggressive and out of touch with other voluntary organizations and local authorities.
- Investing in property is always dangerous particularly when financed by short-term loans. Short-term loans are risky and used when there is a potential high return and guaranteed cash flows to service them. Traditional financial management is to finance long-term acquisitions with long-term finance.
- Friends was overextended against its true asset base of its local groups' income, donations and its freehold property.
- Friends had no flexibility, with an overdraft and most expenditure being revenue on staff and servicing loans.

A different approach is that Friends was right to introduce proper terms and conditions for its staff but the trustees and senior staff needed to have a clear vision of what this would mean for the organization. It might have been better for the organization to divide itself into two different parts; for example, a service agency and a campaigning grass-roots organization. Certainly the business culture was allowed to 'take-over' the charity and it lost its vision. Voluntary organizations are about delivering the best possible service to their beneficiaries. Friends was never a property organization and special projects with housing associations would have allowed Friends to concentrate on its 'core business'. Voluntary organizations are sometimes in competition but they can also build alliances where a 'co-operative' culture of management would be more appropriate.

Providing information

Finding appropriate quantitative and qualitative information is vital to the success of companies as knowledge of their markets provides the basis on which to assess the organization's strategic direction. Does this analysis apply to voluntary organizations?

We would suggest the answer is yes with some very clear differences applicable to voluntary organizations, which involve:

- whether the organization is a fund seeker or grant maker;
- how the organization is legally constituted;
- information requirements and accountability.

Voluntary organizations, which are seeking funds, need to understand their sources of finance. How are those sources performing – are they in decline or are they still growing and are they being maximized? For example, in the mid-1980s government and public concern about HIV/AIDS meant that charities working in these fields found accessing government funds and raising money from the general public relatively easy. By the mid-1990s government funds were no longer available to the same extent and were stagnating or being withdrawn and public interest had moved on.

The profile of popular causes changes continually, for example in the eighteenth century donations to hospitals went into decline but support for victims of piracy was very popular. More recently, charities which help people with drug problems have been traditionally funded by government and trusts as they were not seen as a popular cause for the public to give to – drug addiction being seen as 'self-inflicted'. Public awareness of the drug problem and in particular the exposure in schools has meant that drug agencies can now seek funds more easily from the public. Intelligence about changing profiles of funding is therefore vital to the grant-seeking organization.

The trustees of a registered charity have a legal obligation to make an annual return to the Charity Commission which has become more prescriptive and proactive in requiring the trustees to not just account for the organization's funds but to explain how proactive they have been in achieving the organization's aims. SORP 2000 (discussed in Chapter 3) now has the designation 'reporting by charities' and requires an assessment of risk by the trustees. These reports are public documents, which can be accessed by the public from the Charity Commission or requested direct from the charity who may charge a reasonable fee to supply such information but cannot refuse to supply it – as the trustees of the Diana Princess of Wales Memorial Fund discovered when their affairs were discussed in the *Sunday Telegraph* on 30 May 1999 with comments such as:

> If this was a company, its shareholders would raise some sticky questions about corporate governance . . . to find out why takes a little effort . . . you have to ask for a copy of the full report and accounts.
>
> (Bennett 1999, B3)

Registered charities, no matter what their size, are therefore similar to companies in their disclosure requirements. Voluntary organizations, which are not registered charities or are not registered under other legislation, for example with the Registrar of Friendly Societies, are governed by their constitution document. Such organizations are therefore similar to sole traders or partnerships with a major exception. This exception relates back to the first point of source of finance. If they are seeking funds then the supplier of those funds is likely to demand information from the organization as a condition of finance. For private individuals the supplier of that finance is likely to be a bank and client confidentiality will ensure that the details remain undisclosed. For voluntary organizations the situation is more complex. The supplier of finance will seek information from the organization, which as a minimum will be published accounts and management information, ranging from a simple forecast of financial requirements to a full business plan. In addition, the funder is likely to publish or will make available details of funds it has provided. Public authorities have various disclosure requirements and have public accountability through elected representatives. Grant making by trusts and companies is slightly more complex and not subject to the same public accountability (see Chapter 5 on grants for SORP recommendation on disclosure). Grants to organizations are often disclosed by trusts in their annual reports and companies are required to disclose all donations to charities over £200; however, they do not have to say to whom the donation was made.

Sources of information

As only a minority of voluntary organizations are registered charities, the Charity Commission as a source of information is limited on the entire voluntary sector. Historically the Charity Commission was also a poor provider of information; critical reports on the Charity Commission in the 1980s (Woodfield 1987; NAO 1987), discovered that the Commission's database was paper organized, often out of date and incomplete. The Charity Commission has made great efforts to resolve these problems and the Registrar of Charities is now computerized and the Commission's website provides some elementary information about the numbers by income of registered charities. Owing to these limitations, other providers of information have filled this vacuum. Statistical sources of financial information are provided by:

- Charities Aid Foundation
- Caritas
- Directory of Social Change
- NCVO.

Charities Aid Foundation

The oldest supplier of information, the Charities Aid Foundation began compiling statistics of the largest fundraising and grant-making charities in the late 1970s. By 1988 the eleventh edition of *Charity Trends* was also providing details on corporate donors, surveys on personal giving and commentaries on taxation and government support to the voluntary sector. Annually published and now called *Dimensions*, there are now three volumes covering:

1   Income from government sources

2   CAF's top 500 fund-raising charities

3   Patterns of independent grant-making in the UK.

Caritas Data

Caritas Data is a private organization which publishes the *Dresdner RCM Global Investors Top 3000 Charities 2001* – previously *Baring Asset Management, Henderson Top 2000*, reflecting the name of the principal sponsor – started in the mid-1990s. This is a very large source of data, which is also available on CD, provides five-year details of income and expenditure of top charitable organizations and details of professional advisers and trustees. The publication also provides tables analysing the top 100 charities by different sources of income and statistical material on fund-raising and management costs.

Directory of Social Change

Publishes various surveys and analytical reports including an analysis of grant making by the National Lottery Charity Board.

National Council for Voluntary Organizations (NCVO)

Recognizing the absence of robust statistics on the sector as a whole, the NCVO persuaded the then Central Statistical Office, now the Office for National Statistics, to fund a research project in the mid-1990s to give an accurate estimate of the total income and expenditure of the UK voluntary sector. Originally a large survey was used to collect these first authoritative statistics. Since then it has been updated by maintaining databases of voluntary organizations and using financial data from published sources, most notably organizations' published accounts.

According to the latest edition of the UK Voluntary Sector Almanac (NCVO 2000), the overall current expenditure of the UK voluntary sector, as defined by general charities, is £13.4 billion. General charities employ over 485,000 paid workers and benefit from the voluntary efforts of over three million individuals. Gross current income stands at £14.2 billion (this is lower than the Charity Commission's estimate of over £20 billion primarily due to the double counting, i.e. inter-transfers in the charity sector from charitable trusts to fundraising charities), and general charity assets are estimated to be worth £65.1 billion with liabilities of £4.4 billion.

In addition to providing reliable statistics on the whole voluntary sector, the other goal of the Almanac is

> to provide policy makers, researchers, practitioners and other interested parties with a 'recognisable' and robust economic map of the UK voluntary sector.

> (NCVO 2000, p. 28)

To meet this aim the researchers have developed a conceptual model that places the economic activity of the voluntary sector in a wider context as illustrated:

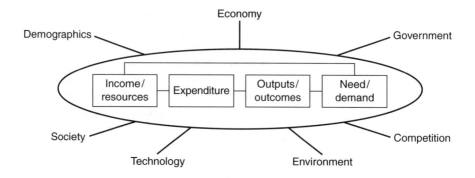

The model should assist the sector and individual organizations with the means to make informed decisions and assist in strategic planning.

Other sources of information

In the 1990s the sector saw the arrival of specific publications focusing on voluntary sector finance and management. The original *Charity Magazine* published by the Charities Aid Foundation has been incorporated into *Charity Finance*, a monthly journal for charity finance practitioners which has quality articles written by leading charity experts. Other charity magazines including *Voluntary Sector* (formerly *NCVO News*), and *Charity Times Third Sector* also feature charity finance articles. *Professional Fundraising*, as its name suggests, focuses primarily on the practice of raising funds. Academic journals, which cover charity research, include *Financial Accountability and Management* (FAM) and *Managerial Auditing Journal*.

In addition, there are sources of information from the various mid-sized firms of chartered accountants who have set up charity units, and most investment firms and solicitors have a regular 'charity newsletter'. The Charity Finance Directors' Group (CFDG) provides its members with regular briefings and has recently embarked on a new venture to establish a benchmarking service, which offers considerable opportunities for charities to improve their practices. The CFDG also publish yearly a *Charity Finance Year Book* which has informative articles and useful data such as model job descriptions and checklists.

Case study/role play – managing a financial crisis

'Victim' is a national 'umbrella body' charity founded in the late 1970s – its history to 2000 is as follows:

- 1975 – Steering group formed by non-statutory crime victim agencies who wanted to share experiences, work together and make sure their voice was heard. Chaired by the former Home Secretary.
- 1977 – First administrator appointed with a grant from the Home Office.
- 1980 – Victim incorporated and registered as a charity.
- 1981 – Management committee elected. Membership comprises twenty-two organizations throughout the UK.
- 1985 – Takes shared premises with the National Crime Statistics Forum (NCSF). The offices are rent-free.
- 1986 – Bill George appointed as director.
- Mid-1980s to mid-1990s – steady growth in activity and staff – matched by growth in service provision aided by the Home Office Voluntary Service Unit.
- 1985 – Victim has seven staff.
- 1987 – The Crime Prevention Unit at the Home Office begins to fund Victim to widen its role in education prevention. In particular, its 'Grannies lock up at night Campaign' is very effective, a personal project of Bill George.

By 1988 Victim has 10 staff, organized to help victim support agencies from its base in London: 85 members.

- 1991 – Victim is organized into three teams with a director and deputy.
- 1992 – Victim is also receiving grants from charitable trusts, staff now 14 and membership 130.

Membership of Victim is approved by the management committee; membership confers on local agencies a degree of 'official approval' particularly for local funding.

Membership fees are £20 per annum. The membership to date has been limited to voluntary groups.

A third of all known voluntary agencies working with crime victims are members.

Individual members from statutory services, primarily probation officers and police, are welcome as providing exchange with non-statutory agencies, but Victim retains its base as a voice for the non-statutory sector.

The management committee has agreed a target of 60 per cent of all voluntary agencies to be members of Victim.

- 1994 – VFM review – As part of its new initiative to seek value for money the government has instructed a review of all national funded organizations. The review undertaken by the Home Office accountant is broadly neutral but is critical of the accounting systems which are still manual and the lack of controls by the management committee. The report recommends the appointment of an honorary treasurer and the establishment of a finance committee.

- 1997 – A second report is undertaken by management consultants paid for at the behest of and imposed on Victim by the Home Office. The report has been initiated by the junior minister and officials following three successive annual general meetings that have seen major criticisms by members over the level and quality of services provided by Victim. This management report is critical of Victim noting:

1   The new finance committee had become a de facto executive; however, it had no authorization power. Its decisions have to always be referred back to the management committee, which meets only quarterly. Despite all members of the finance committee being members of the management committee there was a 'them and us' mentality developed. Increasingly, to get things done, chair's action was taken which further increased the alienation of some members. Committee servicing has become a complex matter with, as one management committee member noted, a mini-version of *War and Peace* arriving every three months of papers. Management committee meetings now last all day and the agenda is only completed by time constraint at the end.

2   The director Bill George has supported the growth of most organizations in the field. He has a national and growing international reputation in the field. He has become highly successful at raising non-statutory funds as the report highlighted, having reduced the proportion of the Home Office core grant to 50 per cent of total expenditure. Funding plans are not widely discussed in the organization. The director takes main responsibility for finance issues. Other staff have little or no contact with funders and have only limited knowledge of funders 'interests'.

3   The chair for the past ten years had been the former Home Secretary who died in 1997. The proposal by the director and some management committee members to appoint the last Home Secretary was not approved, as some wanted Victim to take a more independent line from government, while others thought a former Conservative Home Secretary would not be appropriate with a Labour Government and wanted a closer relationship. The vice-chair – the director of NCSF – has taken on both roles. The vice-chair is due to retire as NCSF director at the end of 1998.

4   Financial systems are still manual, the finance director is in his late 60s and does not want to retire until 70 – two years away because of his personal pension plan. An honorary treasurer has just been appointed. A partner with a leading firm of accountants, she has an intimate knowledge of both charity issues and victims work as she has audited a number of agencies in the field. For a year she was seconded as finance director of the largest agency. She has proposed radical changes in

Victim's systems and clashed personally with the director and chair at her second meeting over information and when the finance director is to retire and be replaced.

5 The deputy director and all but one of Victim's staff have been with the organization for over five years. While there are extensive meeting schedules the management report notes:

  i Meetings being used more for informing staff of decisions than for seeking their contribution.

  ii Meetings being rescheduled or cancelled at short notice, or items presented without adequate notification.

  iii Limited flows of information.

  iv Rivalries between staff. And some protection of contacts and information.

  v Widespread concern at the director's workload; the extent of his contacts and influence make it hard for others to act without consulting him first.

6 The world in which Victim operates is undergoing major changes. Support to victims of crime is now a major issue. The new government is committed to increasing resources for victims of crime. Equally the traditional split of statutory and voluntary agencies in this field is no longer appropriate. With close co-operation should Victim expand to encompass both statutory and voluntary services?

Victim's management committee meets to discuss the report and are presented with a twenty-five-page response written by the director containing both defensive comments and a series of task forces and dates for reports to deal with the issues raised by the consultants. The chair, who congratulates the director on his hard work in preparing such a professional response, dismisses a move by one member of the management committee to open a wider debate. The role of the committee, the chair comments, is to provide support and to assist the director. The two observers from the Home Office on the committee have withdrawn citing conflict of interest.

Nearly two years pass during which the honorary treasurer proposes a new structure based on a small trustee executive and a wider discussion forum with no management power. The current finance director is to retire shortly and a new person in their thirties will be joining with an IT and management accounting background. Sue Johnson, who had been an agency director has become the acting chair – Bill George would still like the former Home Secretary or another suitable national figure. John Gates, also a former director of an agency and now head of National Drugs Action, has become vice-chair.

The proposed new management structure is put before the AGM for approval. Just before the AGM in September 2000 the observer from the Home Office informs the officers and the director that Victim is to have as standard policy a 10 per cent cut in its core grant next year. Furthermore, they have not been satisfied with the response from the last management consultant and a further £40,000 is to be sliced from the grant to pay for another management consultant.

Victim is given two weeks to respond. It is early October 2000 and the new financial year begins in April. Financial information to end of September shows the budget is within 2 per cent correct. Funds available at that date are also given. Victim on behalf of other organizations holds funds for other charities.

The following week the new executive meet. All have been members of the previous management committee. The three officers have been confirmed. The director (Bill) attends the meeting with his deputy and the current finance director and begins with a plan to make some staff redundant and use the provisions when the chair stops him and says 'Before specifics let's look at the whole picture.'

Role play

Scene 1
Three people will play the senior staff (the director, deputy director and finance director). The rest will be the management committee. Take 20 minutes for each side to prepare their strategies and questions. The management committee will then interview the staff.

Scene 2
After the first role-play the 'staff' switch to being the Home Office officials who will meet the management committee. Take 20 minutes to prepare respective briefs. The Home Office officials will then interview the management committee and appraise their plan.

Financial information at 30.9.2000. Unaudited accounts show the 1999/2000 budget to be within 2 per cent accuracy.

	1999/2000(000) £	2000/01 *forecast* £
Income:		
Home Office core grant	256	269
Other grants	143	150
Non-grant income	112	116
Total income	511	535
Expenditure:		
Staff	380	388
Office costs	19	22
Premises	36	37
Printing, etc.	25	30
Travel	18	22
Conferences	20	22
Other	13	17
Total expenditure	511	538

Surplus (Deficit)	0	(3000)
Interest on bank balance	48,000	48,000

Funds information:	£
Cash at bank	538,000
Restricted funds	456,000
Designated funds	38,000
Office equipment provision	5,000
Maternity leave provision	6,000
Redundancy provision	18,000
Accumulated surplus	3,758

Pay scales

Pay rates are negotiated annually with the trade union which are based on local authority scales. Inner London Allowance is currently £2,200 p.a. Staff progress along the scale annually. A 6 per cent contribution to pension is made to all staff.

Director	45–49	44,340–46,539
Deputy director	40–44	41,637–43,821
Assistant directors (3)	35–39	33,898–39,097
Team members (8)	30–34	26,570–31,529
Admin/secretaries	16–22	12,961–15,484

Note: This case study has been prepared for the book. While based on certain events in a number of different agencies and persons the case study does not reflect any existing voluntary organization or persons by this or any other name.

3 Charity accounts –
the background

Introduction

Not all voluntary or non-profit-making organizations are charities. Tax legislation defines a charity as 'any body of persons or trust established for charitable purposes only', but does not define charitable purposes. To find out what are considered 'charitable purposes' one needs to go back to an Act of 1601 and a line of court decisions that have further developed and extended the definition.

The Pemsel case decision (1891) sets out four general headings for charitable purposes, which are still accepted today. These are:

1 the relief of poverty;
2 the advancement of education;
3 the advancement of religion;
4 other purposes of a charitable nature beneficial to the community not falling under any of the other headings.

Where a charity's purposes are within one of the first three headings, they are assumed to be charitable and for the benefit of the community, unless it is shown otherwise, but in the fourth category, a purpose must be shown to benefit the community in a way the law regards as charitable. A purpose contrary to public policy cannot be for the benefit of the community; not only will it not be charitable, but it will be void. Charitable status will not be accorded if the purposes:

- contain an over-element of self-help or
- are not exclusively charitable or
- are substantially political or
- involve profit distribution.

A wide range of purposes have been accepted in the past as charitable; usually this means that similar purposes of new organizations will also be accepted as charitable. These include, for example:

- the relief of sick, mentally or physically handicapped, disabled or old people, the rehabilitation of offenders or drug abusers and similar purposes;
- the provision of land and buildings for public use, such as recreation grounds and community halls;
- the conservation of the national heritage;
- the care of animals needing protection;
- the provision of sports facilities open to the public.

All these purposes are limited and defined by decisions of the courts. The Charity Commissioners for England and Wales (Charity Commission) will give a preliminary ruling on whether proposed purposes are charitable before an organization is actually formed and a formal application for charitable status is made. However, it is worth noting at this stage that the Charity Commissioners have no jurisdiction in Scotland or Northern Ireland. The legislation in Scotland relevant to charities is the Law Reform (Miscellaneous Provisions) (Scotland) Act 1990 whilst in Northern Ireland charities are governed by the Charities Act (Northern Ireland) 1964 and the Charities (Northern Ireland) Order 1987. There is no Charity Commission for either Scotland or Northern Ireland and the charity authority in the former is the Inland Revenue whilst in the latter it is the Department for Social Development.

A charity receives its status by virtue of its objectives and not its legal form. Therefore, a charity can be set up, for example, as a trust, an unincorporated association, a limited company, a friendly society, a housing association or by an Act of Parliament. A trust is normally used where one or more individuals want to settle property that will be used permanently for charitable purposes; this property is effectively what is known as 'permanent endowment'. In simple terms, an unincorporated association is a club whose members aim to achieve a common charitable purpose. A limited company normally will be incorporated as a company limited by guarantee without share capital.

A charity must have a governing document and the nature of this depends on the legal form of the charity. People who wish to form a charity are advised to engage a solicitor to prepare the governing documents, although some model governing documents exist (examples are obtainable from the Charity Commission).

The individuals in charge of running a charity are called trustees in the legislation governing charities, although they may go under other names in the charity's governing document. For example, a charity which is established as a company limited by guarantee has directors who are therefore the trustees.

Trustees of a charity have the duty to ensure that the charity's income is used only for the charitable purposes of the charity and that the charity complies with all the legal requirements imposed on charities. The Charities

Acts 1992 and 1993 made many changes to the law relating to charities, which came into effect in several stages. Their provisions cover charity accounts, charity documents, annual returns to the Charity Commissioners, public collections, the sale of land owned by charities and many other areas. The Charity Commission has produced a guide to the law, *A Guide to the Charities Acts, 1992 & 1993*, which is very clearly written, and charity trustees and administrators are recommended to read it.

Developments leading to the Charities Acts 1992 and 1993

In 1984 the Accounting Standards Committee (ASC) issued a discussion paper on charity accounting. In 1985 the ASC issued an exposure draft (ED38) of a statement intended to provide some uniformity in charity accounts. In 1987 the Woodfield Report, *Efficient Scrutiny of the Supervision of Charities*, commissioned by the government, highlighted a number of deficiencies regarding the monitoring and control of charities by the Charity Commission. In February 1988 the Committee of Public Accounts issued a report, *Monitoring and Control of Charities in England and Wales*, which was highly critical of the way in which charities were monitored and of charity financial management generally. In May 1988 the ASC issued the Statement of Recommended Practice No. 2 (Accounting by Charities) (SORP 2). It is interesting to note that SORP 2 went beyond the requirements of the Charities Acts of 1960 and 1985, something that Woodfield was very much in favour of, as was the Committee of Public Accounts (PAC). In the Summer of 1988 the Charity Commission published *Charity Accounts – Consultation Paper*, seeking views of the sector at large. In September 1988 the Home Office issued a consultation paper *The Regulation of Charitable Appeals in England and Wales*. On 16 May 1989 the government presented its White Paper *Charities: A Framework for the Future* which included many of the recommendations made by Sir Philip Woodfield in his report.

There then followed a considerable period of government inactivity after this flow of public documents. However, those in the charity world, particularly the Charity Finance Directors' Group (CFDG), continued to try and improve charity financial management.

At the beginning of May 1990 CFDG launched a campaign with the slogan 'Charities Act 199?' in an attempt to raise the issue with those MPs known to have associations with charities to try and get the government to act. However, all this came to nothing as *The Times* (July 1990) reported:

> Two Bills put forward by Government departments are thought to have been rejected for next year's programme, they include a Home Office Bill to reform the law covering charities . . .

Towards the end of July 1990 the parliamentary members of the All Party Charities Panel did put down an Early Day Motion in an attempt to get the government to bring forward legislation on charities as soon as possible. Like previous attempts this met with no success.

However, on 5 November 1991 the much sought after Charities Bill was finally published. CFDG in welcoming the Bill expressed sorrow that after 30 years since the last attempt to seriously legislate for charities, discussion on this Bill was to be somewhat curtailed. (By this stage CFDG's campaign had been running for over 18 months and putting that into context, the fact that the second reading in the House of Lords of the Bill was to be on 19 November and the debate was to be completed by 30 November was, to say the least, somewhat rushed.)

Strangely, all the discussion on the Bill took place in a committee of the House of Lords and it eventually went to the House of Commons in the final days just before the 1992 Election. In fact, no discussion took place in the lower house and it was effectively rushed through in well under three minutes on 16 March 1992.

The Charities Act 1992 was effectively a combination of several years' work and was subsequently consolidated into the Charities Act 1993.

Charities Acts 1992 and 1993

As a result of these Acts there was little immediate change in the way in which charity accounts were prepared and presented. However, since 1993 there have been considerable challenges for charity financial management in these areas.

s45 of the 1993 Act requires that every registered charity, over a certain size, should submit to the Charity Commission within ten months of the end of its financial year a full set of accounts professionally audited or independently examined, as laid down under s43.

Accounting records, sufficient to show and explain the transactions so as to disclose with reasonable accuracy the financial position, have to be kept. These records must show details of receipts and payments and of assets and liabilities and have to be kept for a period of at least six years after the end of the relevant financial year. However, if the charity ceases to exist it can, with the approval of the Charity Commission, dispose of those accounting records.

Some charities had to face, for the first time, having their accounts audited, as s43 puts it:

> By a person who:
> is in accordance with Section 25 of the Companies Act 1989 (Eligibility for Appointment) eligible for appointment as a company auditor; or
>
> is a member of a body for the time being specified in regulations under Section 44 below and is under the rules of that body eligible for appointment as auditor of a charity.

The practical effect is that the friendly bank manager of the charity, or whoever had looked at their accounts for years and 'audited' them, probably was no longer eligible. If the charity's gross income or total expenditure exceeded £250,000 for the relevant year or either of the two previous years, then it is no longer good enough, unless of course the individual happens to be qualified as outlined.

However, where the charity's gross income or total expenditure is less than £250,000 but more than £10,000, then it can choose to have the accounts examined independently. This is of course provided that its governing document doesn't call for audit, in which case it would still have to have its accounts audited. s43(3) of the Charities Act defines an independent examiner as 'an independent person who is reasonably believed by the trustees to have the requisite ability and practical experience to carry out a competent examination of the accounts.'

Some charities will have also found for the first time that they had to produce an annual report. This again must be prepared and then submitted to the Charity Commission within ten months of the end of the financial year. This probably meant not much change for the efficient well-run charities but for many thousands of others it created problems. Effectively, for most charities the report and the accounts would be produced as one document.

s42 of the 1993 Act dealing with the Annual Statement of Accounts lays down that a charity's accounts must comply 'with such requirements as to its form and contents as may be prescribed by regulations made by the Secretary of State.' s47 states quite clearly that the public are given the right to request a copy of the charity's most recent report and accounts. Although the charity may charge a reasonable fee for this, it must supply this information within two months of receiving the request.

We have already touched on some of the comments in s42 which also states that where the gross income of the charity does not exceed £100,000 in any year, then that charity need only prepare a receipts and payments account and a statement of assets and liabilities. This of course for the purist accountant is probably an anomaly – how can you have an asset/liabilities statement if you do not do accruals and only produce a receipts and payments account? This figure of £100,000 can be amended at any time by the order of the Secretary of State and where the figure is exceeded then full accrual-style accounts will have to be produced.

Statement of Recommended Practice (SORP) – accounting by charities

Following much consultation the final version of the SORP was issued in October 1995 just before the regulations. Although the Charities SORP had no recommended start date it was suggested by the Charity Commission that charities should adopt it as soon as possible. Accounting practice is such that to present a true and fair view, all standards, SORPs, etc., should be followed from the first accounting period following their production. This effectively meant immediate adoption. This section looks briefly at some of the significant changes from the original 1988 SORP 2.

SORP aim

The Charity Commission's prime aim and objective in publishing the SORP as set out in the document was

> To help improve the quality of financial reporting by charities and to assist those who are responsible for the preparation of the charity's annual report and accounts. The intention is that these recommendations will reduce the current diversity in accounting practice and presentation.
>
> (para 12)

Prescriptive approach

There was considerable debate about this particular approach but it was felt to be the best way to proceed in order to provide simplicity and ensure consistency. One of the principal aims of accounting by charities must be to improve accountability and make comparisons by members of the general public easier. It should also be borne in mind that the regulations, which are in themselves prescriptive, made much of the SORP mandatory.

Words

The formal narrative statement was considerably expanded, which meant that the trustees' report must include information about the charity's objects, activities and achievements as well as a commentary on the financial position of the charity. This reinforced the importance of the annual accounts and reports by strengthening the existing recommendation in SORP 2 (paras 26–28).

Numbers

One change which was probably the most radical of all was the introduction of a 'statement of financial activities' (SOFA). This essentially amalgamated the old income and expenditure account with the reconciliation and analysis of the movement of funds. The main purpose of the SOFA is to bring together all transactions in a single statement so as to present a complete picture which will give a true and fair view of the charity's affairs.

The assessment of the financial position of a charity is quite different to that of a business venture where profit is the main motive. A business raises capital which it uses to generate profits, which it either then distributes to those who contributed the capital, or retains in order to expand its profit-making capacity. On the other hand, a charity administers funds received for the purpose of its charitable objectives. Historically, accounting by charities has been based on a commercial-type profit-and-loss presentation where a surplus or a deficit on the income and expenditure account did not necessarily reflect the actual position of the charity.

This proposal therefore attempted to give the reader an understanding of how the incoming resources have been applied and was a step in the right direction, because it more clearly illustrated the way in which charities operate (paras 22 and 69–165).

Investments

Under SORP 2, investments held for long-term purposes could be shown on the balance sheet at either cost or market value, whilst the 1995 Charities SORP recommended that they be shown at market value under the general heading 'fixed assets' as a separate category. It was felt that market value best represents a true and fair view of the value of these assets to the charity, given the duty of the trustees to administer the portfolio of investment assets so as to obtain the best investment performance without undue risk.

It went on to recommend that if investments were held as current assets, for example where they were to be sold without reinvestment, then they should be valued at the lower of cost or net realizable value in the same way as other current assets (paras 174–182 and 192–198).

As far as the treatment of gains and losses is concerned the Charities SORP recommended a separate section, after the 'income and expenditure section', setting out in full detail both the realized and unrealized gains and losses (para 132).

Overhead costs

The definitions of fundraising and administration costs were amended and improved. It is curious that in SORP 2 although there were several references to publicity costs, these were not defined anywhere. The opportunity was taken to do so by combining them with fundraising (Appendices 1.10 and 1.16).

A new category was introduced so that much of what was reported under the heading of administration would, where appropriate, effectively be described as 'support costs', which are those costs incurred in respect of supporting direct charitable activities (paras 150–153 and Appendix 1.22).

Summarized accounts

Where produced, these have to be approved formally by the trustees and accompanied by a statement from the auditors that they are consistent and accurate by reference to the full detailed accounts. Many charities issue publicity material, containing accounts information, which is often highly abbreviated and partly in graphical or other pictorial form. All such information now had to follow the rules laid out in the Charities SORP (paras 213–222).

Trading activities

The trading results of a charity's subsidiary have to be shown in the main on the face of the SOFA, under the separate heading 'trading activities'. Where only the net income/expenditure is shown then there has to be a full disclosure in the notes showing the profit and loss account for each trading activity. This is an attempt to provide a systematic approach to dealing with trading activities, particularly where this is done through a subsidiary company (paras 121–127).

Although this relates to the SOFA there has to be a full consolidation of assets and liabilities on the charity's balance sheet (para 66).

Branches

This change is one that had a considerable effect on the way in which a number of charities produced their accounts. Accounting for branches was tightened and all branch transactions must be reflected in the charity's own accounts, whether or not the funds were received by the parent charity by the year end. Similarly, all assets and liabilities of the branch should also be incorporated into the charity's own balance sheet.

Many charities did not include all their branches' transactions in their accounts in detail and often the money that the branch remitted to the charity was included net of costs and shown under donations. The Charities SORP effectively recommended a change to this way of operation which led to an increase in the accounting effort required both by the volunteers at branch level and at the head office of the charity (paras 45–49 and Appendix 1.1).

Accounting concepts

In 1988 SORP 2 made little reference to fundamental accounting concepts. The 1995 version makes explicit reference to them, and with the notable exception of smaller charities whose gross income is less than £100,000, all others now have to prepare their accounts in accordance with the accounting concepts of an accrual basis, consistency, going concern and prudence. In the case of those smaller charities which are permitted by law to produce receipts and payments accounts, only the concept of consistency need apply (paras 32 and 33).

'Light touch' approach

The effective removal from the SORP regime of the majority of charities has occurred with the cut-off for the preparation of full accrual accounts set at £100,000 gross income per year. Furthermore, those charities with an annual income of less than £10,000, i.e. the 'light touch' regime, need not have their accounts reviewed (independent examination/audit), nor submit them to the Charity Commission unless they are specifically asked for them.

To allay the fears of many in the charity world, two separate guides to the SORP for these smaller charities were published by the Charity Commission. These charities only need to refer to paragraphs 13–21 of the SORP. The standard format of accounts, shown as an appendix, complies with the recommended practice for receipts and payments accounts.

Glossary

The revised SORP includes a very comprehensive glossary of definitions which has been provided to enable readers not used to certain accounting terms to follow the document more easily (Appendix 1).

Conclusion

The prescriptive approach taken in the revised Charities SORP has undoubtedly changed the way in which many charities manage their finances and led to many more disclosures in the published accounts.

Review of SORP

As promised three years earlier the Charity Commission launched, in September 1998, a review of the SORP to which charities and those interested had until 7 December 1998 to submit their comments and views. The major points on which the Charity Commission requested opinions were:

- **Editorial**. Parts of the SORP need to be rewritten to remove potential ambiguities. There is also scope to improve the layout and the example accounts and to provide some commentary on how the SORP relates to individual accounting standards.
- A number of aspects of **consolidation, branches and combined charities** need to be rethought.
- **Trading**. Apart from consolidation issues when trading subsidiaries are involved, there are more general questions on how to categorize income and expenditure from some types of trading.
- **Accruals accounting for incoming resources**. There is a need for greater detail on how to account for certain categories of incoming resources, particularly legacies.

- **Expenditure classifications**. Further thinking is needed about the nature of administration and support costs and the disclosure requirements for allocated and apportioned expenditure.
- **Measurement and valuation principles,** in particular how these apply to fixed assets (including investments), investment gains and losses and the recognition of liabilities and grants payable within the accounts.
- **Summary income and expenditure account and summary accounts**. The question of when and why these are needed should be clarified.
- **Fund accounting**. Additional guidance is felt to be required in a number of areas relating to the use of restricted and designated funds.
- **Reserves**. Guidance on the disclosure of reserves should be expanded in line with the Commission's leaflet.

The Charity Commission produced in the Spring of 1999 a short report drawing together all the comments that they had received. A committee was appointed with the task of reviewing the operation of the Charities SORP in light of the comments received.

Charity Commission SORP consultation

Generally it was recognized that the SORP had largely met its aims by both improving the quality of financial reporting by charities and reducing the diversity in charity accounting and presentation. Of the 234 respondents, 104 expressed opinions on the general view of the SORP, 77 were supportive, 15 limited that support but only 12 did not approve.

Whilst it was agreed that fundamental changes were not required there was a view expressed that certain areas of the SORP needed clarification, that ambiguities which existed should be removed but that the SORP should not be amended to the detriment of the majority just to please a small minority!

The changes

This SORP has been completely rewritten although there are no major changes to the structure of the accounts nor are there any requirements that should be regarded as difficult. However, because of this rewriting, those preparing and reviewing charity accounts will need to look at all the paragraphs that apply to the charity for whom they are preparing or reviewing accounts. The Charity Commission makes the point that whilst the document is regarded as recommended best practice, charities are at liberty to provide additional information in order to give the reader an enlarged view of the activities and achievements of the charity concerned.

Unfortunately, because of the diversity of the sector, in terms of size, structure and activity, this revised SORP has increased in length.

Additionally, certain sections have been included at the specific request of charities to deal with special situations although there are few, if any charities, to which all parts of the SORP will apply and obviously charities should therefore ignore those sections that do not apply to them. As it is not possible or indeed desirable to be prescriptive on every issue, those who prepare and review charity accounts will, as usual, have to exercise their judgement in certain areas.

This revised SORP is principally a guide for those who prepare or audit or examine charity accounts. Therefore, it has been written in accounting language and as a result may not be easily understood by those who have little or no knowledge of accounting principles and standards. However, trustees are of course ultimately responsible for the resources and finances of their charity as they are reflected in the accounts. Therefore, those trustees who have little or no knowledge of accounting matters will need to seek reassurance themselves on these matters from colleagues, staff or professional advisors who do have the necessary financial and accounting background.

All the anomalies have been removed, particularly those relating to consolidation, the need for a separate income and expenditure account and trading activities. As long ago as September 1997, former Charity Commissioner John Bonds is on record as agreeing in respect of accounting for investment gains and losses that

> If in such a case a charity decides to disclose total investment gains/losses (both realised and unrealised), under one heading 'net investment gains/losses' on the Statement of Financial Activities, the Charity Commission will not raise any objections, nor will it use its power to return accounts for rectification and resubmission, provided that this departure from the SORP is adequately disclosed and justified.
>
> (Bonds 1997)

Therefore this change has been made to the SORP. All issues on which the Charity Commission specifically made it clear that they intended to change or improve have been amended.

Probably the most significant change is in the name of the document. In both the 1988 and 1995 versions it was *Accounting by Charities* which has now become in the 2000 version *Accounting and Reporting by Charities*. This was a deliberate attempt by the Charity Commission to ensure that more emphasis is placed by charities on the Trustees' Report which the Commission felt was not being given the effort it required.

One issue that many would very much like to have seen resolved is that of the inherent inconsistencies between the accounting treatment required by a charitable company and that of an unincorporated charity. These in particular relate to the conflicts between the Companies Act 1985 and the Charities Act 1993. There are also inconsistencies between the reporting thresholds and the need for audit. There are further inconsistencies in areas such as the auditors' duty of whistle blowing which under the 1993 Charities Act only affects unincorporated charities. Although some of the points under this particular issue went beyond the strict parameters of the review, many of these fundamental issues have been addressed.

What's new

A very detailed and self-explanatory new section specifically dealing with charitable companies should resolve all the anomalies and problems flowing from the 1995 Charities SORP (see further Chapter 4). New subsections dealing with transactions with trustees (including their expenses) and connected persons certainly answer all the queries received in response to the Charity Commission request of September 1997.

In the Trustees' Annual Report, trustees are asked to comment on their reserves (the policy, the level and the justification), their investment and grant-making policies and their internal controls (see further Chapter 5). There is very detailed cross-referencing to Statements of Standard Accounting Practice (SSAPs) and Financial Reporting Standards (FRSs) and an appendix which is a summary of all existing accounting standards showing their application to charities (see further Chapter 3).

For smaller charities it is proposed that the threshold for reporting resources expended as set out in the SORP should be increased from £100,000 to £250,000 per year (see further Chapter 3).

Revised/extended

The detailed requirements for narrative information (as distinct from legal and administrative information) in the Trustees' Annual Report have been reduced in order to encourage charities to expand on their activities rather than answer a series of questions (see further Chapter 5).

In the Statement of Financial Activities (SOFA) the presentation of incoming resources and resources expended has been altered to provide a more logical layout and fit in with the way in which charities handle their transactions and prepare their accounts. Incoming resources and resources expended of a similar nature will be grouped together and will be consolidated where there are subsidiary undertakings (instead of summarizing the results of non-charitable trading activities of subsidiary undertakings on a one-line basis). This will make the accounts more transparent (see further Chapter 3).

The rules for recognizing incoming resources have been restated with the emphasis now placed on three factors: entitlement, certainty and measurement. The information on accounting for legacies has been extended and instead of being one paragraph now consists of six paragraphs to more clearly deal with the thorny issue of what to disclose, when to disclose and the accrual situation. The guidance in relation to dealing with intangible income and donations in kind, for example donated facilities, beneficial loan arrangements, donated services or services from volunteers, has been clarified. They now need only be recorded where another party is bearing the financial cost of those resources as supplied and the benefit is quantifiable and measurable.

The section on trading has been completely revised, brought up to date and trading is now more accurately defined as 'operating activities' using accounting rather than taxation rules, with all income from non-charitable trading combined under one heading (see further Chapter 4).

The requirements for disclosing grants are set out more fully with the emphasis on providing the analysis and explanation necessary to understand how the grants made by a charity relate to its objects. Disclosure is required when grants total at least £250,000 in the year or 5 per cent of total resources expended (see further Chapter 4).

The definition of fundraising costs has been improved and replaced by the more correct terminology of 'cost of generating funds'. Again this has become an area that is open to considerable misinterpretation in the four years of accounts that have so far been produced under the SORP. Investment management fees can be included under 'costs of generating funds' provided that they are disclosed separately in the notes to the accounts as applies to all material items of cost under this heading. Accounting for separate funds has been further explained (see further Chapter 4).

The balance sheet section is one area where probably the most radical changes have taken place. However, they are only radical in the extent that there is a considerable extension from what currently appears. This has been done to take account of FRS11, 12 and 15 which deal with respectively 'Impairment of Fixed Assets and Goodwill', 'Provisions, Contingent Liabilities and Contingent Assets' and 'Tangible Fixed Assets'. These three FRSs have all been issued since the 1995 Charities SORP which therefore needed to be updated to take account of them, particularly in relation to inalienable and historic fixed assets, liability accounting and the revaluation of fixed assets (see further Chapter 3).

The section on the Cashflow Statement has been amended and updated to take account of FRS1 which was revised in 1996 after the publication of the Charities SORP (see further Chapter 3). The section on smaller charities has been extended and a greater emphasis placed on accounting aspects (see further Chapter 3). The consolidation of subsidiary undertakings has been expanded to replace the previous section on consolidation and should certainly overcome the problems previously faced (see further Chapter 4).

Charity Commission aim

All charity trustees have a duty to keep proper accounting records for their charity that set out and explain all the charity's transactions. The revised SORP effectively provides guidance on how this should be done annually in relation to the resources entrusted to the charity and the activities it has undertaken. The SORP applies to all charities regardless of their size, constitution or complexity except in those cases where a more specialized SORP applies, such as that for registered social landlords. Therefore, the Charity Commission expects charities to comply fully with this or any other applicable SORP and where they do not then the charity's accounts should identify this and provide a full explanation. Where the Charity Commission feels that the explanation is unsatisfactory or no explanation is given then the matter may be raised with the charity concerned and, in exceptional circumstances, the Charity Commission may institute an enquiry.

Quite clearly the Charity Commission's objective in publishing these recommendations is to improve the quality of financial reporting by charities and to assist those who are responsible for the preparation of the charity's Annual Report and Accounts. The intention is that these recommendations will reduce the diversity in accounting practice and presentation. In all but exceptional circumstances charities preparing accrual accounts should follow this SORP in order for their accounts to give a true and fair view. However, the impact of the SORP will, depending upon the size and complexity of a charity's operation, be different and to help smaller charities in particular the Charity Commission produces a range of simplified guidelines.

General principles

Accounts intending a true and fair view must be prepared on the going concern assumption and the accruals concept and provide information that is relevant, reliable, comparable and understandable. Where charities can choose to prepare receipts and payments accounts then the information must be comparable which is normally achieved through the application of consistent policies. In meeting the obligation to prepare accounts that show a true and fair view, consideration has to be given to the standards laid down in Statements of Standard Accounting Practice (SSAPs), Financial Reporting Standards (FRSs) and Urgent Issues Task Force Abstracts (UITFs) issued or adopted by the Accounting Standards Board which are relevant to the charity's circumstances and accounts. The revised SORP provides guidance and interpretation of the most suitable application of accounting standards for charities but it is supplementary to those standards and does not repeat all of their requirements.

Timing

The Charity Commission committee to review the SORP completed its work in June 2000 and clearance from the Accounting Standards Board was obtained in July 2000. The revised SORP was published on 16 October 2000 and became effective for accounting periods beginning on or after

1 January 2001. However, early adoption was encouraged by the Charity Commission. The SORP 2000, a booklet containing a series of example accounts and a guide to the changes aimed specifically at non-accountants are available on the Charity Commission's website (www.charity-commission.gov.uk).

Research on charity accounts and SORP compliance

A strong argument for consistent principles and practice in charity accounts presentation, as well as recommendations for such principles, accompanied Bird and Morgan-Jones' (1981) survey of charity accounts. They analysed 85 charities' accounts from a list of 1973's 100 largest fund-raising charities, ranked by legacy and gift income, and found a wide variety of practice in many aspects of accounting treatment:

- **Legacies**: often shown on receipts basis, although other income and expenditure shown on accruals basis; in some cases taken direct to balance sheet, or released over years through equalization account
- **Investment income/interest**: mixture of cash and accruals basis, sometimes within same charity
- **Fund-raising**: receipts often shown net of fund-raising costs
- **Branches**: transactions and assets often not consolidated, or inconsistent
- **Consolidation of trading**: some charities consolidated subsidiary activity, some did not; some cases of evidence of related company, but treatment not clear
- **Fixed assets**: wide range of treatments of write-off or capitalization and depreciation
- **Fund accounting**: wide range of treatments of transactions and fund balances, sometimes within same charity
- **Asset valuation**: wide range of valuation methods for investment properties, working properties and investments

Bird (1986) surveyed the published financial statements of 47 large charities for accounting periods ending between December 1982 and December 1983. The survey again found a wide range of accounting treatments, with the following areas showing much the same variety of treatments as in the 1981 study:

- Legacies
- Investment income/interest
- Consolidation of trading
- Fixed assets
- Fund accounting
- Asset valuation

The report concluded: 'The lack of any standardisation of presentation means that it takes the user a long time to discover each piece of information – or to reach the conclusion that it is not disclosed anywhere' (Bird 1986, p. 49).

Ashford (1991, p. 23) did not attempt 'a complete review of charity's conformity with SORP 2', but concentrated on 'accounting policies and particularly the content of the Income & Expenditure account'. The study reviewed 56 charity accounts ending between December 1987 and December 1988, and again found a range of practice similar to that found by Bird. The report concluded that this 'diversity of approaches ... suggests either that charities have a widespread disregard for the recommendations of SORP 2 or more likely, that SORP 2 allows different interpretations' (Ashford 1991, p. 48).

Gambling *et al.* (1990) carried out a survey of the effects of the first version of the Charity SORP, issued in May 1988, on six unnamed charities. It is significant that the authors state in their conclusion:

three of our charities had not heard of either the SORP or the White Paper [on Charities, May 1989] (when asked in October/November 1989).

(p. 33)

Their main conclusions (page 34) can be summarized:

• **Independent examination**: 'It seems unlikely that the independent examiner ... will be able to understand the accounting principles and policies suggested by the SORP, given that the independent examiner need not be a qualified practising accountant and may thus be unfamiliar with complex disclosure requirements.'
• **Fixed assets**: neither capitalization/depreciation nor wholesale expensing were likely to be generally acceptable. They suggested that expensing everything, while disclosing by note fixed assets' cost/valuation, might be more acceptable.
• **Charity's transactions with trustees or employees**: unnecessary.
• **Restrictions on funds and future commitments**: more research was needed on charities' alleged unwillingness to disclose these.
• **Expenditure categories**: classification into administration, fund-raising and publicity would generate controversy and 'more details of what will be involved is needed.'

Hines and Jones (1992, p. 49) carried out 'a longitudinal study of large charities' reporting practices from 1988–90 ... to assess whether or not the SORP actually did have a significant impact upon the accounting practices of UK charities immediately after its introduction.' They reviewed the accounts in a three-year sequence of 40 charities who responded from the top

54 charities – on the basis of voluntary income – listed in the Charities Aid Foundation Charity trends 1985/86.

Their main conclusion was that 'there was no evidence to suggest that SORP 2 had a significant impact upon the accounting practices of UK charities' and continued 'the study found compliance with a selection of the SORP's main recommendations to be steady at about 75 per cent' (p. 63). They went further:

> Since SORP 2 has done little to reduce the diversity of the accounting practices of charities, either a mandatory accounting pronouncement or governmental legislation is required.
>
> (Hines and Jones 1992, p. 63)

Williams and Palmer (1998) examined the state of charity accounting just before it moved into a new era of the issue of the Charities SORP and Accounting Regulations by providing some kind of perspective as to how much charity accounting had changed since the early 1980s using Bird's survey as a benchmark. They carried out a detailed review of 83 charities' accounts, drawn from a sample of 6,000, originally selected for a survey to establish the level of charities' contribution to the economy in 1995/96. Their summary of findings about the distance between charity accounting practice in 1994/95 and the requirements of the new SORP showed a large distance in the following areas:

- **The statement of financial activities**: replaced the old income and expenditure account but was only adopted by a minority of charities.
- **Funds passed direct to reserves**: by 'many charities' – 60 per cent of large and 38 per cent of medium charities passed funds direct to reserves instead of passing them through the SOFA.
- **Restricted resources**: inadequate or no information provided by many charities – 56 per cent large, 88 per cent medium.
- **Grants payable**: a majority of charities not following SORP.
- **Investments**: market value: not used by a majority of charities.

In their conclusions, the authors state 'we have said nothing about auditors in this survey as they were outside its scope, but they are central to the process of improvement of charity financial reporting standards. In too many cases audit opinions mentioned nothing about accounting standards not being followed. Also firms allowed obscure and confusing sets of accounts to be given their *imprimatur*' (p. 278). They ended: 'Finally, it may be that many charities will ignore the new SORP, in which case we will need to see how deep is the resolve of the new Charity Commission regime to enforce its *diktat*' (p. 278).

Fairbairn (1998) undertook a study to assist the trustees of the City Parochial Foundation, a large grant-giving charitable trust, on the process of monitoring grants they had made. One of the primary aims of the study was 'to provide the Foundation with a clearer picture of the need for a continuing financial monitoring role' (Fairbairn 1988, p. 1). To this end, he circulated questionnaires to 70 organizations funded by the Foundation and the Trust for London, and visited 25 of those organizations. Fifty-nine questionnaires were completed and returned. The findings overall suggested widespread and considerable room for improvement in charities' internal financial administration and control. In the section on financial reporting the general findings could have been drawn from the earlier studies: 'Despite the publicity surrounding the SORP, many charities and their auditors had not got the message. There seemed to be an alarming inconsistency in the preparation of accounts. If funders or indeed the Charity Commission were to attempt to use the financial statements for any meaningful assessment they were likely to find them lacking' (p. 5). The report continued: 'some [charities] said they were leaving the SORP for their auditors to deal with – but annual accounts (for 1996/97) . . . showed that there were alarming deficiencies in the understanding of the SORP within many accountancy practices' and 'accounts were commonly signed off with no comparative figures, no separation of restricted funds and a lack of notes to the accounts' (Fairbairn 1998, p. 6).

Lamont's (1998a) report on SORP implementation cited research by KPMG's charities unit on the 'experiences and views' of 319 charities, with income ranging from under £100,000 to well over £100 million. This research showed the following approximate percentages of charities reporting actual or possible departures from the SORP:

- Legacy income   78 per cent
- Grants payable   68 per cent
- Grants receivable   60 per cent
- Investment gains   32 per cent

Lamont concluded that clearly charities were having problems complying with new regulations and that further training was required.

Connolly and Hyndman (2000) reviewed the impact of the SORP on the financial statements of the 100 largest fundraising charities. They concluded:

The results provide evidence that charity accounts have improved significantly since the early 1980s, where improvement is seen in terms of increasing compliance with recommended practice. For example with respect to legacies, Bird and Morgan-Jones (1981) found that approximately half of the charities surveyed either credited legacies directly to reserves (thus bypassing the income and expenditure account) or split them between revenue and reserves. It was suggested that such treatments were used to reduce the revenue result and give the appearance of being in need of funding. Both SORPs provided clarity about the correct accounting treatments and recommended much clearer and more obvious disclosure of legacies. The analysis of the 1996/97 accounts showed 92 per cent of charities following the recommended treatment of the revised SORP (1995). Similar patterns are seen when considering other dubious accounting treatments. Bird and Morgan-Jones found 22 per cent of charities expensing fixed assets on acquisition and of those which capitalised, 40 per cent did not subsequently depreciate. The figures for 1996/97 show almost 100 per cent compliance on both these counts.

(Connolly and Hyndman 2000)

A problem, which the authors identify, was in their sample, which focused solely on large fund-raising charities, which because they are seeking funds from the public, and are subject to the greatest scrutiny, are more likely to comply and promote best practice than charities which do not seek funds from the public.

The top 100 fund-raising charities identified by the Charities Aid Foundation since the mid-1980s have also been subject to numerous research studies and, as the authors themselves acknowledge:

generalisations beyond this group should be made with caution.

(Connolly and Hyndman 2000, p. 98)

The latest research study on SORP compliance of 125 top charities (Palmer *et al.* 2001) discovered a number of major divergences from SORP compliance, mirroring the findings of earlier research. This study found that, while a number of divergences are revealed in accounting policies and other notes to the accounts, hardly any are specifically disclosed *as departures from the SORP*. It was noted that the signing off of so many non-compliant accounts leaves unanswered the question of whether the audit firms do not understand the SORP requirements, or do, but do not apply them as rigorously as one might hope. It also questions whether the Charity Commission's reliance on the adequacy of auditors' reports, particularly for many small- and medium-sized charities, can be justified. The research identified the need for further study into the monitoring of SORP implementation and suggested that it would be useful to extend the research into the reasons behind non-compliance, in particular asking the following questions:

• To what extent is it ignorance of the requirements – on the part of charities and auditors?
• To what extent is it resistance, and, if so, is the resistance well thought through or merely unwillingness to change?
• How can charities – and the Charity Commission – rely on audit firms getting it right?

The Charity Commission claims to be generally happy with the larger charities (Ashford 2000) but concluded on SORP compliance:

> Few accounts the Commission has seen follow both the spirit and the letter of the SORP in every respect. But for the better ones, any shortcomings that are there don't give us great cause for concern (and the auditors have normally signed an unqualified report). With this greater consistency the Commission can now start doing what the SORP intended: stop worrying about the accounting and concentrate on what is happening in the charities behind the accounts. It is becoming much easier to spot problems and issues of concern and even to start building up pictures of what the accounts often look like for different groups of charities. The large task of improving the consistency of the accounts of smaller charities will continue.
>
> (Ashford 2000, p. 95)

4 Published accounting standards

Introduction

What is the bottom line when there is no bottom line? One of the biggest problems with charity accounting is that from a reporting point of view it needs to be significantly different from commercial accounts reporting and given the accounting regime in the United Kingdom this has not been possible. Considerable changes have taken place over the past ten to fifteen years in an attempt to distinguish more clearly between a set of accounts produced for a commercial organization and that produced for a charity. We have seen the development from receipts and payments to income and expenditure to the Statement of Financial Activities (SOFA) and in this chapter we will look at this in some detail. We will also make the point that when it comes to other accounting statements, such as the balance sheet and cashflows, there are few if any differences between the way in which a commercial organization reports and charities report, although the gap is widening. However, first we will take a look at the thorny question of who charity accounts are actually prepared for.

Stakeholder reporting

The debate about stakeholders and stewardship in the charity world has been around for some considerable time (Leat 1988; Vinten 1989) but it effectively started to come to a head with the publication of the draft revised Statement of Recommended Practice, as it then was, in 1993. The Charity Commission committee spent some considerable time debating the issue of stakeholders, in particular in relation to the audience for the accounts for which it was effectively producing the Charities SORP (Palmer 1995). This exercised the minds of the committee considerably. As a result, no firm conclusions were reached except a consensus that the accounts were not just being produced solely for the benefit of the Charity Commission. This decision probably resulted in the Commission requiring auditors and independent examiners to 'whistle blow'.

The House of Lords debate on the Charities Bill in 1991 had discussed who were the recipients of charity reports and accounts. We need to remember that this subject is not just about the financial affairs of charities. This matter is about reporting generally.

All those with an involvement in charity, commonly described as stakeholders – be they donors, beneficiaries, trustees, employees, creditors, grantees, etc. – have the right to expect that the resources entrusted to a charity are being used cost-effectively and efficiently. It must therefore be part of the reporting procedure to ensure that this happens.

Thus it is probably sensible at this stage to define what is meant by stakeholders, if of course this is possible! Put very simply, it is everyone with any interest whatsoever in the particular charity. This, therefore, is what makes stakeholder reporting so difficult a topic and very different perhaps from the corporate sector and even the public sector. Quite clearly, the tighter you define stakeholders then the easier the reporting becomes.

Bruce (1994) makes the point that stakeholders are a 'target group of people who are crucial to a charity marketing approach'. He goes on, however, to define stakeholders as just one of four classes of charity customer, the other three being beneficiaries, supporters and regulators. However, these are probably only really classes of stakeholders rather than a stakeholder being a class of charity customer. This definition illustrates the vagaries of opinion in the charity world that exist on this particular topic.

Wise (1995), seems to be agreeing with the earlier definition of stakeholders, and not with that of Bruce, when he makes the point:

> Businesses exist for the benefit of their shareholders. Charities exist for the benefit of their beneficiaries. But, in both cases it is recognised that regard must be paid to other stakeholders if the primary stakeholder interests are to be best served.
>
> (Wise 1995, p. 32)

Whether or not the beneficiaries, supporters, regulators or customers are stakeholders is probably irrelevant. What remains important is that whatever definition is accepted, one does need to report to all these groups.

Indeed, all charity accounts and the reports thereon do have a constant and well-informed readership in the officials of the Charity Commission and those of the Inland Revenue and HM Customs and Excise as well (particularly in the latter two cases in Scotland and Northern Ireland). All these bodies demand copies of financial statements and can, and do, demand further explanation of matters which they find unclear. Charity trustees therefore may find it useful to prepare the trustees' report as if it were addressed to these officials in the first instance.

From the research listed in Chapter 3, reporting generally by charities has improved over the past few years. This must be encouraged and charities need to be far more open than they have been in the past about their activities, for example by explaining how they are achieving their objectives.

The SORP goes to great lengths to set out the sort of information that it wishes to see in the trustees' annual report, particularly of a narrative nature, as Wise (1995, p. 106) states:

> Strategic review of performance should involve a balanced view of stakeholder perspectives and activities within the charity.

Research projects cited in Chapter 3 into the financial reporting by charities often tend to highlight the problem of stakeholder reporting, which they perceive to be peculiar to the charity world but which is becoming less so as more and more companies are finding that they too need to take account of their customers, suppliers, staff, and so on.

Mattocks suggests:

> The purpose of a charity's report and accounts should serve as a medium between the charity and the public. Donors (potential or otherwise) should be properly informed about the position of a charity. A charity's annual report and accounts are therefore public documents and should not require professional skills to examine them (i.e. those of a professional accountant).
>
> (Mattocks 1992, p. 78)

This is a very sensible and logical conclusion as too often the only public reporting done by a charity is through its annual report and accounts which are often meaningless, because of the way in which they are presented, to all but the very informed, qualified reader. This is certainly one area where charities could learn from the corporate world where accounts have become much more informative and far easier to read than the average set of charity accounts. Charities must go on improving their reporting to all those who have an interest in the operation of the charity, not just to meet legal requirements but to ensure that they continue to enjoy public support.

Accounting for smaller charities

As the SORP puts it: 'a smaller charity is one which due to its size does not have to adopt all the requirements of this SORP.'

Receipts and payments accounts

The majority of charities are relatively small with very simple structures and no control of other charities. The vast majority of these have cash and deposit accounts but few other assets. For these small charities, currently defined for these purposes as those with a gross income or total expenditure for any one year of less than £100,000, accounts may be produced on a receipts and payments basis. This is provided of course that the charity is not a limited company and attention should also be paid to the governing document as to its instructions relating to the preparation of accounts. Even so, it is recognized that the trustees of smaller unincorporated charities may still feel happier preparing annual accounts for the various funds of their charity on the more traditional cash basis.

The only fundamental accounting concept that has to be applied will be that of consistency of accounting treatment. In other words, the way in which the accounts are produced each year should be consistent with the year before. Obviously the accruals concept will not apply and neither will there be a need for prudence or 'the going concern basis concepts to be used'.

The SORP recommended what it described as 'functional classification for reporting of costs', that is to show in the SOFA what has been expended on charitable objectives, publicity and fund-raising, and management and administration costs. However, the regulations make it clear that smaller charities who have not opted to use accrual accounting as the basis for reporting their figures will not have to provide a functional classification split of costs. In other words, in the receipts and payments account they will continue to show expenditure on the natural classification basis, for example salaries, wages, and so on.

A number of matters need to be disclosed in the annual report if not shown by way of note to the accounts. These include grants of £1,000 or more to institutions, payments to trustees by the charity or its subsidiary, trustee indemnity insurance and any ex-gratia payments made by the charity stating clearly the authority under which they were made.

As the amounts involved for a small charity are, in aggregate, quite small in relation to the whole of the sector, regulation as to the method of production is dispensed with. However, to demonstrate compliance with the terms of trust, each legally distinct fund administered by the charity will normally need to be accounted for by a separate receipts and payments account. The same result can also be achieved by grouping the funds together in a combined account and using notes to analyse the individual funds.

As the SORP 2000 itself makes clear, the receipts and payments accounts and the statements of assets and liabilities (Charity Commission 2000, Section 3.2.2) may be organized in any way which the trustees feel is appropriate. There is therefore considerable flexibility here but anyone producing receipts and payments accounts should make certain that they have read thoroughly and understood paragraphs 350–356 of the SORP 2000.

Statement of assets and liabilities

A statement of assets and liabilities will be needed. This effectively is a list of the cash and non-cash assets and liabilities of the charity as at the period end-date of the receipts and payments account. The Charity Commission guide *Accounting for the Smaller Charity* sets out on page 32 an example of the type of statement required. Where the charity has legally distinct funds, for example an endowment or special trust fund, then the assets and liabilities of each fund must be distinguished from each other in the statement of assets and liabilities. It is not necessary to place a value on the assets that the smaller charity owns as at the balance sheet, unless of course it is felt that the valuation is essential to a meaningful description of the asset.

Notes to the accounts

For the smaller charity which is preparing accounts on the receipts and pay-ments basis there will effectively be no need to produce any notes to the accounts as required by the SORP 2000; however, it is recommended that these are prepared where doing so would increase the user's understanding of the accounts. The revised SORP 2000 does recommend that notes on related party transactions, trustee remuneration and information on significant non-monetary resources should always be given. However, where the smaller charity opts to prepare accrual accounts then it will have to comply with the regulations and follow the SORP in producing notes to the accounts.

Accruals

The concept of accruals, which is one of the four fundamental accounting concepts, means that, for the purpose of charities, the incoming resources or funds and the expenditure of those resources or funds are accrued. That is the income is recognized when earned as in the case of revenue or when receivable as in the case of gifts, donations, bequests, grants, etc., and for expenditure when it is incurred, not as for receipts of payments when money is received or paid.

The accruals basis of accounting matches activities and their income against the costs incurred so that both are usually included within the same accounting period, using prudent estimates where necessary. It would not be prudent, for example, to take credit for contract income without a corres-ponding accrual in the accounts to cover any further costs expected to be incurred in completing the contract.

To give another example, if from one year's revenue a charity purchases all of its stationery on a bulk discount order to cover the next three years then the accounting treatment will be different for receipts and payments and an accruals basis. For simple receipts and payments accounts the absence of sta-tionery costs in years 2 and 3 might not be at all obvious from studying the year's accounts. The uninformed reader may even think that the charity does not require any stationery.

Under the accruals method the stationery costs will be apportioned to each year, by regarding the cost of any substantial year-end stocks as prob-ably either a prepayment of stationery for future use to match them with the activities of that year or as stock in hand. Therefore, the accounts would in any year be adjusted to show the required true and fair view of the charity's financial activities and position.

Thus, one introduces the idea of debtors and creditors. As an example, where a Gift Aid donation has been received from an individual and the tax repayment applied for but not received by the year end, it would under accrual accounting be accrued for and shown as a debtor. Thus, if the donation was a net £78 with tax to be recovered at £22 under accrual accounting the figure shown in the accounts in the year would be £100 whilst, at least in the first year, under receipts and payments basis it would just be £78.

This accrual concept therefore matches income with expenditure so far as their relationship can be established or justifiably assumed and deals with it accordingly in the SOFA of the period to which it relates. However, this is provided that the accruals concept is not inconsistent with the prudence concept, in which case the latter will prevail.

With accrual accounting one will therefore have a balance sheet and the purchase of fixed assets will go to the balance sheet and be written off over a period of time. Hence, we have the charge of depreciation in the SOFA when it is produced on an accruals basis which will not apply when the accounts are produced on a receipts and payments basis. This section's review has, of course, been a somewhat oversimplified description of the particular kind of accounting procedure which is necessary when preparing accrual accounts.

Change in basis of accounting

Where because of size or decision of the trustees the charity changes from producing its accounts on a receipts and payments basis to full accrual accounting or vice versa, then the corresponding amounts for the previous financial years should be restated on the basis of the new accounting policy.

Special aspects

The SOFA in the accounts of a smaller unendowed charity which holds no funds on 'special trust' (i.e. which must be spent on specified purposes – restricted) and has no fixed asset revaluation gains/losses will look no different from the old income and expenditure account except for the addition of brought forward and carried forward fund balances. Receipts and payments accounts for the smaller charity after the 1995 SORP were very little different in their format from those before the SORP.

One major change, however, is that as a result of Section 47 of the Charities Act 1993 the trustees must, within two months of any written request and subject to payment of any reasonable copying fee they may require, provide any member of the public who makes the request with a copy of the most recent accounts prepared.

Endowments and special trusts administered as part of the charity have to be accounted for in such a way that it can be seen from the accounts that the terms of trust are being complied with. Branches or local groups controlled by the charity and which raise funds in the name of the charity on its behalf need to be accounted for by inclusion in the charity's accounts.

Obviously, non-monetary benefits provided to a smaller charity will present accounting problems. They cannot, quite clearly, be shown in receipts and payments accounts but have to be when accrual accounting is carried out. However, assets, such as property, which have been received as a gift for the benefit of the charity should appear in the year-end statement of assets and liabilities where receipts and payments accounts are produced. All tangible benefits which the charity receives or provides should in any case be suitably described in the annual report in a way which will indicate their value and importance to the charity.

Where the smaller charity carries out charitable trading either through the charity or through an operating activity subsidiary then information on this should be shown separately in the accounts.

Evolution of the Statement of Financial Activities (SOFA)

The traditional income and expenditure account treatment had for some time led to complaints that it did not reflect or fully explain all the financial activities of the charity. Therefore, it was considered that the very nature of the raising and using of charity resources required a different approach from that of the business community.

Charities do not usually have shareholders, even those that are companies, so such matters as distributable profit (dividends) or the retention thereof do not arise. Moreover, those who provide the resources for charities do not usually expect a monetary return on their donations, but more of a warm glow! However, the users of a charity's financial statements do need to be able to assess the services that the charity is providing, primarily through its charitable expenditure and its ability to continue to provide those services.

The accounts should also show how the trustees have carried out their duties and ensured that their responsibilities have been met during the year. Whilst it may be that the bottom line, surplus or deficit, provides some of this information, any presentation which focuses only on the bottom line tends to ignore the fundamental differences between accounting for charities and for the business sector. What is the bottom line when there is in effect no bottom line?

Charities, except those that are effectively trading, are not usually in the business of directly matching income and expenditure. Therefore, they are not working towards a particular year-end date. In other words, to place undue emphasis on the bottom line at a particular point in time can be misleading as income and expenditure in any one period are not often directly linked, for example grants received this year may be for projects to be carried out in the following year or indeed over a number of years.

Furthermore, unfortunately, the traditional income and expenditure account with its distinction between revenue and capital does not always adequately explain a charity's activities. Businesses primarily invest in fixed assets to generate future profits whilst, of course, a charity may be investing in fixed assets as part of its charitable activity (primary purpose), for example equipping a cancer research laboratory, building an old people's home, acquiring lifeboats, building kennels. This difference is extremely important to certain charities where a significant proportion of their annual expenditure is of a capital nature.

In any particular year a charity may use part of its income to purchase fixed assets for its charitable activities and since this expenditure is of a capital nature it will not be shown in the income and expenditure account. This could therefore lead to a surplus on the income and expenditure account and give a misleading impression. Unfortunately, the SOFA still does not include capital expenditure, whether of a charitable or other nature, and therefore judging the charity on the bottom line criteria will continue to be misleading in these circumstances where there is significant charitable objective spending of a capital nature.

Disclosures

Foremost amongst the recommendations of the SORP was the introduction of the statement of financial activities (SOFA). This is a way of showing, in summary form for the year, all the charity's funds, all its incoming resources, all its revenue expenditure, all transfers between funds, all recognized and unrecognized gains and losses on investments and how the fund balances have changed since the last balance sheet date.

This comprehensive primary accounting statement should show what funds the charity has and how they have been used. Of course, it may be necessary to add appropriate additional information in the notes to the accounts, wherever necessary, to bring out some special feature, for example the equipping of a medical research laboratory or the effectiveness of a particular fund-raising campaign or significant branch activities.

However, the SOFA is not as radical as it sounds. As we will see it essentially amalgamates the old-style income and expenditure account with the reconciliation and analysis of the movement of funds.

Reasoning

The SOFA recognizes that charities do not usually have just one single indicator of performance which is comparable to the bottom line for business. As well as considering the changes in the amounts of the net resources of a charity, it is important to consider the changes in the nature of those resources. As a result, both the SORP and the regulations recommended a primary statement that records the resources entrusted to a charity and reflects the financial activities thereof.

The SOFA is effectively divided into two parts, a statement of operations and a statement of other changes in net assets. However, many charities' accounts show that the distinctions based on operations tend to be somewhat arbitrary and are dependent on the impossible task of trying to match a charity's income and expenditure when, as we have seen, in most cases no such match is possible or even desirable. Therefore, the SOFA moved away from giving undue emphasis to the bottom line based on matching and dropped the use of the words surplus and deficit. It focuses instead on the periodic measurement of the changes in both the nature and amounts of all the net resources of a charity.

Format

A columnar format was scheduled in the 1995 regulations, unlike the 1988 SORP 2 where this presentation was merely recommended, so there has been no choice but to comply. The minimum required is one column for unrestricted funds, one for restricted funds, one for permanent endowments and one for the total for the year. Therefore, this required separation of income and expenditure streams between the types of funds for the first time for many charities. There is also a fifth column showing the comparative total for the previous period but it is not a legal requirement to have to show comparatives for each type of fund.

However, where there have been no movements in any particular fund or the charity does not have that type of fund, then it is not necessary to include that column. In other words, columns will only need to be included where the actual funds exist and there has been movement on them. This columnar approach can be added to; for example, unrestricted funds can be split between general purpose funds and other unrestricted funds. Whilst, of course, funds may be summarized in this way, if there is more than one restricted fund then details should be shown in the notes to the accounts.

Historically, prior to 1995 many charities either combined all funds together and just showed effectively what is now the total column or produced separate income and expenditure accounts for each fund without any total for all funds. Both these methods of reporting were effectively ruled out in 1995 as the SOFA must be in the prescribed columnar format.

This format also introduced standard headings for each row (i.e. line) such as incoming resources, charitable resources expended, cost of generating funds, etc., which has helped to make charity accounts more comparable. Again, as the SORP makes clear, this information will always be required, but if there has been no movement on a particular heading in the year or previous year then that heading need not be included.

Functional classification of expenditure means that instead of disclosing expenditure by type, i.e. natural classification – cost centre such as rent, rates, light and heat, salaries etc., expenditure will be described by its nature, such as charitable expenditure, cost of generating funds, etc. This helps the reader to understand what the charity is doing and how much it is spending on these particular activities.

Finally, the SOFA encompasses a statement of gains and losses covering both realized and unrealized gains and losses for investment assets but only realized gains and losses for tangible assets.

Statement of Financial Activities – example

Arts Theatre Trust Limited

Consolidated Statement of Financial Activities (including an Income and Expenditure Account) for the year ended 31 March 2001

	Notes	Unrestricted funds £'000	Restricted funds £'000	Total funds 2001 £'000	Total funds 2000 £'000
Incoming resources					
Incoming resources from operation of theatre and arts centre	3	1,200		1,200	1,259
Incoming resources from activities for generating funds	4	549		549	296
Donations		12	79	91	79
Investment income		18	1	19	16
Total incoming resources		1,779	80	1,859	1,650
Less cost of generating funds	4	337	2	339	280
Net incoming resources available for charitable application		1,442	78	1,520	1,370
Charitable expenditure					
Cost of operation of theatre and arts centre		1,209	81	1,290	1,230
Managing and administering of the charity		150	2	152	113
Total charitable resources expended	5	1,359	83	1,442	1,343
Net movement in total funds or the year (net income and expenditure)	5	83	(5)	78	27
Total funds brought forward		1,294	17	1,311	1,284
Total funds carried forward	14, 15	1,377	12	1,389	1,311

This SOFA includes all gains and losses recognized in the year. All incoming resources and resources expended derive from continuing activities.

Balance sheet

The balance sheet of a charity must show the state of affairs at the end of the financial year.

Introduction

The 1995 Charities SORP did not introduce many changes to the balance sheet although the changes to the recognition of income and expenditure and fund accounting, for some charities, had a considerable effect on the size of the figures that then had to be included. For instance, the writing back of deferred, restricted income included originally under creditors and treated as a restricted fund carried forward greatly strengthen the balance sheet.

There had been many arguments about what a balance sheet is supposed to represent. As long ago as April 1993 the Accounting Standards Board (ASB) produced a discussion paper on 'the role of valuation in financial reporting'. There was a problem in UK accounting in that there was no consistency in valuation practice. This particularly affected the valuation of assets which may appear in the balance sheet at current revaluation, a previous revaluation or original historic cost. The ASB saw this as an unsatisfactory situation and suggested that a prescriptive approach should be followed, using one of three options.

The 1995 Charities SORP effectively moved well ahead of all of that debate and provided considerable guidance on balance sheet valuation, although it still essentially accepted general accounting principles as does the 2000 version. It is perhaps worth bearing in mind that the only reference in the regulations to the SORP occurs in relation to the valuation of assets and liabilities where it clearly states that the SORP should be followed.

Presentation

The funds of a charity should be grouped together in the balance sheet according to their type, distinguishing between endowments, other restricted funds, designated and other unrestricted funds as the SORP itself explains. Further analysis of major individual funds needs to be given, as appropriate, in the notes to the accounts.

The assets of the charity should be analysed in the balance sheet between fixed and current assets. The fixed assets section should show separately those for charity use and those for investment, and for current assets these should be analysed between current and long-term elements with the total (if material) of any provisions for liabilities or charges shown separately. The totals for both short-term and long-term creditors should be sub-analysed in the notes.

In addition, the assets and liabilities should be analysed in a way that enables the reader to gain a proper appreciation of their spread and character. The balance sheet must be approved by all the trustees as a body but need only be signed by one of them on behalf of all of them. It must, of course, always be dated.

Example

Arts Theatre Trust Limited
Consolidated and Charity Balance Sheets as at 31 March 2001

	Notes	Group 2001 £'000	2000 £'000	Charity 2001 £'000	2000 £'000
Fixed assets					
Tangible assets	10	830	824	830	824
Investments	4	–	–	1	1
		830	824	831	825
Current assets					
Stocks	11	217	213	203	212
Debtors	12	207	206	272	206
Cash at bank and in hand		423	319	314	319
		847	738	789	737
Creditors: amounts falling due within one year	13	242	195	185	195
Net current assets		605	543	604	542
Total assets less current liabilities		1,435	1,367	1,435	1,367
Creditors: amounts falling due after more than one year	15	46	56	46	56
		1,389	1,311	1,389	1,311
Funds					
Unrestricted funds					
General	16	1,210	1,263	1,210	1,263
Designated	16	167	31	167	31
		1,377	1,294	1,377	1,294
Restricted funds	17	12	17	12	17
		1,389	1,311	1,389	1,311

Approved by the board on 13 June 2001 and signed on its behalf by

....

S. A. Bloggs, Chairman

Checklist

1   Are the assets of the charity subdivided between fixed assets and current assets?
2   Have the fixed assets been subdivided into:
    i   Intangible assets?
    ii   Tangible assets for the charity's use?
    iii   Inalienable and historic assets?
    iv   Investments?
3   Have fixed assets been divided between those used in direct furtherance of the charity's objects and those which are used for some other purposes such as the generation of income?
4   Have current assets been divided into:
    i   Stocks and work in progress?
    ii   Debtors?
    iii   Investments?
    iv   Cash at bank and in hand?
5   Are the liabilities divided between current and long-term liabilities?
6   Is there a heading for net current assets or liabilities?
7   Have the assets and liabilities been analysed in a way that enables a proper appreciation of their spread and character?
8   Is there a heading for total assets less current liabilities?
9   Is there a heading for provisions for liabilities and charges?
10   Has the figure for net assets been given?
11   Have the charity's funds been divided into:
    i   Unrestricted income funds?
    ii   Income funds which are restricted as to their use?
    iii   Endowment funds?
12   Where the use of any income is time conditional, has it been disclosed as 'deferred income' on the balance sheet, with suitable explanation in the notes?
13   For assets for which there is no readily identifiable market price has a reasonable approach to valuation/revaluation been adopted?
14   Have revaluation increases to assets acquired for charity use been added to the appropriate fixed asset account where applicable?
15   Where there has been a permanent diminution in the value of a fixed asset has this been appropriately recognized?
16   Have liabilities been correctly identified and recognized, differentiating between amounts payable within the next year and amounts payable after more than one year?
17   Where there is an asset related to the liability has this been referred to?
18   Has the balance sheet been approved by the trustees, as a body, and signed by one of them on their behalf?
19   Has the date of approval been stated?

Cashflow statement

Requirement is dependent on the size of the charity, i.e. the need to refer to FRS 1. Attention should also be paid to the governing instrument of the charity as this may require a cashflow statement.

History

A cashflow statement may be required for some charities in order to conform to statements of standard accounting practice (SSAP) and financial reporting standards (FRS). In accordance with SSAP 10 'statements of source and application of funds', the 1988 SORP 2 recommended that charities should prepare a source and application of funds statement. However, SSAP 10 had at this stage already suffered from many criticisms and between 1975 and 1989 it was twice considered for revision, but no changes were made.

Developments internationally requiring the preparation of cashflow statements led to the Accounting Standards Committee to issue in July 1990 an exposure draft which subsequently became the first financial reporting standard, published by the ASB in 1991. This is FRS 1 'Cashflow statements'. As the cashflow statement is considered to be a primary statement, it should be accorded the same prominence in the accounts as the SOFA and the balance sheet.

On 31 October 1996 the ASB published a revised version of FRS 1, the accounting standard on cashflow statements. This revision replaces the original FRS 1, issued in September 1991, and follows on from FRED 10, published in 1995, which detailed the proposed changes. The new standard applies to company accounting periods ending on or after 23 March 1997.

FRS 1 requires a genuine cashflow statement, the concept of 'cash equivalents' having been omitted. There is a definition of cash, to include cash in hand, deposits and overdrafts repayable on demand. The FRS has a section dealing with the management of liquid resources which will include, for example, cashflows relating to short-term deposits and other items previously regarded as cash equivalents.

The order and headings for cashflows have been restructured and the reconciliation between the cashflow statement and the balance sheet has been altered to focus on the effect of cashflow on net debt (borrowings less cash and liquid resources). Under certain strict conditions cash inflows and outflows can now be netted off.

FRS 1

Currently a cashflow statement should be prepared if in either its present or its previous financial year two or more of the following size qualifications were met:

> Gross income in the year in excess of £2.8m.
> Balance sheet total in excess of £1.4m.
> More than 50 employees.

Special provisions apply to small groups and in cases where a charity is within the size qualification in some years but not in others. The figures may alter from time to time (Companies Act 1985 Sections 246–249).

SORP

The major difference between FRS 1 and the SORP is that whilst the cashflow should comply with the requirement of FRS 1 it will not include movements in endowments from 'operating activities' as these should be treated as increases or decreases in the financing section.

Effectively cash donations to endowments should be treated as additions to endowments. The receipts and payments from the disposal and acquisition of investments should be shown gross in the 'capital expenditure and financial investment' section of the cashflow statement. The very rare payments made out of permanent endowments should be shown as a decrease in the 'financing' section and transactions which do not result in cashflows should not be reported in the cashflow statement (para 275).

Exemption

Charities, whether or not incorporated under the Companies Act, are exempt from FRS 1 if they satisfy the small company limits for the purposes of filing abbreviated accounts with the Registrar of Companies at Companies House. However, attention should be drawn to the reasons for excluding a cashflow statement from their accounts, in the notes to the accounts.

Homeless International does just this and draws the reader's attention, in its accounting policies, to the fact that a cashflow statement has not been prepared on these grounds. Many other charities also take advantage of the exemption but without providing the reasons why, although in most cases these will be obvious.

Example

The ABC Charity
Consolidated Cashflow Statement for the year ended 31 March 2001

	Notes	2001 £'000	2000 £'000
Net cash inflow from operating activities	20	2,090	595
Capital expenditure and financial investment			
Payments to acquire tangible fixed assets		(1,990)	(1,000)
Proceeds from sale of tangible fixed assets		130	170
Purchase of investments		(1,200)	(865)
Proceeds from sale of investments		2,300	915
		(760)	(780)
Cash inflow/(outflow) before increase in liquid resources and financing	20	1,330	(185)
Financing			
Finance lease payments		(40)	(40)
Management of liquid resources			
Increase in short-term deposits		(400)	(200)
Increase/(decrease) in cash in the year	20	890	(425)

Statement of changes in resources applied for fixed assets
for charity use for the year ended 31 March 2001

	Unrestricted Funds £'000	Restricted Funds £'000	Totals 2001 £'000	Totals 2000 £'000
Net movement in funds for the year	3,065	(810)	2,255	400
Resources used for net acquisitions of tangible fixed assets	(1,100)	(400)	(1,500)	(590)
Net movement in funds available for future activities	1,965	(1,210)	755	(190)

The ABC Charity
Cash flow information for the group

	2001 £'000	2000 £'000
(a) Reconciliation of changes in resources to net inflow from operating activities		
Net incoming resources before revaluations	2,155	150
Gain on sale of tangible fixed assets	(20)	(30)
Depreciation	380	270
Decrease in stocks	100	450
Increase in debtors	(765)	(225)
Increase/(decrease) in creditors	240	(20)
Net cash inflow from operating activities	2,090	595

	2001 £'000	2000 £'000
(b) Reconciliation of net cash flow to movement in net funds/debt		
Increase/(decrease) in cash in the period	890	(425)
Cash outflow from decrease in lease financing	40	40
Cash outflow from increase in liquid resources	400	200
Movement in net funds and debt in the year	1,330	(185)
Net funds and debt at 1 April 2000	3,020	3,205
Net funds and debt at 31 March 2001	4,350	3,020

(c)   Analysis of net funds/debt

	1 April 2000 £'000	Cashflow £'000	31 March 2001 £'000
Cash at bank and in hand	200	890	1,090
Liquid resources	3,000	400	3,400
Finance leases	(180)	40	(140)
	3,020	1,330	4,350

Disclosure of accounting policies and notes to the accounts

Introduction

The statement of accounting policies must be the most appropriate to give a true and fair view and be detailed enough to cover all material items (para 277).

Accounting standards

True and fair view accounts should follow the standards laid down in SSAPs and FRSs that have been issued or adopted by the Accounting Standards Board. Any departures must be justified with a full explanation otherwise it may be deemed not to be true and fair (paras 279–281).

Accounting policies/notes

Examples of matters on which the accounting policies should be explained where the amounts involved are material include:

- Donations
- Grants payable and receivable
- Costs of generating funds
- Charitable expenditure
- Investment assets
- Valuation, capitalization and depreciation of fixed assets
- Commitments not yet met
- Use of designated funds.

Notes

This is probably the most comprehensive part of the SORP and the 2000 version has taken the opportunity to group together all of its accounting policy notes in one clearly defined section (paras 282–291). However, comments on general accounting notes remain scattered throughout the text!

Checklist (extract)

- Have tangible fixed assets been analysed into:
    - Freehold interests in land and buildings?
    - Leasehold and other interests in land and buildings?
    - Plant and machinery?
    - Fixtures, fittings and equipment?
    - Payment on account and assets in the course of construction?
- Are investment assets and income therefrom analysed between:
    - Investment properties?
    - Investments listed on a recognized Stock Exchange, including ones valued by reference to such indices?
    - Investments in subsidiary and associated undertakings or in companies that are connected persons?
    - Other unlisted securities?
    - Cash held as part of the investment portfolio?
    - Other?

- Where values are determined otherwise than by reference to readily available market prices has the name and qualification of the valuer been given?
- Where there are contingent assets and liabilities has the following information been given:
  - The amount, or estimated amount?
  - Its legal nature?
- Is there a description of the nature and purpose of all of the charity's significant capital and income funds that are subject to legal restrictions as to their use?
- Is there an indication whether or not sufficient resources are held in an appropriate form to enable each fund to be applied in accordance with restrictions imposed?
- Has the name of each subsidiary and particulars of the charity's shareholding, or other controlling interest, been given?
- Has the number of employees whose emoluments fell within each band of £10,000 from £50,000 upwards been given?
- Has the auditor's or independent examiner's remuneration been analysed between:
  - Audit or independent examination services?
  - Other services?
- Where ex-gratia payments are made otherwise than as an application of funds for charitable purposes has the total amount or value of the following been given:
  - Payment?
  - Non-monetary benefit?
  - Other expenditure of any kind?
  - Waiver of rights to property to which charity is entitled?
- Where indemnity insurance has been purchased, is that fact and the costs involved given?
- Where a trustee or a person with a family or a business connection with the trustee has received remuneration, directly or indirectly, from either the charity or a company which any such persons control, has that fact, the name of the recipient, the source and the amount been given?
- Where trustees have been reimbursed for any expenses incurred have the following been stated:
  - Aggregate amount?
  - Nature of the expense?
  - Number of trustees reimbursed?
- Where gifts in kind have been brought into account has the basis of valuation been disclosed?
- Has the basis and principles used for the allocation of costs been disclosed clearly?
- Have particulars of any material departures from the SORP and the reasons therefore been given?
- Is there an analysis of the major items of the cost of generating funds?

Summary financial information and statements

Introduction

Summary financial information and statements are those derived from the full annual accounts of the charity and expressed in any form, for example extracts, graphs, tables, etc., which purport to be or represent the accounts of the charity. Such forms of the accounts, where produced by charities, have to be approved formally by the trustees and accompanied by a statement from the charity's auditors that they are consistent and accurate by reference to the full detailed accounts. Many charities issue publicity material which contains accounts information, often highly abbreviated and partly in graphical or other pictorial form. Such information has to follow the rules laid out in the revised SORP (paras 292–297).

Content

The SORP makes it clear that as the style will vary considerably from charity to charity it is not practicable to give detailed recommendations on the content. It does, however, set out some general principles (para 293). The full annual report and accounts must always be produced irrespective of the circulation of any summary financial information. Thus, even if all interested parties receive a copy of the summary financial information the full report and accounts must be available (para 294).

All such abbreviated accounts should be accompanied by a statement signed on behalf of the trustees explaining that they are a summary of information extracted from the annual accounts and they should contain information which relates both to the SOFA and the balance sheet (para 295). All summarized accounts should state the date on which the annual accounts, of which they are a summary, were approved. In addition, for those charities registered in England and Wales it will also be necessary to state whether the full annual report and accounts have been submitted to the Charity Commission (para 295).

If summary branch accounts are produced then it must clearly be stated that the summary is for the branch only and has been extracted from the full accounts of the main charity, giving the name of that charity. The summary financial information and statements should also give details of how the full annual accounts, the external examiners' report (as applicable) and the trustees' report can be obtained.

Incorporated charities

Charitable companies have to follow these recommendations and in addition must make clear in the accompanying statement whether or not the accounts have been sent to the Registrar of Companies (para 292). Many charities are still producing incorrect summarized information. Greater care must be taken in producing these, now that the SORP and regulations are fully effective.

Other summary financial information

The SORP makes it clear that any other summary financial information in whatever form it is produced which does not include information on the SOFA and the balance sheet must be accompanied by a statement signed on behalf of the trustees showing clearly the:

- Purpose of the information
- Whether or not it is from the full accounts
- Whether or not these accounts have been audited, independently examined or subject to a reporting accountant's report
- Details of how the full annual accounts, trustees' report and external examiners' report (as appropriate) can be obtained.

SORP exercise

During the year 2001 Age Concern Wivelsfield (ACW) received or spent the following income:

1 Received: £100,000 in respect of a health authority contract for the running of a project to give respite support. The following expenditure on this project has been incurred:

	£
Salaries	2,000
Travel	1,000
Professional fees	5,000
	8,000

2 Received: £50,000 in respect of a grant from the local authority, which has given ACW the money towards the costs of running an education programme. Of this sum £10,000 has been spent by the end of the period.

3 General donations and Gift Aid income of £80,000 were received. From this the sum of £5,000 was spent on general charity expenditure.

4 ACW incurred running costs as follows:

	£
Fund-raising and publicity	20,000
Management and administration	30,000

5 Interest was earned on the unspent funds as follows:

	£
Health project	5,000
Local authority	2,000
General donations	3,000

6 The local authority provided free use of its premises. Were the charity to have paid for the premises it would have cost £10,000 per annum.

7 ACW received a donation of a minibus from local businesses. The minibus was valued at £15,000.

8 After taking investment advice ACW with the opening cash balances purchased £20,000 of UK equities. At the year end these were valued by their broker at £30,000. Income in the year was £1,500 on the investments.

9 A grant of £20,000 was received to fund a case worker for support services to carers in the borough for the year to 31 March 2001, by the year end £15,000 had been paid.

10 Of the general donations received of £80,000 ACW decides to designate £10,000 for repairs and renovations.

Further information

The charity's opening balance sheet position was as follows:

	£
Fixed assets	10,000
Cash at bank and in hand	30,000
Net assets	40,000
Represented by:	
Unrestricted funds	40,000

The depreciation policy is 25 per cent reducing balance

Compile appropriate financial statements for ACW for 2001. (Note: You will need to construct the cash book for the year in the first instance.)

SORP ACCOUNTING EXERCISE
Age Concern Wivelsfield
Cash Book
for the year ended 31 December 2001

	£	£	
Balance brought forward at 1 January 2001	30,000		unrestricted
Health authority contract – Income	100,000		restricted
Health authority contract – Salaries		2,000	restricted
Health authority contract – Travel		1,000	restricted
Health authority contract – Professional fees		5,000	restricted
Education programme – Income	50,000		restricted
Education programme – Expenditure		10,000	restricted
General donations	80,000		unrestricted
General charity expenditure		5,000	unrestricted
Fund-raising and Publicity		20,000	unrestricted
Management and Administration		30,000	unrestricted
Interest – Health project	5,000		restricted
Interest – Local Authority	2,000		restricted
Interest – General donations	3,000		unrestricted
Purchase of investments		20,000	unrestricted
Support services to carers	20,000		restricted
Carers' salaries		15,000	restricted
Income on investments	1,500		unrestricted
Balance carried forward		183,500	
	291,500	291,500	

SORP ACCOUNTING EXERCISE
Age Concern Wivelsfield
Statement of Financial Activities
for the year ended 31 December 2001

	Unrestricted	Designated	Restricted	Total
Incoming resources				
Donations and gifts	105,000			105,000
Grants			65,000	65,000
Activities in furtherance of ACW's objects			100,000	100,000
Investment income	4,500		7,000	11,500
Total incoming resources	109,500		172,000	281,500
Less cost of generating funds	20,000			20,000
Net incoming resources available				
for charitable application	89,500	–	172,000	261,500
Resources expended				
Direct charitable expenditure	11,250		33,000	44,250
Management and administration				
of the charity	40,000			40,000
Charitable expenditure	51,250	–	33,000	84,250
Net incoming/ (outgoing) resources				
before transfers	38,250		139,000	177,250
Transfers between funds	(10,000)	10,000	–	–
Net incoming/(outgoing) resources	28,250	10,000	139,000	177,250
Gains/(losses) on investment assets	10,000			10,000
Net movements in funds	38,250	10,000	139,000	187,250
Fund balances brought				
forward at 1 January 2001	40,000	–	–	40,000
Fund balances carried				
forward at 31 December 2001	78,250	10,000	139,000	227,250

SORP ACCOUNTING EXERCISE
Age Concern Wivelsfield
Balance Sheet
for the year ended 31 December 2001

	£	£
Fixed assets		18,750
Investments		30,000
		48,750
Current assets		
Cash at bank and in hand	183,500	
Creditors: amounts falling due in one year	5,000	
Net current assets		178,500
		227,250
Represented by:		
Restricted funds		139,000
Unrestricted funds		78,250
Designated funds		10,000
		227,250

Funds analysis

	B'f	Income	Expenditure	C'f
Restricted funds				
Respite support	–	105,000	8,000	97,000
Education programme	–	52,000	10,000	42,000
Case worker	–	15,000	15,000	–
Unrestricted funds	40,000	109,500	71,250	78,250
Designated funds				
Repairs and renovations	–	10,000	–	10,000
	40,000	291,500	104,250	227,250

Restricted funds balances are represented by cash

SORP ACCOUNTING EXERCISE
Fixed asset note

		£
Balance brought forward		10,000
Donation of minibus		15,000
Total		25,000
Depreciation	25% RB	6,250
Balance carried forward		18,750

All fixed assets are for the unrestricted use of the charity

Investments

	£
Acquired in the year at cost	20,000
Unrealized gain	10,000
Market value at 31 December 2001	30,000

Analysis of direct charitable expenses

	£
Health authority	8,000
Education programme	10,000
Depreciation	6,250
General charitable	5,000
Carers' salaries	15,000
	44,250

Analysis of staff costs

None of the employees received remuneration in excess of £40,000.

None of the trustees received any remuneration. No trustees received reimbursement for any of their expenses.

Analysis of creditors

Creditors falling due within one year relates to the deferred income of a grant received to fund a case worker for support services to carers for the quarter to 31 March 2002.

5 Issues in charity accounting

Introduction

This chapter looks particularly at some of the problems faced by the accountant in producing charity accounts. As we outlined in the previous chapters there are significant differences between accounts prepared for a commercial organization and those prepared for a charity. Many of these differences are enshrined in statute but others have arisen because of the particular needs of charities to express themselves in ways that make the accounts more understandable from a layman's point of view. In particular we will look at fund accounting, recognition of income, the differing types of expenditure by a charity, branches and trading activities.

Fund accounting

There is a common impression that the Charities SORP in 1995 introduced fund accounting. Quite clearly this is not the case. Fund accounting has been in existence for some considerable time (Vatter 1947) and stems from trust law which predates any charity Acts. However, prior to the implementation of the Charities SORP, many charities did not comply with that trust law.

The main purpose of the accounts is to give an overall view of the total incoming resources during the year and how they have been spent with the balance sheet to show the overall financial position at the year-end. There are additional requirements for charities that have to account for more than one fund under their control. The accounts should provide a summary of the main funds, differentiating in particular between the unrestricted income funds, restricted income funds and endowment funds. The columnar format of the Statement of Financial Activities (SOFA) is designed to achieve this.

Charities need to account for the proper administration of the individual funds in accordance with their respective terms of trust and accounting records must be kept in a way which will adequately separate transactions between different funds. Some charities may hold one or more restricted funds, some of which may be permanent or expendable endowment funds.

Depending on the materiality of each, the notes to the accounts should group the restricted funds under one or more headings.

Unrestricted income funds

These are also sometimes known as general funds. They are expendable at the discretion of the trustees in furtherance of the objects of the charity. Some trustees have the power to declare specific trusts over unrestricted funds and where this power is available and exercised the assets affected will form a restricted fund and the trustees' discretion to apply that fund will be legally restricted. Designated funds form part of restricted funds (see next section).

Designated funds

Where part of an unrestricted fund is earmarked for a particular project it may be described as designated, as a separate fund. However, that designation has an administrative purpose only and does not legally restrict the trustees' discretion to apply the fund. In other words, trustees will still have the right to use those funds in furtherance of the objects of the charity. The precise purpose of all designated funds should be stated in the notes to the accounts.

Restricted funds

Restricted funds are subject to specific trusts declared by the donor(s), or with their authority (e.g. in a public appeal). They can only be used for the purposes for which they are given. Restricted funds may be income funds that are expendable in furtherance of some particular aspects of the objects of the charity. Or they may be capital funds, where the assets are required to be invested, or retained for actual use. It is therefore essential that the donor's wishes are followed as regards the income received and the way in which it is expended. Income must be applied for the purposes for which it has been given and where restricted income is temporarily invested prior to application then any income or gains derived from that investment will be added to the restricted income fund in question.

Endowment funds

A fund where there is no power to convert the capital into income is known as a permanent endowment fund and must generally be held indefinitely. This concept of 'permanence' does not necessarily mean that the assets held in the endowment fund cannot be exchanged, nor does it mean that they are incapable of depreciation or loss. What it does mean is that the permanent endowment fund cannot be used as if it were income.

Trustees may have the power to convert endowment funds into expendable income, this type of fund is described as expendable endowment. Where this is the case and the power is utilized then the funds will either be restricted or unrestricted dependent upon whether the original gift permitted general expenditure or restricted it to specific purposes. However, in the case of a permanent endowment fund holding assets, whilst these may be sold the proceeds have to be reinvested and cannot be used as though they were revenue. Effectively this sale and repurchase is described in the SORP as 'exchange' and whilst this may lead to a gain or loss, that gain or loss is of a capital, not revenue, nature. Therefore, the gain or loss becomes part of or a reduction of the capital and in the SOFA is shown below the line in the movement of funds section.

Fund assets

Any gains or losses made on the disposal of an asset forming part of a particular fund will then accrue to that fund. Likewise, of course, depreciation of fixed assets held in a particular fund will be a charge against that fund. It is therefore important for trustees to ensure that the assets and liabilities held in the fund are consistent, for example there is no point in investing in long-term securities if, because of donor restrictions, the funds have to be applied in the short term.

Accounts presentation

The treatment of movements of funds should not be affected by the type of fund involved. This means, for example, that restricted and unrestricted incoming resources receivable at the same time should be accounted for in the SOFA at the same time. This should also reflect the principal movements between the opening and closing balances on all the funds of the charity. The SOFA should be analysed between unrestricted income funds, restricted funds and endowment funds (permanent and expendable combined).

The notes to the accounts should provide information on the structure of the charity's funds so as to disclose fund balances and the reasons for them differentiating between unrestricted income funds (general and designated), restricted income funds, and permanent and expendable endowment, as well as identifying any material individual funds within them. In particular, the assets and liabilities representing each type of fund of the charity should be clearly summarized and analysed between those funds.

The restrictions imposed upon each fund and details of how they have arisen along with the purpose should be clearly stated in the notes. This disclosure should indicate whether or not sufficient resources are held in an appropriate form to enable each fund to be used in accordance with any restrictions. Any funds in deficit should always be separately disclosed and an explanation given in the trustees' annual report. Additionally, explanations should be provided for any unusual movement in any of the funds and material transfers between different funds and allocations to designated funds should be separately disclosed without netting off. Separate sets of statements may, if required, be produced for each major fund linked to a summary. It is for the trustees to decide on the most suitable form of presentation, bearing in mind the complexity of the funds' structure and the need to avoid confusion between the movements on the various funds.

Fund accounting SORP disclosure checklist

- Do the accounts properly show the administration of the individual funds in accordance with their respective terms of trust?
- Are restricted funds accounted for separately?
- Where applicable, are endowment funds accounted for, distinguishing between income and capital?
- Is the treatment of movement of funds accounted for in the SOFA at the same time?
- Are individual fund balances and the reasons for them suitably available.
- Is there a description of the nature and purposes of all of the charity's significant funds?
- Is there an explanation of the nature of transfers out of, and allocations to, designated funds and the reasons for them?
- Are the assets and liabilities analysed between the funds?
- Is there an indication whether or not sufficient resources are held in an appropriate form to enable each fund to be applied in accordance with restrictions imposed?
- Are all funds in deficit separately disclosed and is the matter referred to and explained in the trustees' annual report?
- Is there a description of endowment funds which analyses them between permanent and expendable?
- Are funds, other than funds used in carrying out the charitable objectives, retained by subsidiaries shown under an appropriate separate heading in the consolidated accounts?

Incoming resources

Introduction

As the SORP makes clear, all incoming resources becoming available to the charity during the year should be recognized in the SOFA. This would include all income belonging to the charity regardless of its source or of the purpose to which it is to be put or has been put.

The value of all resources accruing to a charity should be recorded in its SOFA provided it is prudent to do so. The practicality of this needs to be looked at and income should not be recognized until any conditions relating to its receipt have been met. Three factors are paramount: entitlement, certainty and measurement. Legal enforceability is of paramount importance and charities using the accruals basis should not include income where there is an uncertainty as to their entitlement.

Conditions and restrictions

If a charity receives income which is subject to restrictions then the income should be recorded in the accounts in full, albeit in a restricted fund column. The charity needs to recognize this income as if there has been a transfer of economic benefit from the donor to the charity.

This is distinct from incoming resources received subject to certain conditions. Conditions create barriers that must be overcome for the income to be recognized. Timing (e.g. a three-year grant) is one such example of a condition. In this situation the next two years are a condition to be overcome and this income should therefore be deferred. In this case the notes to the accounts should analyse the movement between incoming resources deferred in the year in question and income released in relation to earlier years.

Where charities receive funding by way of capital grants to finance the purchase of fixed assets, there was a potential conflict as to how SSAP 4 and the SORP require the accounting treatment. This is now resolved by the revised SORP that indicates that funds received for the restricted purpose of providing fixed assets should be accounted for immediately as restricted funds. However, there is no general rule in relation to the treatment of the fixed assets acquired with the funds and this will depend on the basis on which they are held. The fixed asset may be held in a restricted fund or an unrestricted fund dependent upon the terms attached to the gift.

Legacies

Put simply, legacy income must be included in the SOFA unless it is incapable of financial measurement. Effectively, this means that the legacy will have been received or is reasonably certain that it will be received and that the value of it can be measured with some degree of reliability. This is certainly one of those cases where the factors of entitlement, certainty and measurement come into play. As an example there will be reasonable certainty and obviously entitlement once the charity has had a letter from, say, the solicitors dealing with an estate advising them that a payment of legacy will be made or that property has been bequeathed and will be transferred.

However, at this stage it may not be possible to measure in financial terms the amount of the legacy and therefore until that can happen it should not be included in the accounts. Once a charity receives a payment on account or a letter advising that such a payment will be made then this amount should be treated as receivable and included in the accounts. This would be the case even where the letter is received after the end of the financial year but it is clear that it had been agreed prior to the year end. It is unlikely in practice that entitlement, certainty of receipt and measurability conditions will be satisfied before the charity has been advised.

Assets left to a charity, such as investments, property, etc., should be valued and brought into the account at that value. Where the charity has been notified of material legacies which have not been included in the accounts, this fact and an estimate of the amounts receivable should be disclosed in the notes to the accounts.

Often the charity will be informed that they are the beneficiary of a will some time before probate. At this point it is often difficult to quantify the final amount the charity will eventually receive and so it cannot be included in the accounts for that particular accounting year. If the charity does know the amount it will be in receipt of by the time the accounts are finalized, then an amount should be included in the accounts for this.

Intangible income

A charity may receive assistance in the form of donated facilities, donated services or beneficial loan arrangements. Such assistance is generally referred to as 'intangible income'. Such intangible income should only be included in the SOFA if the charity would otherwise have had to purchase the donated facilities, the benefit is quantifiable, material, and where the donor is paying the costs involved. An equivalent amount should be included in the SOFA as expenditure under the appropriate heading. Details of amounts falling under this heading should be disclosed in the notes to the accounts.

Some charities receive substantial amounts of voluntary help. Such help should not be accounted for in the SOFA, but should be dealt with in the notes to the accounts or in the trustees' annual report.

Gifts in kind

In summary, the SORP effectively states that incoming resources in the form of gifts in kind should be included in the SOFA in the following ways:

> Assets given for distribution by the charity should be recognized as incoming resources for the year only when distributed.

> Assets given for use by the charity (e.g. property for its own occupation) should be recognized as incoming resources when receivable.

Where a gift has been made in kind but on trust for conversion into cash and subsequent application by the charity, the incoming resource should normally be recognized in the accounting period when receivable. However, in certain cases this will not be practicable (e.g. second-hand goods donated for resale in charity shops). In these cases the income should be included in the accounting period in which the gift is sold.

In all cases the amount at which gifts in kind are brought into account should be either a reasonable estimate of their value to the charity or the amount actually realized. The basis of any valuation should be disclosed. Where material, an adjustment should be made to the original valuation upon subsequent realization of the gift.

Other income

Income from investments such as dividends, interest and property rents should be included under the heading 'investment income' in the SOFA. This, however, should not include capital returns, i.e. capital growth. The notes to the accounts should show this gross investment income analysed between the different types of investment held as laid down in the SORP dealing with the balance sheet; that is, investment properties, investments listed on a recognized Stock Exchange, investments in subsidiary or associated undertakings, other unlisted securities, cash held as part of the investment portfolio and any other investments.

Incoming resources from the government and other public authorities can be the result of grants, contracts or service agreements. The SORP recommends that such incoming resources should be treated in a similar manner to other incoming resources and included under the relevant heading in the SOFA. Thus grants will normally be included under 'donations, legacies and similar incoming resources' whilst payment for contracts/service agreements, i.e. fees, would normally be included under 'activities in furtherance of the charity's objects'. Any conditions imposed would obviously need to be taken account of particularly where these effectively turn the incoming resource into restricted income. Again the notes to the accounts should give a full description of the sources of any material incoming resources by category.

Any income which the charity has not been able to categorize under the specific headings set out in the SORP will be regarded as 'other incoming resources'. In all cases this should be very much in the minority and it is probably true to say that many charities will not need to make any use of this category. As the SORP itself puts it: 'the most common example is the gain on the disposal of a fixed assets for the charity's own use'. The treatment of income from trading activities and branches of the charity are dealt with separately later in this chapter.

Netting off

All incoming resources, the SORP makes clear, as far as practicable should be reported gross. This means, in particular, that expenditure on fundraising should not be netted off against the funds raised but should be separately disclosed. The SORP accepts that on occasions this may not be practicable and in these cases the reason for netting off should be given. It is also recommended that if the netting off is material then an estimate of the gross funds raised and the deducted expenditure should be given in the notes.

Expenditure

Introduction

Specifically charitable expenditure will comprise all the costs incurred by the charity in meeting its objectives and should in the SOFA be analysed between grants payable, direct costs, support costs and management and administration costs. These costs should also include the depreciation of fixed assets that are used wholly or mainly for charitable activities including projects. This analysis should be further explained in the notes to the accounts so that the reader can understand how the charity spends its resources on its various activities. Where applicable and the amount is material then it is further recommended that support costs are shown separately in the SOFA.

Grants

In the business world generally, expenditure is usually treated as not being incurred until consideration for the expenditure has passed, in other words until something is received in exchange for the expenditure. However, in the case of grant expenditure relating directly to charitable activity, no exchange is involved and this creates problems since it is not possible to match the expenditure with the receipt of goods or services, as neither occurs.

The SORP explains that a grant is a payment made by a charity to an institution or an individual to further the objects of the charity. Grants can be repayable to the charity in certain circumstances. There is therefore an obligation created by agreeing to make a grant. Not all obligations are legally binding, particularly where there are conditions involving future and uncertain events and there are uncertainties about passing and receiving the economic benefit promised.

In the period following the issuing of the Exposure Draft of the SORP there was considerable debate about the disclosure of grants payable in a charity's accounts. The SORP reached a very sensible compromise on this issue. It recommends that if explanation is needed of the grants then the analysis may be shown in the notes to the accounts, as part of the trustees' report or by means of a separate publication.

Whilst information on grants payable clearly should and must be available to anyone who requires it, there is no need to clog up the annual accounts with this information, provided the information is readily available in some other format. Many charities do already provide this information in a separate published document. As the revised SORP points out, additional disclosure will not be applicable where the total grant expenditure made by a charity does not exceed 5 per cent of the total expenditure of that charity. In such a case none of the grants will be regarded as material.

The SORP makes clear that the analysis need not cover grants to individuals but must cover those to institutions in detail. Thus for both individual and institutional grants analysis should be given that discloses the total number and the total value of the grants given for different charitable purposes. Additionally, for institutional grants the trustees are required to provide more detail in order to convey a proper understanding of the charity's grant-making activities. Effectively in all cases grants to any one institution in any one accounting year where the total value is at least 2 per cent of total institutional grants in that year should be disclosed although there is no requirement to disclose any grants which are below £1,000 in total. Otherwise the number of grants shown should cover at least the 50 largest institutional grants.

Cost allocation

The definitions of fund-raising and administration costs have been amended from those that appeared in the 1995 SORP and the former has been widened considerably and renamed 'cost of generating funds'. The revised SORP has taken the opportunity also to review where administration and fund-raising costs should be shown in the SOFA. Obviously costs will still need to be recorded by their 'natural classification' but, as with the 1995 SORP, are reported by their 'functional classification'.

The regulations make clear that those charities whose gross income does not exceed £250,000 will not have to provide a 'functional classification' split of costs. Instead they may choose to use a 'natural classification', e.g. salaries, wages, rent, rates, etc. In other words, the preparation of 'functional classification' of costs only applies to those charities whose gross income is in excess of £250,000 per annum.

Support costs

In the Glossary support costs are defined as:

> 'Support costs' of charitable activities comprise costs incurred directly in support of expenditure on the objects of the charity, and can therefore be considered as part of total expenditure directly relating to the objects of the charity. Such costs will include all services (either at headquarters or through a regional network) which are identifiable as wholly or mainly in support of the charity's project work or other charitable expenditure (excluding management and administration costs) if – but

only if – they are an integral part of the cost of carrying out the direct charitable objectives of the charity.

The Cancer Research Campaign's objective is the furtherance of research into the causes of cancer. To achieve this objective it makes grants to universities, institutes, hospitals, etc., where research is being carried out. It has at its headquarters a scientific department whose activities, whilst not engaged directly in research, are to assist those who are carrying out the research. Costs of this activity would therefore be correctly allocated to support costs.

Cost of generating funds

The revised SORP defines this as those costs actually incurred by a charity (or by their agent) in raising funds from whatever source. This will include costs incurred in getting in donations, legacies, carrying out fund-raising activities, investment management costs and similar costs. It may also include the costs associated with raising funds for providing goods and services in the furtherance of the charity's objects but it should not include any of the costs of carrying out those activities. For example, the cost of applying for a lottery grant could be regarded as a cost of generating funds.

Obviously the publicity costs associated with fund-raising or raising the profile of the charity should be included under this heading but it will not include publicity costs incurred in furtherance of the charity's objects. Where material, the different categories of the costs of generating funds should be shown either on the face of the SOFA or in the notes to the accounts. An analysis of the major items of expenditure should be given in the notes to the accounts linked, wherever possible, to the incoming resource categories reflecting the funds raised.

Management and administration

Nothing excites the media more than charities overspending on so-called 'overheads' (for further discussion see Chapter 8). Although most of the costs of running a charity can be identified as belonging to either cost of generating funds or support costs, there will always remain costs that are incurred in connection with the management of the charity's assets. These are organizational as opposed to project administration costs and include compliance with constitutional and statutory requirements. Further examples of these costs are:

- Expenditure on trustees, management and annual general meetings.
- Compliance with constitutional and statutory requirements, e.g.
  - i Annual audit fee
  - ii Most legal fees
  - iii Valuation fees.

- Management of the charity's assets.
- Organizational management.

Unlike the 1995 SORP these costs will now be shown as part of the charitable expenditure. However, there should continue to be a clear analysis of all the main items of expenditure on management and administration in the notes to the accounts.

Conclusion

Whilst making it clear that it is not practicable to define precisely what should be included under each heading as each charity's circumstances would be different, the Charities SORP does make it clear that the basis for the allocation should be disclosed in the accounting policies. Items of expenditure which involve more than one 'functional classification' should be allocated on a reasonable and consistent basis to the various 'functional classifications', e.g. cost of generating funds/support. Expenditure incurred on activities falling directly within any one functional classification should not be apportioned to any other functional classification.

Trading – operating activities

Introduction

The underlying principle in respect of the bringing in of trading figures into the accounts is that netting off of income and expenditure should be kept to a minimum. One area in which this principle may significantly affect charity accounts is the reporting of fund-raising income, particularly from shops. In the past, many charities often normally only brought in the net figures. As a result of the 1995 SORP the income and expenditure in respect of charitable trading such as sale of donated goods has been shown gross, that is separately under the appropriate incoming resources and resources expended headings.

However, sales by shops of bought-in goods through trading subsidiaries could be shown net because this was regarded as a non-charitable activity. As most charity shops sell both donated and bought-in goods, this treatment could become very complicated. This position is now changed by SORP 2000.

Effectively for the purposes of analysing incoming resources from operating activities, such income should be analysed between that which is derived from activities in furtherance of the charity's objects and that which comes from activities specifically undertaken for generating funds. Obviously in the accounts any charity should seek to further explain the activities that it carries out and expand the headings accordingly.

All incoming resources received for activities that are in the nature of a payment for the provision of goods or services should be combined together under the relevant activity. Thus income from trading and grants or donations that have conditions that make them similar in economic terms to trading income, such as a service agreement with local authorities, should be aggregated. However, grants to fund core activities continue to be regarded as donations and should be included under the heading 'donations, legacies and similar incoming resources'.

Checklist

1 If a charity's operating activity is primary purpose trading or ancillary thereto, then exempt from income tax and corporation tax under the Income and Corporation Taxes Act (ICTA) 1988.
2 If work in connection with trade carried out by beneficiaries or ancillary thereto also exempt from income tax and corporation tax under S.505 ICTA 1988.
3 Fees/grants from government or public authorities for goods/services under 1 and 2 above.
4 For trading types 1 and 2 above carried out by a charity show income/expenditure gross in SOFA.
5 Separate heading required in SOFA for type 1. To type 3 above as 'activities' in furtherance of the charity's objects.
6 If trade carried out by subsidiary for benefit of charity then the subsidiary must show results using normal accounting rules.
7 Show separately in SOFA any payments by subsidiary to charity.
8 Trading results of subsidiary will only be accounted for by charity in charity's consolidated SOFA of the charity group.
9 If trading subsidiary carrying out primary purpose trading then its reserves should be included in the group balance sheet as 'trading funds' as part of the group's unrestricted charitable funds.
10 If occasional trading permitted is usually fund-raising (e.g. jumble sales) then show gross in SOFA under 'activities for generating funds'.
11 Sale of donated goods should be shown gross under 'activities for generating funds'.
12 For 10 and 11, operating costs should be shown in SOFA under 'cost of generating funds'.

Economic mix

Wherever possible, the incoming resources and resources expended to each different type of activity should be segregated; indeed this may have to be done for tax purposes. Charity trustees should consider the balance of the activities being undertaken to determine the most appropriate place to include the incoming resources from such enterprises. One example given in the SORP is that of a charity shop that sells mainly donated and bought-in goods but also sells goods made by the beneficiaries and uses the premises for providing information about the charity. In other words there is a mix of economic activity. In this case it would be acceptable to class all the incoming resources from the shop under 'activities for generating funds' although there is clearly a mix and some of the income is coming from 'activities in furtherance of the charity's objects'.

It is important that the presentation adopted and the disclosure in the notes are sufficiently detailed to understand the main activities and distinguish the assets and liabilities and transactions of the charity from those of its subsidiary/ies.

Branches

Introduction

The 1995 SORP attempted to sort out the problem of accounting for branches. The major change from the 1988 SORP 2 was one which had a considerable effect on the way in which a number of charities produced their accounts. Accounting for branches was tightened and all branch transactions then had to be reflected in the charity's own accounts, whether or not the funds were received by the parent charity by the year end. Similarly, all assets and liabilities of the branch also had to be incorporated in the charity's own balance sheet.

Many charities did not include all the branches' transactions in their accounts in detail and often the money that the branch remitted to the charity was included net of costs and shown under donations. The 1995 SORP effectively recommended a change to this way of operation which led to an increase in the accounting effort required both by the volunteers at branch level and most certainly at the head office of the charity.

Definition

SORP 2000 Glossary describes a branch as:

(a) simply part of the administrative machinery of the main charity; or

(b) a separate legal entity which is administered by or on behalf of the main charity and whose funds are held for specific purposes which are within the general purposes of the main charity. 'Legal entity' means a trust or unincorporated association formed for a charitable purpose. The words 'on behalf of' should be taken to mean that, under the constitution of the separate entity, a substantial degree of influence is exerted by the main charity over the administration of its affairs; or

(c) in England and Wales, a separate legal entity not falling within (b) which the Charity Commission has directed under section 96(5) or 96(6), the Charities Act 1993 should be treated as part of the main charity for accounting purposes.

This is very little change from the definition in the Glossary to the 1995 SORP and is still perhaps a bit wordy, but if a branch is not within any one of these three definitions then it can probably be said to be autonomous, particularly where it is a separate legal entity, and as such these organizations would prepare their own accounts which will not form part of the main charity's.

Autonomous branch?

Branches are entities effectively set up to conduct the business of the charity and often to fund-raise on its behalf. To take this a bit further, if, for example, the branch:

- uses the name of the main charity within its title;
- exclusively raises funds for the main charity and/or for the main charity's local activities;
- uses the main charity's registration number to receive tax relief on its activities;
- receives bank interest gross;
- obtains zero rates for VAT purposes on certain purchases;
- is perceived by the public to be the main charity's local representative;
- receives support from the main charity through advice, publicity materials, etc.

then it will certainly not be autonomous and its affairs should be accounted for as part of the charity.

Accounting

The 1995 SORP clearly recommended and this is repeated in the 2000 version in that

> All branch transactions should be accounted for gross in the main charity's own accounts. Similarly all assets and liabilities of the branch including, for example, funds raised but not remitted to the parent charity at the year end, should be incorporated into the charity's own Balance Sheet. This provision need not apply where the transactions of the branches in aggregate are not material to the charity's accounts.
>
> (SORP 2000)

Whilst of course this is but a set of recommended practices, we have seen that much of the Charities SORP has been enshrined in law in the regulations flowing from the Charities Acts and this is certainly true of branch accounting.

Funds raised by a branch for the general purposes of the main charity will be accounted for as unrestricted funds in the accounts of the main charity. Funds raised by a branch for specific purposes of the main charity will need to be accounted for as restricted funds in the accounts of the main charity. Funds held for the general purposes of a branch, which is a separate charity, should usually be accounted for as restricted funds in the accounts of the main charity.

(SORP 2000)

However, separate legal entities that may be known as branches but which do not fall within the definition of a branch should prepare their own annual report and accounts and if they are connected to charities the relationship should be explained in the trustees' report. Where the branch is not a separate entity and its accounts form part of the accounts of the reporting charity, it may well be in the interest of local supporters and beneficiaries for additional accounts to be prepared covering only that branch.

Role of branch treasurers

A bit more work for them as the argument put forward is that any money raised using the charity's name belongs to the charity and that the branch is acting as custodian in a trustee capacity. It therefore follows that any income and expenditure of the branch should be reflected in the charity's own SOFA with the minimum of netting off. Similarly, at the year end all that which the branch has in cash or assets, as well as what it owes, i.e. liabilities, should be incorporated into the charity's own balance sheet. In order to achieve this, some form of annual accounting return is required from the branches so as to provide the analysis needed.

Overseas branches

Some charities operate outside the UK through a branch network which in the main carries out the activities of the charity, although some will also do fund-raising. Most of the issues raised are not much different for overseas branches than they are for UK-based branches although there are some significant ones to be taken into account.

Prior to the 1995 SORP there appears to have been one of two ways in which charities accounted for these branches. First, where the branch was clearly within the control of the UK parent, and this meant that it accounted for the activities within the parent's accounts. In this case, money sent from the UK would not be regarded as expenditure until it was actually used, but merely a transfer from one bank account to another.

The second type of operation is one where the overseas activity was not carried out by an arm of the UK-based charity. Effectively, here, as the funds left the UK they were leaving the control of the charity and would therefore be regarded as grants to overseas charities.

However, there are further complications in that in many cases the overseas organization is run jointly by two or more charities. It is therefore extremely important to determine the legal status of overseas operations. Quite clearly, if they are part of the whole then they must be accounted for in the normal way in which branch accounts of charities are dealt with under the SORP. Local laws, of course, will have to be taken into consideration and it may well be that in addition to incorporating the figures in the UK charity's accounts, a separate overseas set of accounts for each country will need to be produced.

6 Regulatory framework and audit requirements

Regulatory framework

The much delayed publication of the accounting rules resulting from Part VI s42 of the Charities Act 1993, the *Charities (Accounts and Reports) Regulations* 1995, was issued by the Home Office in October 1995.

So what was new?

- A detailed statutory framework for the maintenance of accounting records and for the preparation of charity accounts and annual reports.
- A statement of financial activities (SOFA) as the basis of accounts.
- A statutory requirement for charity audit, mainly for larger charities, and less rigorous independent examination for smaller charities.
- A new 'light touch' regime for the smallest registered charities.

The limits for unincorporated registered charities are:

Annual gross income	Type of accounts	Type of review
Below £10,000	Receipts and payments	None
Above £10,000 and below £100,000	Receipts and payments	Independent examination
Above £100,000 and below £250,000	Accruals	Independent examination
Above £250,000	Accruals	Audit

In addition, charities with annual income of less than £1,000 which do not have a permanent endowment need not register with the Charity Commission. Those charities with annual income of less than £10,000, i.e. the 'light touch' regime, need not submit a copy of their accounts to the Charity Commission unless they are specifically asked for them. All registered charities with annual income in excess of £10,000 have to submit a copy of their accounts to the Charity Commission.

All registered charities, however, have to submit an annual return to the Charity Commission. For the smaller charity this is a fairly simplified document merely to keep the records straight. Any charity can choose to impose upon itself more rigorous rules than the table sets out, e.g. a charity with an income of less than £250,000 can, if it wants, elect to have its accounts audited rather than independently examined.

Independent examination is of course a less onerous form of scrutiny than audit, both in terms of the depth of work that is to be carried out and the qualification necessary to undertake such work. The examiner is not required to form an opinion as to whether the accounts show a true and fair view but reports instead, based on the examination carried out, whether specific matters have come to his or her attention. However, many charities will, because of their own constitution/trust deed, still require audit whatever their size. This is a problem that the trustees have to resolve if they want to make use of the independent examination procedures.

Changes in company law as regards audit and audit exemption are likely to have left some charities with a problem. In the table produced earlier the threshold for audit at £250,000 is the same whether the charity is incorporated or unincorporated. However, below that figure there is a problem. Charities that have an income in the range £10,000 to £90,000, if they are unincorporated, require an independent examination but if they are incorporated, they require no verification by an auditor or preparer of audit exemption reports.

Annual income	Unincorporated charity		Incorporated charity	
	Audit	Independent examination	Audit	Audit exemption report
Less than £10,000	No	No	No	No
More than £10,000 to £90,000	No	**Yes**	No	**No**
More than £90,000 to £250,000	No	Yes	No	Yes
More than £250,000	Yes	No	Yes	No

The table above sets out the situation with the inconsistent problem area clearly highlighted. This matter still needs to be resolved and discussions are still continuing between the Charity Commission and the Department of Trade & Industry (DTI). The situation might have deteriorated following the proposal from the DTI in early 1997 to abolish the 'accountant's report' for businesses with turnover between £90,000 and £350,000 (the threshold for audit for non-charitable companies). Fortunately, the DTI listened to the Charity Commission and to the charity sector generally and agreed not only to exempt charities from this new ruling but also to look at ways of reviewing the existing anomaly. As the official 1997 DTI Report stated:

The current arrangements will be retained for those charities which have chosen to incorporate, pending an *early consultation* on options for harmonisation of the financial reporting requirements under charities legislation on the one hand and companies legislation on the other.

The italics are added as the report was issued early in 1997! All incorporated charities have of course to produce their accounts on the accruals basis and comply with company law regulations.

Certain of the recommended changes to the SORP required changes to the Regulations and therefore, the Home Office issued for discussion Draft Regulations on Charity Accounts and Reports on 22 February 2000. Comments on these Draft Regulations had to be submitted by 30 April 2000 to the Charity Commission. The consultation document was very technical but in summary it covered:

- whether to raise the annual income threshold for simpler arrangements for preparing annual reports and accounts from £100,000 to £250,000;
- how best to cover governance arrangements and investment and reserves policies and practices in the annual report, at least for larger charities;
- how to make the detailed analysis in the accounts of incoming resources less prescriptive;
- how to revise the expenditure analysis to bring it in line with the Exposure Draft of the SORP;
- how to cover historic or inalienable assets, for reflecting in a recent accounting standard and the Exposure Draft of the SORP;
- how to revise the rules on related party transactions in the light of a recent accounting standard and the Exposure Draft of the SORP;
- how to make various other minor and technical changes to maintain consistency with the Exposure Draft of the SORP;
- whether to make a minor amendment on the rules on accounts scrutiny to allow the Charity Commission to give a dispensation at an earlier stage;
- where exactly to draw the boundary of the special accounting regime for Common Deposit Funds and non-pooling scheme Common Investment Funds;
- how to carry out technical updating of the rules for registered social landlords and certain designated education institutions, including making explicit that the accounts for these bodies must give a true and fair view; and
- whether provision needs to be made for any additional classes of charity to be allowed to treat accounts prepared under some other statutory accounting regime as also being their accounts for the purposes of the charity accounting regime; and whether that treatment should be conditional on the alternative accounts giving a true and fair view.

The Charities (Accounts and Reports) Regulations 2000 were laid before Parliament on 25 October 2000 as Statutory Instrument 2000 Number

2868. The Regulations came into force on 15 November 2000 for statements of accounts prepared by the charity trustees of a charity in respect of the financial year that began on or after 1 January 2001. Where the trustees wished, earlier adoption could have been undertaken and had to be if the trustees had not either approved the accounts of the charity or authorized the signature on the annual report for accounts ended before that date by 15 November 2000. The Regulations follow very closely the Statement of Recommended Practice (SORP) and in particular have dealt with all the issues raised above.

The charity audit – some important aspects

Introduction

The charity audit is an audit of stewardship and there is a considerable overlap between the role of the external auditor and the charity finance director.

There is no such thing as a private charity, secrecy is out and a greater openness is required. All those with an involvement in a charity – the modern parlance describes them as stakeholders, be they donors, recipients, trustees, employees, etc. – have the right to expect that the resources entrusted to the charity are being used cost-effectively. It must therefore be part of the audit to ensure that this happens.

Requirements

Until the Charities Act 1993 there was no statutory auditing requirement for charities. The Charity Commissioners did, however, have power under Section 8 (3) of the Charities Act 1960 to

> Require that the condition and accounts of a charity for such period as they think fit shall be investigated and audited by an auditor appointed by them.

Section 22 (4) of the Trustee Act 1925 empowers trustees

> In their absolute discretion, from time to time, but not more than once in every three years unless the nature of the trust or any special dealings with the trust property make a more frequent exercise of the right reasonable, cause the accounts of the trust property to be examined or audited by an independent accountant.

In addition, obviously certain charities may have to have an audit. For example:

- Those incorporated under the Companies Acts.
- Those incorporated under the Industrial and Provident Societies Acts.
- Charitable Housing Associations.
- War charities or charities for disabled, governed by the War Charities Act 1940.
- Charitable Friendly Societies.

Both the Woodfield Report (1987) and the White Paper *Charities a Framework for the Future* (1989) proposed forms of audit or examination according to the size of charities. There followed a Bill debated in the House of Lords towards the end of 1991 from which emerged the Charities Act 1992 now mainly consolidated into the 1993 Act.

The audit requirements specified therein set out that if a charity's gross income or total expenditure in any of the following:

a   relevant year;
b   financial year of the charity immediately preceding the relevant year; and
c   financial year of the charity immediately preceding the year specified in paragraph b;

exceed £250,000 then the accounts will have to be audited by a person who:

i   is in accordance with Section 25 of the Companies Act 1989 eligible for appointment as a company auditor; or
ii   is a member of a body for the time being specified in the regulations still to be laid out and is under the rules of that body eligible for appointment as auditor of the charity.

The need to be eligible as a company auditor implies that the same considerations of independence apply. Ethical guidance is also relevant.

Where the annual gross income or total expenditure is effectively less than £250,000 in any of the specified years, then the accounts have to be independently examined by a person who in the opinion of the trustees is reasonably believed to have the requisite ability and practical experience to carry out a competent examination of the accounts. Alternatively, of course, they can if they wish still have the accounts audited.

Charity audit is automatically higher risk than other audit due to the level of public interest and often press interest in charity accounts (Bennett 1999).

Some overall considerations

Charities exist not to generate profits but to meet an identified charitable objective. Financial performance is not therefore measured by surplus or deficit, and success and operational performance is measured differently in a charity from that of a commercial organization.

The primary purpose of the charity is paramount. Accounting systems therefore must reflect the activities of the charity and provide sufficient information to control and manage those activities. Accounting by charities is reflected in the Charities SORP and not driven primarily by FRSs/SSAPs. Therefore, in considering the appropriateness of these financial reporting standards it must be remembered that they have been prepared to deal with business enterprises where the motive is profit and not with charities where the motive is certainly different.

One example is SSAP 4, which deals with the treatment of government grants and lays down some specific rules about accounting for capital and revenue grants. As far as charities are concerned, this difference of treatment is anomalous and therefore led to a recommendation under the Charities SORP which many auditors may find awkward. What is quite clearly a true and fair view for a non-profit organization may not be so for a profit-orientated organization.

Audit scope

The scope of the audit can depend on the status of the charity which will also determine the type of any report that has to be given. Charities are governed in many different ways:

- as a company probably limited by guarantee;
- as a Trust;
- as an unincorporated association;
- by Royal Charter;
- by a specific Act of Parliament; or
- under one of the various acts relating to Friendly, Industrial and Provident Societies and Housing Associations.

It is essential that any auditor or independent examiner should know and understand the legal structure of the organization and recognize what is included within the audit scope.

The purpose of an audit must be to provide independent confirmation of the financial affairs of an organization. Obviously, therefore, the terms of the auditors' appointment should determine the actual scope of the audit and the nature of the report required. The requirements of a charity audit became clearer following the publication of the accounting regulations and the Auditing Practices Board guidance Practice Note 11 – *The Audit of Charities*.

As we have seen in business operations, the auditors will be required to express the opinion that the accounts give a 'true and fair' view. This concept has been debated, often hotly, in many forums and there continues to be an expectation gap between that which the trustees or the staff of the charity think they are receiving from the audit and what the auditor thinks is being provided. Therefore, it is vital that the scope of the audit is clearly defined in the usual letter of engagement, which it is important that the auditors are willing to discuss with the client.

As well as commentating on the accounts, the auditors should also review the trustees' report. The production of such a report is a legal requirement and it is therefore necessary to ensure that the information in this report is consistent with that given in the financial statements. As many in the charity world are prone to exaggeration – but then which company chairman or director is not – this can sometimes lead to problems.

Audit should provide

The charity should get more from the audit than just a management letter and it is essential that the auditors are seen as part of the team. There certainly must not be an attempt by the auditors to 'highjack' the accounts which are those of the charity. Quite clearly, independence has to be maintained but empathy is important. So from the point of view of the charity, what should the audit provide? This should include as a basic minimum:

- independent review;
- value for money;
- more than just a checking of the figures;
- innovative ideas;
- practical advice.

Not surprisingly, little of the training of a chartered accountant seems to involve any understanding of how a business works, let alone how a charity does. Certainly there is nothing on charity and trust law. To be truly effective it is therefore important that the charity audit team specializes and gains this experience by repeated involvement. However, it would be quite wrong for any charity to stand the cost of this learning curve and therefore quite clearly there is a need for further detailed charity audit and accounting training.

Like many organizations, but perhaps more so than in the industrial world, the annual report and accounts are used by a charity as part of its public relations and it is therefore important that the auditor provides advice on presentation.

Fundamentals of an effective audit

The specific guidelines on charity audits, which flowed out of the Charities Act 1993 after the accounting regulations, were published on 22 October 1996. The guidelines, published as Practice Note 11 – *The Audit of*

Charities, take the form of commentary on factors to be considered by auditors in order to meet the requirements of the Auditing Practices Board's Auditing Standards when undertaking the audit of a charity's financial statements. It also provides background information on the regulatory and legal framework relating to charities in the UK. At the time of writing (June 2001) the APB is reviewing the Practice Note in light of the revised SORP, Regulations and its own operating effectiveness.

Besides its relevance to auditors, the Practice Note contains much that would be of interest to trustees and others involved in the management of charities, and should help them to gain a better understanding of both the auditors' work and the way in which charities can benefit from the audit process. The application of auditing standards is no different in the case of charities than in the case of other organizations.

The Practice Note sets out special considerations relating to the audit of charities which arise from individual Statements of Auditing Standards (SASs) and where no special considerations apply no comment is made. The following SASs are included:

SAS 110   Fraud and error.
SAS 120   Consideration of law and regulations.
SAS 130   The going concern basis in financial statements.
SAS 140   Engagement letters.
SAS 160   Other information in documents containing audited financial statements.
SAS 210   Knowledge of the business.
SAS 220   Materiality and the audit.
SAS 300   Accounting and internal control systems and audit risk assessments.
SAS 400   Audit evidence.
SAS 410   Analytical procedures.
SAS 420   Audit of accounting estimates.
SAS 440   Management representations.
SAS 450   Opening balances and comparatives.
SAS 460   Related parties.
SAS 470   Overall review of financial statements.
SAS 510   The relationship between principal auditors and other auditors.
SAS 600   Auditors' reports on financial statements.
SAS 610   Reports to directors or management.
SAS 620   The auditors' right and duty to report to regulators in the financial sector.

The purpose of this practice note is very clearly to provide guidance on the application of auditing standards when auditing a charity, rather than a general commentary on such audits. The approach taken has therefore been to consider the various SASs issued by the APB and to provide guidance on matters specific to the audit of a charity's financial statements. There is therefore an attempt to incorporate, within this framework, all the major issues which are likely to need particular application of judgement by auditors. More specifically, the five key areas covered are:

- factors affecting auditors' assessment of risk;
- analysis of relevant law and regulations;
- controls over key aspects of a charity's income and assets;
- matters to be reported directly to the Charity Commission; and
- content of report on financial statements.

The fundamentals of an effective audit should be to:

- understand the activity;
- identify key areas;
- assess risk;
- plan;
- monitor progress;
- report.

It is vital that the auditor knows the organization and understands fully what its mandate and mission is. The auditor should know where the money comes from, where it is going to and the systems within the organization for controlling income, expenditure, staff resources, etc.

Quite clearly one will start by identifying those key areas within which the charity operates, both in its fund-raising and operating field. Some of these have considerably more risk than others and it is here that concentration on the sensitive areas is essential. Charities are forever changing the way in which they fund-raise, as new innovative ideas come forward and the business will change, often dramatically, from year to year.

Therefore, it is important that audits should be planned and structured in a way that takes account of this, but also assists the management of the charity in the task of both maximizing the resources available and ensuring that they are applied to achieve the charitable objectives as cost-effectively as possible. Monitoring progress then becomes vital, and one of the complaints frequently heard from charity finance directors is that they never know what is happening whilst the audit is in progress and that, worse still, the reports at the end of the charity audit seem to take far too long to arrive.

Auditing income

There are as many types of charity, probably more, than there are types of business. Charity is not just one industry but many complex ones. The main difference in audit approach has to be due to the nature of voluntary income which is so different from the turnover of a 'normal' for-profit enterprise as to make it extremely difficult to audit. Obviously there will not be a sales invoice for a donation although of course there should or could be a receipt. Quite clearly in the case of legacy income, despatch notes and invoices will be unheard of; however, there should be an audit trail via a chain of letters to and from the executors of the legacy. Only when a charity goes into trading activity are there likely to be any profit margins.

Much, probably most, of the income of a fund-raising charity will be unsolicited and this leads to considerable difficulties in verification of completeness. Obviously it will be quite easy to audit what is there but very difficult to confirm that it is all there. However, attempts must be made to do this. It is extremely important for the auditor to ascertain in relation to income:

- What was its origin?
- What restrictions, if any exist, on its use?
- What is its nature?

Why are these questions important?

The consideration of these three questions should, in the case of the origin, allow judgements to be made about whether it is all there and how to audit it. For example, taking legacy income one needs to look at whether it is a pecuniary legacy, specific bequest or part of the residue. Have there been any interim payments? Have inheritance tax and capital gains tax implications been taken care of? What about tax on dividends received? Here it should be a fairly easy and straightforward process to audit the correspondence between the charity staff and the executors of the will and, where necessary, examine the wills concerned.

Second, any money received in trust must be used for the purpose for which it was given. The restriction principle is paramount here and any unspent restricted income has to be carried forward and separately identified in the accounts. The use of restricted funds is very tightly controlled and needs to be easily identifiable in the accounts. Paperwork supporting legacy income should be reviewed to ensure that the terms of the will do not stipulate the setting up of a restricted fund with a specific purpose.

Recognition of the nature of the income is vital. Charities are governed by strict rules in what they can and cannot do. Contrary to popular misbelief, there are many tax implications for charities, for example the raising of funds is in itself not a charitable objective and consequently trading is usually outside the scope of activities that can be carried on by a charity. Thus if it has carried out this business within the charity it is essential that this is looked at in considerable detail.

Grants should not be recognized until the conditions for receipt have been met. If there is a likelihood of the grant having to be repaid then it should be treated as a contingent liability. Grants restricted to future accounting periods should be deferred and recognized in the future accounting period to which it relates, and the basis for apportionment should be explained in the notes to the accounts. Grants for immediate financial support and assistance should be recognized immediately in the SOFA. A description of the sources of material grants, by category, should be disclosed in the accounts. By category refers to whether the grant, for example, is local authority or government department.

The possibility of there being gifts in kind will need to be reviewed with the client. A valuation will need to be established where the gift is capable of measurement. If material, the gift should be disclosed by way of a note and an accounting policy showing the basis of valuation incorporated. Some other possible examples of evidence that can be reviewed to verify the figures in the books are:

- published literature;
- minutes of meetings – particularly fund-raising committees;
- membership records – where applicable;
- comparison of events' income with entrance fees, etc.;
- Gift Aid records;
- internal notice boards;
- correspondence from donors;
- comparison of raffle/lottery proceeds with details of tickets sold (e.g. stubs);
- attendance at occasional functions.

Auditing expenditure

This of course is somewhat more straightforward. Generally, the audit of expenditure is a control over the purchases, payments and creditor cycle. Additionally, with a charity it is, however, important that a check is made to ensure that payments are within its charitable objective purposes.

The audit approach should therefore check the adequacy of controls over:

- analysis;
- allocation and matching with income;
- ordering procedures;
- creditors' records;
- commitments;
- value for money.

For restricted funds there will be a need to ensure correct use of the income for the purposes intended. Endowment funds need to be very carefully looked at. Under Trustee Law the trustees of a charity or trustees' family or business connections are not allowed to benefit from their involvement in the charity in any way. This includes remuneration, beneficial loans, gifts or services. Any such benefit must be disclosed in the accounts by reference to the source, the recipient and the amount. Exceptions to this are where the constitution permits it. The fact that the trustees have received no remuneration must be stated in the accounts.

Many charities pay their trustees expenses in respect of their attendance at meetings. Under the SORP the number of trustees in receipt of expenses should be disclosed, together with the total of the expenses and an indication of what the expenses are for. In most cases, this will be for travel and subsistence. If the trustees have received no reimbursement that fact must be stated.

Trustees are liable for the consequences of the charity if it can be proved they acted in breach of trust. The Charity Commission is able to take proceedings in court to recover from the trustees personally. In order to guard against this, insurance has recently been made available on the market by which trustees can insure themselves against such a claim. In the instances of such insurance being taken out, the fact that the insurance has been purchased and the costs incurred need to be disclosed in the accounts.

The normal payroll work undertaken in the course of an audit will need to be done. However, in addition to this the number of employees whose emoluments were in excess of £50,000 needs to be disclosed in the accounts. The banding by which this is shown is different to the old Companies Act requirement as the banding of the remuneration is £10,000 and not £5,000. If no employees received remuneration in excess of £50,000 this fact needs to be stated.

Some charities make material payments of grants. Where this is the case the name of the recipient institution and the aggregate amount of the grant made to that recipient in the accounting period needs to be shown. The definition of material depends on the size of the charity. If the proportion of expenditure spent on grants is less than 5 per cent then no disclosure needs to be made. Where disclosure is required, all grants made over £1,000 in this instance should be disclosed. In the case of a large grant-making organization this can be restricted to the largest 50 grants.

If the trustees consider the disclosure of this information to be detrimental to the charity or the recipient, this information may be withheld but the full amount of all the grants made should be disclosed. In cases of grants made to individuals, only the aggregate value and the number of grants should be disclosed.

Audit evidence

The auditor should give special attention to the possibility of:

- understatement or incompleteness of the records of income;
- overstatement of expenses, in particular cash grants;
- misanalysis or misuse in the application of funds;

- misstatement or omission of assets;
- the existence of restricted or uncontrollable funds in foreign or independent branches.

Internal controls

Large charities will, or rather should, have internal controls appropriate to any large enterprise. The auditors should look for and encourage the charity to implement internal controls and reporting systems in keeping with the scale of operations. In considering internal controls, the auditor should bear in mind any related reporting requirements. For example, the Friendly Societies Act 1992 requires that the audit report has a statement to the effect that a satisfactory system of control over transactions has or has not been maintained. Obviously the smaller the charity, the weaker the internal controls are likely to be, and here the use of volunteers and trustees in ensuring that all procedures have been correctly followed is advised.

Review of financial statements

As normal, the auditor should consider whether the accounting policies adopted are appropriate to the specific objectives, activities and constitution of the charity. In particular, the auditor should consider the basis of:

- disclosing income from fund-raising activities (i.e. net or gross);
- accounting for income and expenditure (accrual or cash basis);
- the capitalizing of expenditure on fixed assets;
- apportioning overhead expenditure;
- accounting for income from donations and legacies;
- considering the possible exposure to taxation.

Going concern

Charities without significant endowment or accumulated funds will often be dependent upon future income from voluntary sources in order to meet the financial commitments arising from the continuation of their activities. Thus the review of the financial statements may lead the auditor to question whether a going concern basis of accounting is appropriate. However, before forming a conclusion on the matter, the auditor should take account of the amount of, and trends in, income and expenditure since the accounting date, any forecast and representations by management as to future income and expenditure and (where relevant), the market value of the charity's tangible assets.

Statutory reports

There is, in fact, no common report possible for all charities because they will all be constituted differently and will be governed by many differing rules and laws. For example, the auditors' report on the financial statements of a charity registered under the Companies Act will continue to be determined in accordance with the provisions of that Act and addressed to the members of the charity. However, the auditors' report on the financial statements of a charity registered under the Acts relating to Friendly, Industrial and Provident Societies will be in a different form and addressed to the charity itself.

Summary financial information and statements

The statement which accompanies the summarized accounts must also show clearly whether or not the full annual accounts have at the date of issuing the statement been audited or independently examined. In those cases where they have been, then there has to be a statement from the auditor or independent examiner giving their opinion as to whether or not the summarized accounts are consistent with the full accounts. Practice Note 11 – *The Audit of Charities* gives the following example:

Auditors' statement to the Trustees of XYZ charity

We have examined the summarised financial statements set out in pages ... to ...

Respective responsibilities of trustees and auditors

You are responsible as trustees for the preparation of the summary financial statements. We have agreed to report to you our opinion on the summarised statements' consistency with the full financial statements, on which we reported to you on (date).

Basis of opinion

We have carried out the procedures we consider necessary to ascertain whether the summarised financial statements are consistent with the full financial statements from which they have been prepared.

Opinion

In our opinion the summarised financial statements are consistent [are not consistent] with the full financial statements for the year ended 31 December 19xx [in the following respects . . .]

Registered auditors   *Address*
Date

This statement will also have to make it clear whether the full accounts were unqualified or not. If the report and accounts were qualified then the statement accompanying the summarized accounts should give enough details to enable the reader to appreciate the significance of the qualification. A full repeat of the auditors' or independent examiners' report will not be necessary.

Whistle blowing

This 'whistle blowing' duty is a provision designed to increase public confidence by giving the auditor or independent examiner of an unincorporated charity the right and duty to report certain facts direct to the Charity Commission. This will occur if, acting in their capacity of auditor or independent examiner, they find evidence of deliberate or reckless misconduct by one or more trustees, especially action (or often more appropriately inaction) which puts the property of the charity at risk.

Auditors are not required to change the scope of their work to discover whether or not reportable matters exist. The duty arises if something is discovered whilst carrying out their audit which in their opinion is judged to be of 'material significance'. The APB Practice Note, commenting on SAS 620, sets out in some detail the three main types of material significant matters likely to be reportable:

1   a significant inadequacy of the arrangements made by the trustees for the direction and management of a charity's affairs;
2   a significant breach of a legislative requirement or of the charity's trusts; or
3   circumstances indicating a probably deliberate mis-use of charity property.

Audit management report

This is still not used as frequently in the charity world as elsewhere and it is vitally important that it is, so that the charity can derive full benefit from it. The report should not be just a catalogue of what is wrong, and it should certainly not be destructive criticism. What it should be is helpful, pointing out the weaknesses and providing ways of overcoming them whilst at the same time suggesting ideas for building on the strengths.

The report should of course describe the standard of the accounts and the systems on which they are based, paying particular attention to controls in existence. The charity's attention should be drawn to departures from best practice within the charity sector and from the law. Any known changes, e.g. revised Charities SORP, should be highlighted for the benefit of the charity client. As referred to earlier, often these, when they are produced, arrive late, are produced well after the accounts have been signed off, and quite frequently so far into the following year as to be useless as a tool for planning improvements.

Conclusion

Both the management of the charity and the auditors should recognize and expect that the auditors can, and should, do more than just provide an audit report. Relationships with the charity will frequently tend, certainly with the larger charities, to be with the executive management and it is essential that the auditors also meet with the trustees or at least those who have financial responsibility. The Charities Act effectively came about because of the increasing demand from the public that charities be properly controlled and efficiently managed. It is therefore essential that auditors should contribute to this.

Independent examination

Introduction

The decision on whether a charity needs audit or independent examination depends on its size. To meet the requirements of the Charities Act 1993 all charities with an income in excess of £250,000 will require audit, whether independent examination is required for a smaller charity or not depends on the legal status of the charity. Unincorporated charities with an income of £250,000 or less can have an independent examination unless their constitution specifically requires an audit. Incorporated charities with an income up to £90,000 do not require audit and those with an income within the range £90,000 to £250,000 are entitled to an audit exemption report.

What is an independent examination?

It is a less onerous form of scrutiny than audit, both in terms of the depth of work to be carried out and the qualification necessary to undertake such work. It does not lead to the expression of an opinion that the accounts show a true and fair view. Instead, it highlights whether certain matters have been brought to the reviewer's attention. The work must include the following procedures:

- obtaining an understanding of the activities and structure of the charity to plan appropriate examination procedures;
- checking that the election for independent examination is valid;
- recording the procedures carried out and the conclusions reached;
- comparing the accounts with the accounting records to ensure they are in accordance with one another;
- reviewing the accounting records to identify gross failures to maintain proper records;

- carrying out an analytical review to identify unusual items or disclosures in the accounts, obtaining explanations and, if necessary, obtaining additional verification of the amounts involved;
- checking that the format and basis of preparation of the accounts accords with the requirements of the Regulations.

In addition, where accounts are prepared on the accruals basis, the independent examiner must check them for compliance with the Regulations in terms of format and content, review accounting policies, estimates and judgements, enquire about post balance sheet events and compare the accounts with the trustees' report to make sure they are consistent with each other.

The independent examiner should inform the Charity Commission, in writing, if they have reasonable cause to believe that one or more of the trustees has been responsible for deliberate or reckless misconduct in the administration of the charity.

Who can be an independent examiner?

The Charities Act 1993 defined an independent examiner as 'an independent person who is reasonably believed by the trustees to have the requisite ability and practical experience to carry out a competent examination of the accounts.' It went on to define independent as having 'no connection with the charity's trustees which might inhibit the impartial conduct of the examination.'

Therefore, the independent examiner should be competent and familiar with accountancy methods but need not be a practising accountant. Someone with a professional qualification, especially a qualified accountant, is strongly recommended by the Charity Commission. This is particularly so for the larger charities or where accruals accounting is adopted.

The independent examiner's report

The content of the report is determined by the Regulations. It must state:

- the name and address of the examiner and the name of the charity;
- the date of the report and the financial year to which the relevant accounts relate;
- reference to the report being carried out under Section 43 of the Charities Act 1993;
- whether or not matters have come to the independent examiner's attention which give him/her reasonable cause to believe that:
  - proper accounting records have not been maintained;
  - the accounts do not agree with the accounting records;
  - where accruals accounts are prepared, the Regulations for form and content of the accounts have not been complied with;

- whether or not any matter has come to his/her attention which should be referred to in the accounts;
- by exception, if there have been any of the following:
  - material expenditure or action contrary to the trusts of the charity;
  - withholding of information or explanations due to him/her;
  - where accruals accounts are prepared, inconsistencies between the accounts and the trustees' report.

The report must be signed by the independent examiner and must state any relevant professional qualifications or professional body of which they are a member. The recommended reporting requirements are set higher than the compliance reports for companies under the deregulation regime.

Conclusion

The *Directions and Guidance Notes* (CC63), a revised version of CC56, published by the Charity Commission on 'The Carrying Out of an Independent Examination' should certainly be read by all charities who are going to be independently examined and must be read by those carrying out such examinations.

Trustees' annual report

Introduction

The charity world has frequently tended to express its accountability and measure its effectiveness in purely financial terms. This approach is obviously only part of the picture and cash is often only a poor proxy for value. Charity accounts too rarely contain qualitative information that is essential for a full understanding of the figures. The information that is needed is not how much has been spent but how much has been achieved in affecting the issues being addressed and meeting the charity's objectives. The trustees' report, along with the sometimes glossy annual review, can successfully carry out this function.

Stakeholders need to know how the charity is succeeding in its aim to achieve its particular objectives. There will be a break in the special relationship between the stakeholder and the charity, even in cases where the stakeholders want to support the objectives of the organization. In fact, the charity is not in some way accountable and cannot demonstrably satisfy the various stakeholders' different requirements.

It is essential that the trustees' annual report is designed to provide some basic information relating to the charity, its trustees and officers and a concise but comprehensive review of the charity's activities. The trustees' report should therefore provide detailed written information that should tie in with the expenditure headings in the accounts that follow. It should also provide other qualitative non-financial indicators, for example as the charity ChildLine does by showing the number of children counselled.

Charities Act 1993

Section 45 makes it quite clear that:

> The charity trustees of a charity should prepare in respect of each financial year of the charity an annual report containing:
>
> (a) such a report by the trustees on the activities of the charity during that year; and
> (b) such other information relating to the charity or to its trustees or offices;
>
> as may be prescribed by regulations made by the Secretary of State.

Regulations

The requirements in relation to the annual report are set out in the 2000 Regulation 7(3) as follows:

1   in the case of any financial year of a charity in which neither its gross income nor its total expenditure exceeds £250,000, a brief summary of the main activities and achievements of the charity during the year;
2   in the case of any financial year of a charity in which its gross income exceeds £250,000 –
   a   be a review of all activities, including –
      i   material transactions, significant developments and achievements of the charity during the year in relation to its objects;
      ii   any significant changes in those activities during the year;
      iii   any important events effecting those activities that have occurred since the end of the year and any likely future developments in those activities; and
      iv   where any fund of the charity was in deficit at the beginning of the financial year, the steps taken by the charity trustees to eliminate that deficit; and
   b   contain a statement as to whether the charity trustees have given consideration to –
      i   the major risks to which the charity is exposed; and
      ii   systems designed to mitigate those risks; and
3   in either case, be dated and signed by one or more of the charity trustees, each of whom has been authorized to do so.

SORP

The 1995 SORP recommended that the formal narrative statement be considerably expanded. This meant that the trustees' report had to include information about the charity's objects, activities and achievements as well as a commentary on the financial position of the charity. However, despite this, it did not appear to be happening so the revised 2000 SORP reinforced the position by restating the requirements.

The detail for the narrative information has been reduced in order to encourage charities to expand on their activities and achievements of their objectives. In particular, trustees are asked to report on their reserves (the policy, the level and the justification) and, where applicable, their investment and grant-making policies as well as the effectiveness of their fundraising activities. Trustees should also provide a statement confirming that the major risks to which the charity is exposed have been reviewed and systems established to minimize those risks.

To paraphrase the SORP, it is the trustees' responsibility to prepare, in respect of each financial year, accounts and notes which comply with the SORP and a report setting out the narrative information required. This report should describe what the charity is trying to do and how it is achieving its objectives. For those charities that are incorporated, to avoid duplication, the trustees/directors should ensure that their annual report as trustees includes all those matters that are required to be included in the statutory directors' report.

Trustees are advised to include any additional information that they are required by law to report, and they should confirm that the accounts comply with the current legal requirements, the requirements of the charity's governing document and the requirements of the revised SORP. The report and accounts have to be approved by the trustees acting together dependent upon their governing document. Both the report and the accounts should be signed by at least one of the trustees who has been authorized to do so by the trustee board. Obviously the date of approval needs to be given. Any trustee who considers that the report and/or accounts should not be approved, or should not have been approved, should report this matter to the Charity Commission along with any concern which they were unable to resolve with their fellow trustees.

Whenever a full set of accounts is distributed by the charity it must have attached to it the trustees' annual report together with the audit/ independent report on the accounts. To summarize, the trustees' annual report should:

- explain the objects of the charity
- provide a description of the organizational structure of the charity
- explain how decisions are made
- include a statement regarding the relationship between the charity and related parties/other charities with which it co-operates

- provide a review of the activities of the charity
- include a statement of the charity's policies, e.g. on reserves, investments and grant making
- where funds are in deficit provide an explanation of why they are in deficit and the action that has been taken
- include a statement confirming that major risks to which the charity is exposed have been reviewed and systems have been established to minimize those risks.

There also has to be a statement setting out the legal and administrative details, either as part of the report or as a separate section in the report and accounts. These include such obvious things as the full name of the charity, a list of the trustees and the method of appointment/election, the address of the principal office, the name and addresses of principal advisers, an indication of the nature of the governing document, details of specific restrictions and a summary of any specific investment powers.

It is important that trustees, when preparing the trustees' report, appreciate the balance between clarity and brevity. Some reports are too long and detailed and are therefore not read, whilst others are so short that they may merely raise more questions than they answer and will not meet the requirements as set out above. As we have clearly seen, the regulations under the Charities Act 1993 stipulate the minimum requirement of the trustees' annual report whilst the SORP itself provides further recommendations.

7   Management accounting

Introduction

Income from dedicated supporters, grants or investment is not like making and selling a product. These traditional income sources have not previously required voluntary organizations to undertake costing and budgeting. As one Christian overseas charity accountant commented: 'if we are short we ask the congregations'. A number of factors have begun to change this attitude:

- Government funding and in particular the contract culture;
- the competition for funds;
- increased scrutiny of how funds are spent;
- the SORP.

Understanding what an activity costs and having a clear perspective of what the organization wishes to achieve – break even, surplus or planned deficit – are vital if a voluntary organization is to both survive and deliver services effectively. Without understanding its cost structure and preparing financial forecasts, a voluntary organization is unlikely to survive. As management improves in voluntary organizations (Bruce 1994; Hind 1995; Courtney 1996; Hudson 1999), they see budgeting as a process which helps the aims of the organization and involves the whole organization participating. Budgeting can be a useful communication technique both within the organization, particularly when it is 'bottom-up', and in meeting the requirement of a funder.

Cost accounting

Most simple costs are the financial value(s) of the resources used to develop a service. You need to be clear of the full range of resources which go into a service and their financial value.

When calculating costs it is useful to do so against two dimensions:

- the type of expenditure;
- the site (project) at which the activity occurred – referred to as a 'cost centre'.

This is also useful for control purposes as it allows reports comparing the budget against the actual activity to be compiled during the year and at the year-end.

Costing a service

Unit costs are the simplest and most common way to cost a service or organization. They recognize the cost of one part or 'unit' in a service. Depending upon the nature of the activity, this could be a cost per service user, per component or per staff member. This is important as it:

- helps you to gauge the relative efficiency of parts of your service compared to other parts or to that provided by another organization;
- helps you to prepare tenders for contracts and to decide the appropriate fee to charge.

A useful model for costing a service has been described by Osbourne (1996):

1 Identify and describe the components of a service.
2 Decide upon the relevant service units to which a cost is to be attached – make sure this is meaningful. An appropriate unit for residential care might be a cost per night while for a nursing service it might be a cost per hour.
3 Identify the key implications of these costs upon the various elements of a service – different costs have different implications. A member of staff not only has a salary but also national insurance, pension and issues of training and support, etc.
4 Finally, calculate the unit cost for the service – dividing the total cost of the service by the most appropriate measurement. Also entered here are the overhead costs of the organization.

Overhead costs

These are costs which are incurred by the organization as a whole, and are usually apportioned to the different cost centres. There is no one method of dividing these costs, but the most simple and common is called absorption costing which is to spread all the cost into the centres.

In separating out overhead costs for absorption, it is useful to think of the total costs at each cost centre as comprising four elements:

1 Direct costs of the service.
2 Indirect costs which are incurred in support of the service and are usually carried out within, or linked to the service itself – heating/lighting of office for the service.

3　Overhead costs which are the costs of the headquarters and central services of the organization – chief executive's salary, etc.
4　Capital related costs – interest repayments or depreciation upon any equipment.

The benefits of absorption costing are:

1　It makes sure that the full costs of an organization are absorbed at the service level, so that overhead costs are not a drain upon other incomes or reserves.
2　It ensures that an organization can receive the maximum amount of income to cover its costs.
3　It can lead to greater accountability of the central services of an organization to the services that are funding them.

Problems with absorption costing have been noted by Osbourne (1996) to be as follows:

1　Absorption costing can lead to inefficiency in central services, as they have no incentive to minimize or control their costs.
2　Competitive edge can be blunted if another organization bidding for a contract has 'leaner costs' or is not working on an absorption model.
3　Can cause resentment among service managers who may feel they are supporting the central services to the detriment of their own service.

Two alternatives to dealing with overhead costs are:

1　Workload charging – central services charge a fee for their services directly to other parts of the organization.
2　Service load agreements – a level of service is agreed at a predetermined price.

Unit costs and analysis – a warning

There are limitations to unit costs when used to evaluate or compare different services and cost centres. Comparison on costs alone is not sufficient, as other elements can obscure differences, for example:

- the complexity of the needs being met and in the quality of the service being provided;
- the accommodation a service is operating from, which could affect its costs;
- significant regional differences in salaries or costs for a national organization;
- how different services may be treating their costs.

Activity-based costing

Dissatisfaction with traditional costing methods, and in particular the application of overhead costs, led to the development of activity-based costing (ABC) in the 1980s. What makes ABC different is that it takes the perspective that overheads do not just occur and have to be allocated in some formula, but instead are real costs caused by activities or cost drivers. The dynamic approach of ABC is that instead of thinking of overheads as rendering a service to units of cost, it sees overheads being created by cost units. Thus overheads should be charged according to the costs which have caused them. The advantage of ABC is that it replaces the arbitrary nature of overhead apportionment, which can be inefficient and cause conflict with the direct service operations of a voluntary organization with a more transparent system. Advocates of ABC argue that overhead costs can be analysed and cost drivers identified. Park (1997) illustrates the use of ABC for a service charity running a number of educational establishments for children with specific disabilities:

> The products being provided are placements at one of the schools, nurseries or training centres. Under ABC the costs would be allocated to the type of placement and not by cost type. In this example direct allocation of costs to the product is impossible, hence keys also need to be identified which reflect as closely as possible the true cost of the service. To determine the most appropriate key(s) will require the involvement in, and commitment of, the staff who do the actual work. Illustrated is the revised allocation of costs together with the possible keys:

Breakdown by cost type	*Allocation key*	*Breakdown by product/activity*
Payroll staff salaries	Time spent per activity	School A
Computer processing costs	Number on payroll	School B
Bank charges	Number on payroll	Nursery A
Materials	Number on payroll	Training centre, Secondary resource A, Fundraising, etc.

> Then, depending upon the level of additional detail required the costs can be further broken down, for example:

School A   Routine processing of salaries
            Modification of salaries
            Responding to employee queries, etc.

> Once the business processes have been determined and the basis of allocation of costs agreed, provision of costs by business process gives management insight into both the level and the nature of the cost.

In defining a business process there is an implicit assumption that a business process or product must have an owner. When one is looking at a product this is clearly identifiable – the customer. However, these relationships also exist within an organization. It is the recognition by the service provider and the customer of their respective positions, roles and responsibilities which underpins ABC. These roles are not necessarily mutually exclusive. Again, using the example of a payroll department, this department is both the customer of the information technology department for the running of the computerized payroll, and the service provider of payroll information to the sites and employees.

Critics of ABC argue that analysis of overheads in order to identify the cost drivers is time-consuming and the cost savings associated do not justify it. Bashir (1999) and Park (1997) outline the specific problems associated with ABC application to the voluntary sector. They both conclude that ABC is primarily relevant to very large charities, which could justify the expense involved in having the sophisticated computer systems to provide the information to undertake ABC analysis. However, as a one-off analysis exercise ABC can be used by all voluntary organizations.

Cost behaviour

The basic principle of cost behaviour is that as a level of activity rises, so costs will usually rise. The problem is, in what ways do costs rise, and by how much, as the level of output increases? Costs can be divided into fixed and variable:

- A fixed cost is one that does not change with outputs, for example a professional salary or rental of a telephone line.
- A variable cost does vary with a level of output, for example a sessional worker as sessions increase or telephone charges as you make a call.

You can also have costs that are a mixture of the two; for example a second telephone line. Here your fixed costs increase stepwise:

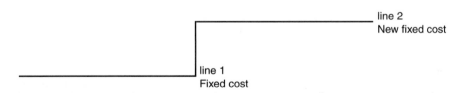

line 2
New fixed cost

line 1
Fixed cost

Salaries can also have a fixed element and then a variable element, i.e. overtime payments. These are called semi-fixed or mixed costs.

Example

Reviewing the need for vehicles at its projects, three different mileage uses are proposed ranging from 15,000 to 25,000 to 40,000 miles. What are the costs of vehicles at these different rates?

The following information is obtained per vehicle:

1   Vehicle leases are £3,000.
2   Petrol and oil cost 10p per mile.
3   Tyres cost £400 per set to replace. They require replacement at 25,000 miles.
4   Fixed maintenance costs are £175 per annum.
5   Tax and insurance are £300 per annum.

Answer

The costs can be divided into fixed, variable and mixed (step) costs.

	£ per year
Fixed costs are:	
Leasing charge	3,000
Maintenance	175
Tax, insurance	300
	3,475

Variable costs are:	
Petrol and oil	10p per mile

Step costs are:	
Tyre replacement at 25,000 miles.	
Therefore at:	15,000 miles no cost
	25,000 miles £400
	40,000 miles £400

The estimated yearly costs then are:

	15,000 miles £	25,000 miles £	40,000 miles £
Fixed costs	3,475	3,475	3,475
Variable costs (10p per mile)	1,500	2,500	4,000
Step costs	0	400	400
Total	4,975	6,375	7,875

Break-even analysis

In calculating a budget your income and expenditure may be exactly equal, that is you 'break even'. A voluntary organization tendering for a local government contract may wish this. In reality the actual accounts will probably be a small surplus or deficit but in tendering for the contract you wish to ensure that you are not going to make a loss. Break-even analysis is used to assess whether a particular activity should be undertaken.

To use break-even analysis you must understand the concept of contribution. This is calculating how much of your variable income less expenditure is required to cover your fixed costs.

Example

A voluntary drug counselling service is financed by fees of £500 for every client seen. The organization has certain fixed costs. In preparing the budget, it would be useful to know at what point does the variable income less variable expenditure cover the fixed costs.

The costs are as follows:

Annual fixed costs	£462,500.00
Variable cost per client	£17.50

Calculation
Contribution per client £500−£17.50 = £482.50
Break-even point = £462,500/£482.50 = 958 clients

The project requires 958 clients to break even, in other words to cover its fixed costs.

To calculate the break-even point you need first to work out the contribution per unit. This is done by taking the variable costs away from the variable income per unit. If total fixed costs are then divided by this contribution per unit, the number of units needed to break even will be found.

Budgeting

A budget is a plan translated into money for a defined period of time. The time period is usually one year. The budget is prepared after the organization has clarified its aims and objectives and produced a variety of action plans to achieve them. The purposes of a budget are:

1   To co-ordinate different activities (departments) towards a single plan
2   To communicate and set targets
3   To maximize and allocate resources
4   To identify financial problems
5   To establish a system of control by having a plan against which actual results can be compared
6   To compel planning.

Budget planning

Setting a budget involves translating plans into pounds. Parts of the plan can be calculated with precision while other aspects are more estimation. Before calculation can take place a number of key decisions will have to be made. These include:

Balancing   Does the budget have to be balanced, i.e. one that aims to produce no surplus or loss? Such a decision will have other implications for the financial management of the charity in relation to the level of reserves the organization holds and, if a deficit is planned, what are the implications for the liquidity, the cash flow of the organization, i.e. will it be able to pay salaries?

Timing   Budgets must be completed to a deadline that allows time for planning. This also includes ensuring that the timing matches the decision-making process of funders. Realistic dates also need to be set to allow both those contributing to the budget and those doing the calculations and co-ordination (the finance department) to have sufficient time to complete their tasks.

Evolution   During the year events can occur which require a radical change. Budgets can then become unrealistic or inaccurate. Budgets can and should be changed to reflect new circumstances otherwise in an original or unaltered state they could continue to signal a problem even though it has been resolved. An alternative is to keep the original budget but provide a note explaining the circumstances; however, this course of action can be ineffective for monitoring and control purposes. A better way is to set up a flexible budget system.

Accountability – allotting responsibility   The planning process will have helped to clarify who has the power to affect various parts of the budget. As far as possible action plans will only have been provided by those who carry responsibility for delivering the service and the general rule is to push the financial authority down to that level. For example, a drug rehabilitation charity may have decided to cut the number of places it offers in hostels by providing more help through detached support workers to people in their own homes. The detached workers' co-ordinator would have been consulted as to the feasibility of extending services and an extra cost agreed. The co-ordinator then becomes a budget holder, responsible for providing the agreed level of service within that cost.

Zero basis versus incremental   Many budgets are drawn up yearly by simply applying a percentage increase to the items originally agreed. This is referred to as 'incremental' budgeting. This method is criticized as it fails to consider whether items are still relevant and the amount allocated appropriate. It also does not recognize inefficiency and mistakes in one year will continue to be repeated. An alternative is to assess every budget item as if for the first time; this method is called 'zero-based' budgeting. In practice, incremental budgeting is the most widely used. This is because many items and activities, particularly in service-providing voluntary organizations, are so fundamental to the organization that they will continue each year, particularly if they are contract funded. In addition, to review every line item would require so much time that it would, if achieved, be self-defeating as the cost saving would probably not be justified. This is not to say that you should dismiss zero-based practices. What you should do, as part of your overall management activities, is to review your activities regularly and, where appropriate, apply a zero-based method on those items.

Types of budget

Budgets should be drawn up according to the needs of the organization. The basic budget is an estimate of incomes and expenditures for the forthcoming year. A relatively simple voluntary organization with a few sources of income and one expenditure activity may just require one budget. More financially complex organizations will require a master budget, which is supplemented by a series of budgets on different activities created to meet specific planning and assessment needs. These might be departmental-type budgets, which will be amalgamated to form the master budget, or different types of budgets, for example projections on the cash needs of the organization or the capital (longer-term) needs.

Budgeting in most organizations is a cyclical activity revolving around the financial year:

1 The finance department/officer provides a plan and budget worksheets to budget holders some six months before the budget is due to start.
2 Budget holders will then compile the respective budget for their activity and return it to the finance officer responsible.
3 The finance officer responsible will then combine all the budgets and create a master budget and the Chief Executive/Management team in larger organizations will then discuss this some three months before the start of the new year.
4 The budget will then be reviewed and approved by the management committee.

In smaller voluntary organizations this activity is usually informal. Larger, more complex organizations, particularly those with branches, may have a more formal procedure usually outlined in a budget manual, a formal written document that explains the purpose of the budget and the formal procedures, and the time frame to be followed.

Many voluntary organizations are dependent on just one source of income. In service delivery organizations this may be a statutory funder and in such cases the voluntary organization is well advised to follow the format of the funder. This format may not be suitable for control purposes. In such cases, the organization is advised to develop the budget format that best suits their needs and then using a spreadsheet to convert this into the funders' format. Larger organizations with many different funders can use the same process, remembering of course to keep a clear trail and reconciliation between the two different documents. If such exercises are required they should be viewed as a compliance cost of meeting the needs of the funder.

A common misconception about budgets is that once set they cannot be changed. In part this comes about because the term 'fixed budget' is used by cost accountants. The term 'fixed budget' in fact means that the budget has been prepared on one estimate of income and expenditure at one level of activity – for example that an advice service will see 100 people a week or a hostel will be 80 per cent occupied. Unforeseen events can occur which are beyond an organization's control. Should the budget then be changed to reflect these changed circumstances? We would suggest that they should. In addition, where the service activity can be quantified then a flexible budget should be prepared instead of a fixed budget. The differences between the two (Bashir 1999, p. 63) are as follows:

Fixed budget	*Flexible budget*
Compares dreams at a point in time to the reality of current situation	Presents realistic statistics based on changing circumstances
No time spent on revisions	Requires continual updating
Wastes funds expended on programmes that are discontinued or found to be ineffective	Continual maximization of resources
Encourages unreasonable expectations	Positive context for accomplishment

Later in this chapter we calculate and use for control purposes a flexible budget.

Preparing forecasts

Voluntary organizations have a variety of income sources, some of which are relatively easy to predict, and others more problematic; for example, a local authority three-year contract versus a mass appeal to the public. Expenditure can also prove relatively easy to calculate or, as for example with capital projects such as building works or installing a new computer system, have 'hidden' problems.

Forecasting is a process that ranges from asking simple but practical questions such as 'this is what it cost last year, how much next year?' to the gathering of intelligence about the organization's micro and macro environment. For example, the changes in the charity tax regime have seen charities losing income through the withdrawal of Advanced Corporation Tax, but potentially gaining income with the flexibility of Gift Aid without limits. A charity with an investment portfolio would therefore be looking at a decline in income stream while an active fund-raising charity with supporters who are prepared to Gift Aid their donations would see an increase.

There are many techniques that can be used to ensure that forecasts are as accurate as possible. Two quantitative techniques used in the business environment which charities could use are time series analysis and regression analysis.

Time series analysis   Data over months and years are obtained and compared. This can be extremely useful in analysing donations where seasonal or cyclical fluctuations or long-term underlying trends can be identified. For example, a charity reviewing its donations over three years:

20 × 1   £480,000
20 × 2   £495,000
20 × 3   £510,000

without further investigation may assume that for the following year a further increase of £15,000 to £525,000 would be achievable. Investigations of monthly figures, however, reveal:

Month	*20 × 2*	*20 × 3*	*Cumulative 20 × 3*	*MAT 20 × 3*
	£	£	£	£
January	37,000	41,000	78,000	499,000
February	39,000	45,000	86,000	505,000
March	40,000	47,000	133,000	512,000
April	41,000	48,000	181,000	519,000
May	42,000	44,000	225,000	521,000
June	41,000	41,000	266,000	521,000
July	41,000	39,000	305,000	519,000
August	38,000	37,000	342,000	518,000
September	41,000	38,000	380,000	515,000
October	42,000	41,000	421,000	514,000
November	43,000	40,000	461,000	511,000
December	50,000	49,000	510,000	510,000
	495,000	510,000		

It is clear from the moving annual total (MAT) that the upward trend in collections was reversed in summer 20 × 3 and that unless it is possible to change the situation, collections in the forthcoming year will be substantially down.

Regression analysis This is a quantitative technique which checks any underlying correlation between two variables; for example, donations from the public and Christmas. You would expect donations to increase during the Christmas festivities when a culture of goodwill is promoted. However, all other charities are also doing the same, people have other things to spend their money on than giving to charities, particularly if they have young children. Therefore, if you are not a particularly 'warm cause charity' or the profile of your supporters are parents with young children then Christmas may not be the best time for your organization.

Internal appraisal of the organization involves the use of reality audits such as a position audit which examines the current state of an organization with respect to issues such as its tangible assets, i.e. investments, relative to intangible assets such as the charity's 'brand' image and position in the market. For example, the charity 'Guide Dogs for the Blind' is very well known. But how high on name recognition is 'Canine Partners for Independence'? Commercial media organizations undertake market analysis, which can identify public perception broken down by region, age, sex, etc., of a charity and its position relative to others. Techniques such as SWOT (strengths, weaknesses, opportunities and threats) analysis can be used to appraise income sources.

Budget preparation must also take into account timing differences between the receipt of income and the payment of expenditure. Some costs, such as insurance premiums, are only paid annually and income from, for example, government grants is paid quarterly, possibly in arrears. This phasing of the budget is important because, without it, useful comparisons between actual and budgeted income and expenditure will not be possible.

Structuring the budget

All budgets by the time they are issued to managers are split into lines. Each line is effectively an authorization to spend or a target to achieve. Budgets also have columns, which split the authorization into time periods. Additional columns, once the budget is operational, allow comparisons to take place between what was expected to happen and what actually happened and the difference between the two expressed in money or percentage terms. These reports may be monthly or usually for a board of trustees are issued quarterly.

In addition, a cash flow budget is constructed. The cash budget shows the total expected outflows (payments) and inflows (receipts) during the year. It is vitally important that this budget is prepared so that the organization is aware of shortages and surpluses during the year. A known cash shortage can be planned for and resolved by, for example, arranging an overdraft. It would be wrong to assume that if the organization is in surplus, it does not have a problem. Idle cash means that the opportunity to earn interest is lost.

For example, for surplus cash of £250,000 and potential earnings with inflation at 2.5 per cent:

	Gross return	*after inflation*
In a normal current account	£0	(6,250)
In an interest paying current account at 1%	£2,500	(3,750)
In a deposit account flow to a current account at 4%	£10,000	3,750
On a money market account at 6%	£15,000	8,750

It should also be noted that surpluses shown on a budget or accounts statement and cash surpluses are not the same for the following reasons:

1   Cash may be paid for the purchase of fixed assets, but the charge in the income and expenditure account (for charities the Statement of Financial Activities) is depreciation, which is only part of the asset's costs.
2   When a fixed asset is sold there is a profit or loss on sale equal to the difference between the sale proceeds and the 'net book value' of the asset in the balance sheet at the time it is sold. For example, if an asset originally cost £50,000 and depreciation of £35,000 has been charged since its purchase, its net book value will be £15,000. If it is now sold for £11,000 there will be a loss on disposal of £4,000. This loss would be recorded in the accounts, but the effect on the sale would be to increase the organization's cash by £11,000.

Budgets and budgetary control

Budgetary control is the practice of establishing budgets, which identify areas of responsibility. They are usually allocated according to the plan of activities and the strategic aim it seeks to meet. An individual manager is responsible for this budget (e.g. Appeals Director) and it is the responsibility of the finance department to provide a timely report of comparing actual results against budget from which the manager responsible can either take corrective action or have reassurance that everything is going to plan.

The most important aspect of budgetary control is variance analysis which involves the comparison of actual results during a common period (for operational managers usually a month, for trustees perhaps quarterly) with budgeted expectations. The differences between actual results and expected results are called variances.

Small variances are obviously to be expected and do not require special comment – indeed to avoid overwhelming managers with unnecessary information it may be appropriate to provide exception reports, that is reports which show only large variances. Variances need investigation to determine their cause and to decide what action might be taken to get the organization back to the plan. One important distinction to make is whether the variance is:

- *Controllable* – in other words due to factors within the organization which can be rectified by the management, or
- *Non-controllable* – due to factors outside the control of the organization. Large non-controllable variances may require a rethink of the plan.

Example

A hospice's expenditure on drug supplies for month 3 is £32,000 against a budget of £28,000. Possible reasons for this might include:

1   Price increases by usual supplier – may be *controllable*. The person responsible for purchasing should try competitive suppliers.
2   Unexpected world prices rise for all aspirin-related drugs – *non-controllable*. Drug budget may need revising for remainder of year.
3   Spoilage of supplies due to inadequate storage conditions – *controllable*. Storage problem needs resolving but this may require additional expenditure.
4   Use of expensive branded drugs instead of cheaper alternatives – may be *controllable*. Hospice needs to look at policy.

Note that although budget holders may be required to account for why the variance has occurred, it is not necessarily their actions which have caused it. The point of the control process is to facilitate appropriate action, not to find someone to blame.

The wrong approach to budgetary control is to compare actual results with a fixed budget. As we discussed earlier, a fixed budget does not mean that the budget is kept unchanged. Revisions are made if required. Instead it means that the budget has been prepared on 'one' estimate of income and expenditure at one level of activity, for example that a homeless night shelter will have 100 rough sleepers or a cultural centre will have 300 visitors per day in the summer months. No plans are made which show the resulting effect on income and expenditure if the numbers are higher or lower than this. For control purposes you can imagine the problem if the numbers are 20 per cent higher or lower than this.

A flexible budget recognizes both the existence of these problems and the different behaviour of fixed and variable costs. It therefore allows you to relate your input to your output levels for a matching activity in the same period.

Example

An advice service may decide on a day caseload ratio of one advisor to twenty clients. The assumption is that sixty people will use the advice centre on any one day and therefore three staff are required. The budget makes this assumption but experience shows that actual numbers may be less. The organization should then prepare a contingency plan for the break-even point at which it would keep three advisors. Below that figure, say 48, you would only have two advisors. So the client adviser ratio would increase to 24:1.

The advantage of flexible budget planning is that you can identify problems in advance and have an action strategy available if they do arise. In this case you could have planned alternatives for spare capacity of advisors – for example researching and writing booklets or have flexible conditions of service for the third advisor.

Fixed versus flexible budgetary control – a worked example

A disabled person's charity has a trading subsidiary – a wood workshop – which makes children's rocking horses for local authority children and foster homes at a set price. Budgeted results and actual results are shown for May 20X1.

	Budget (a)	Actual (b)	Variance
Rocking horses made	100	150	50
	£	£	£
Income (a)	10,000	15,000	5,000
Expenditure:			
Materials	3,000	4,250	(1,250)
Wages	2,000	2,250	(250)
Maintenance	500	700	(200)
Depreciation	1,000	1,100	(100)
Rent and rates	750	800	(50)
Other costs	1,800	2,500	(700)
Total costs (b)	9,050	11,600	(2,550)
Surplus(Deficit) a−b	950	3,400	2,750

Notes

1   In this example, the variances are meaningless for the purposes of control. Costs were higher than budget because there were 50 per cent more rocking horses made. The variable costs would be expected to increase above the budgeted costs. There is no information to show whether control action is required for any aspects of income or expenditure.

2   For control purposes, we need to know:

   a   whether actual costs were higher than they should have been to produce 150 rocking horses;

b   whether actual income was satisfactory from the sale of 150 rocking horses;

c   whether the number of rocking horses made and supplied has varied from the budget in a good or bad way.

The correct approach to budgetary control is to:

i   identify fixed and variable costs

ii   produce a flexible budget.

In our example we have the following estimates of cost behaviour:

a   materials, wages and maintenance costs are variable;

b   rent, rates and depreciation are fixed costs;

c   other costs consist of fixed costs of £800 plus a variable cost of £10 per rocking horse made and distributed to the local authorities.

The budgetary control (variance) analysis should be:

	Fixed budget (a)	Flexible budget (b)	Actual (c)	Variance (b) − (c)
Rocking horses made	100	150	150	
	£	£	£	£
Income	10,000	15,000	15,000	0
Expenditure:				
Variable				
Materials	3,000	4,500	4,250	250
Wages	2,000	3,000	2,250	750
Maintenance	500	750	700	50
Semi-variable costs:				
Other costs	1,800	2,300	2,500	(200)
Fixed costs				
Depreciation	1,000	1,000	1,100	(100)
Rent and rates	750	750	800	(50)
Total costs	9,050	12,300	11,600	700
Surplus	950	2,700	3,400	700

Discussion

1   In producing and distributing 150 rocking horses, the expected surplus should have been not the fixed budget surplus of £950 but the flexible budget surplus of £2,700. Instead the actual surplus was £3,400, £700 more than expected. The reasons for this improvement is that costs are lower than expected as the projected income on 150 horses was exactly as expected.

2 Another reason for the improvement was that the local authorities took all the rocking horses produced. As the cost of producing each unit was less than the price paid by the local authority, a surplus (contribution) was made on each rocking horse. What would have happened if the local authority had not taken and paid for the additional rocking horses?

3 Understanding costs and in particular the difference between fixed, variable and semi-variable costs is vitally important in understanding finance and budgetary control reports. Issues requiring further investigation are:

a The wages did not rise in exact proportion (controllable variance) and are £750 less.

b The other variable cost element (controllable variance) is over by £200.

4 The fixed costs are non-controllable and do not require any more attention from the manager's perspective.

Communicating and computerizing financial information

Finance departments and their managers are no longer bookkeepers hidden away in the back of the building surrounded by dusty ledgers. Instead, they are responsible for a whole host of duties and one of the most important of those is communicating financial information for decision making. The advent of computerization in accounting has been one of the major reasons why the finance officer now has such a dynamic role. Previously, manual systems would take a long time for everything to be calculated and checked to make sure it balanced. Then, from those balances, a separate report would be compiled to produce budget information. Properly set up, a computer system can produce the financial information within days of a month end. Depending on the package and the system design and the organization's requirements, a report produced directly or separately using a spreadsheet can then be supplied to managers. It is now only the smallest and simplest of voluntary organizations which would not benefit from computerizing its accounting function and using spreadsheets to model and plan their future.

Costing volunteering

It is estimated that charities have over 3 million unpaid workers and they contribute the equivalent of almost 1.5 million full-time jobs (NCVO 2000, p. 6). The economic value of this activity has been estimated at £12 billion of which more than £7 billion is either in terms of direct service work or administrative support, the remaining £4 billion relating to voluntary fundraising. These are staggering figures, but of equal interest to us when we have undertaken training on costing in voluntary organizations was why volunteer time had not been valued?

We believe voluntary organizations do not cost volunteer time because it is seen as a 'non-monetary measure' – a free resource – which challenges the fundamental accounting concept of materiality. In addition, 'Estimating the monetary value of volunteering is difficult' (Hedley and Davis Smith 1994, p. 8). We do believe that costing volunteering time should be an activity undertaken by organizations as:

- externally, particularly in costing contracts, it demonstrates the true input value of the voluntary organization;
- internally, it focuses the voluntary organization's attention on how valuable this resource is, and therefore should be ensuring this precious asset is both cared for and being effectively used.

There are numerous methods to value volunteering which have attempted to resolve the methodological problems of how you cost the many different types of volunteer activity, volunteers with different experiences and qualifications and measuring time (Karn 1982; Brudney 1990; Ellis 1996).

Finlow (1999) discusses the different approaches undertaken – for example in imputing a volunteer's time, what value rate should be used for a standard minimum wage, a standard average wage or some equivalent? – and the different costing methods – opportunity cost, replacement cost or an output-based approach.

The literature on volunteer value seems to be united in opposition to the use of the minimum wage or a standard wage, which is believed to undervalue volunteering (Ellis 1996), and recommends the equivalency model (Karn 1982) which involves undertaking the following process:

1   Evaluate job title
2   Calculate true equivalent cost
3   Calculate equivalent hours worked
4   Calculate equivalent days off
5   Calculate equivalent hourly rate.

However, this method does require an investment by the voluntary organization in undertaking such analysis and as Finlow (1999) comments:

> Any charity involved in local government tendering would be laughed at if a submission were made with rates so much in excess of the national minimum.
>
> (Finlow 1999, p. 22)

We believe a pragmatic stance should be taken by voluntary organizations to costing volunteering. They should show the minimum wage replacement cost in tendering for a statutory service contract and the equivalency rate where appropriate. The merits of this approach are that the minimum wage method is relatively easy and cheap to calculate. The equivalency method quite rightly demonstrates the real value of volunteers.

Costing volunteering is an area which is still relatively unexplored and further research is required on costing methods and attitudes by stakeholders, particularly funders, when such methods are used.

Conclusion

Understanding costs and having a costing system is vital to all voluntary organizations. Planning and budgeting are essential if the organization is to have a clear direction and be able to appraise whether it has achieved its objectives and aims.

Illustrative exercises

Exercise 7.1

The importance of forecasting in setting up a subsidiary

'Support' was established as a parent support group for children who were born with severe disability. When the charity was formed, the life expectancy of children was not expected to go beyond early teens. Advances in drug treatment have meant that the children can now expect to live into adulthood. Furthermore, limited movement has opened the possibility that some form of work experience could also be offered. The management committee of Support has decided that 'diversification and expansion' is appropriate and set up a working party to explore opportunities. Support currently has a long-term reserve of £100,000 invested in 7 per cent government stock. The working party was chaired by a prominent IT company Chief Executive whose own disabled daughter was now eighteen. He proposed that the charity should set up a trading subsidiary for an initial outlay of less than £40,000, which would employ the 'children' to undertake simple manual tasks in the assembly of microchips, which could then be sold. He offered to donate free a part of his own factory space for ten years and the time of a manager to run the subsidiary. His commercial accountant has prepared the following estimates for the subsidiary to start on 1 July 200X:

1   Equipment £35,000.
2   Initial materials stock £28,000 which will be replaced monthly with a stock maintained of £28,000 at the end of each month.
3   Sales were expected to be £20,000 per month for the first 3 months and £30,000 per month thereafter representing a profit margin of 33.3 per cent above cost of materials.

4　Suppliers have agreed to give one month's credit and customers will be given 2 months' credit.
5　Monthly expenses paid out in cash will be £4,600.
6　Insurance payable at the start £1,000.
7　Depreciation estimated at £6,000.
8　Legal costs for the formation of the company will be £950 to be paid for in August.

At the trustees meeting the Chief Executive said how much he liked the idea but that a proper business plan should be drawn up. They suggested that the finance officer of Support should assist this process by providing:

a　A month by month estimate of the cash requirements of the subsidiary for the first six months.
b　A financial forecast for the first six months outlining the commitment of Support.
c　A report to the trustees of Support on financial and other related implications.

Answer to Exercise

1 Cash budget
Support subsidiary estimate of cash requirements July to December 200X

	July	August	September	October	November	December
Income:						
Sales	0	0	20,000	20,000	20,000	30,000
Expenditure:						
Equipment		35,000				
Stock:						
Initial		28,000				
Replacement		15,000	15,000	15,000	22,500	22,500
Expenses	4,600	4,600	4,600	4,600	4,600	4,600
Insurance	1,000					
Legal		950				
Total	5,600	83,550	19,600	19,600	27,100	27,100
Deficit for month	5,600	83,550			7,100	
Surplus for month			400	400		2,900
Cash requirement	5,600	89,150	88,750	88,350	95,450	92,550

2 Forecast

Income and expenditure for the first six months

	£	£
Income:		
Sales		
(3 × £20,000) + (3 × £30,000)		150,000
Less cost of sales (3/4 × sales)		112,500
		———
Trading surplus/Gross profit		37,500
Expenditure:		
Expenses (6 × £4,600)	27,600	
Insurance	1,000	
Legal cost	950	
Depreciation	3,000	32,550
		———
Surplus/Net profit for period		4,950
		———

Forecast Balance Sheet

	£	£
Fixed assets		
Equipment	35,000	
Less depreciation	3,000	32,000
	———	
Current assets		
Stock	28,000	
Debtors (2 × £30,000)	60,000	
	———	
	88,000	
Deduct: Current liabilities		
Creditors	22,500	65,500
	———	———
		97,500
		═══
Financed by:		
Profit		4,950
Loan from Support		92,550
		———
		97,500
		═══

3 Report from Finance Officer

On the forecast cash flow, the maximum estimate of cash requirement from the charity to the company will be £95,450. The subsidiary will also require long-term financial support from the charity as the forecast balance sheet identifies. The issue for the charity is therefore: is it part of its charitable activity or is it an investment activity? Discussing the investment option first. The net profit from the venture is estimated at 3.3 per cent (1). The return on the capital required from the charity for a period of six months is 5.3 per cent (2), which is equivalent to 10.6 per cent (3) per annum and compares favourably with other forms of investment. This also represents a premium of 30 per cent for the higher risk involved in this venture rather than leaving the funds invested in government stocks. Put simply in cash terms, we currently have £100,000 invested in 7 per cent stock, which gives us an income of £7,000 per annum. Our cash return in net profit from the subsidiary for the first year is estimated at £9,900, an increased cash return of £2,900. Of course in government stock our money is completely safe although inflation is eroding it. How safe is the venture? For example, how do we know the chips will sell and what contracts have been confirmed? This should be part of the business plan.

A number of accounting and regulatory issues also need review. The Statement of Recommend Practice (SORP) on charities will not be applicable as, I understand, the assets and donations are being made to the trading subsidiary and not to the charity. If this is not the case, then further consideration will be required. A formal loan agreement or share issue will be required between the subsidiary company and the charity (see section on Trading Activities in Chapter 10). We need to check Support's trust deed to see if such a loan is possible. We will require permission from the Charity Commission and the Inland Revenue. If, as the proposal suggests, it is within the charity's objects, then the investment will be shown on the charity's balance sheet as a subsidiary held primarily for the charity's own use and for its functional purposes. If the proposal is not within the charity's main objects, then it should be both classified and justified as an investment fixed asset as outlined earlier. It is the decision of the trustees as to whether they wish to use the charity funds for this purpose. An alternative would be to seek a loan arrangement with a bank or explore what support exists from government or trusts for this venture.

Finally, in reviewing the estimates there are some other concerns, which require further investigation. For example, the monthly cash payments. Are these not actually wages and therefore the term 'children' is not really appropriate? There are potential tax and National Insurance implications. The very generous offer by the chairman of the Opportunities Committee also needs to be subject to a formal agreement, both to cover the charity if anything was to go wrong, as well as to demonstrate transparency in Support's relationship with its trustees.

Notes:
(1) Calculated as £4,950 (net profit)/£150,000 (sales).
(2) Calculated as £4,950/£92,550 (cash requirement).
(3) Assuming profits are generated at the same level throughout the period.

Exercise 7.2

Understanding overhead costs in tendering to run a day centre

Following reorganization, Any Council now comprises two main urban areas at either end of its boundary separated by countryside. One of the urban areas is the County Town and has an active and large Age Concern organization – ACCT. The other smaller urban town has services provided by the former council. Aware of its responsibilities, the new Council has asked ACCT if it would like to run the same services. It currently gives a grant of £80,000 to ACCT. The new services will be half the current size and it has offered a grant of £45,000, that is more than half the current grant recognizing the additional costs involved in the second project. The Council will transfer its current building rent free to ACCT. The Council is looking for a quick response as the current staff have also tendered for the work. There are no 'TUPE' responsibilities as the Council will redeploy existing staff if ACCT takes over.

The current ACCT organization has a large purpose-built building owned by the organization, which accommodates 150 people daily in a variety of activities, advice, medical, etc., services. The building has an average 80 per cent capacity use. The budget of ACCT for the current year is:

Income:	£
Council grant	80,000
Insurance/services	10,000
Donations	17,000
Catering profit	13,500
Investment	5,600
Total	126,100
Expenditure:	
Staff	104,000
Costs	22,000
Total	126,000
Surplus	100

Notes on budget – staff costs (inclusive of NI, etc.).

1 A director £25,000 – who has advised that a Centre manager at £22,000 will need to be appointed and they would expect a 10 per cent salary increase to reflect new responsibilities.
2 A secretary £15,000 – two-thirds of whose time is spent on direct services at the current Centre and has estimated that admin costs at the other Centre will be £7,500.
3 A finance officer £20,000 – who has advised that they would require no additional help as the new computer system has given them spare capacity; however, they would expect a salary increase.

4   Service co-ordinators (both part-time at £10,000 each).
5   A catering manager £12,000 – who has advised they would need an assistant at £10,000.
6   Service session staff £12,000; volunteers' expenses £4,000.
7   Building running costs £10,000, the new centre will be half in size.
8   Office, admin audit £8,000, a further £2,000 would be required for travel, audit, etc., for the new Centre.
9   Investment income: ACCT currently has funds of £80,000 in a 7 per cent fixed interest account.
10 Lunchtime meals are charged at £1.00 and the tea/coffee sessions at 25p per session. A profit of 30 per cent is made on catering. The Centre and catering services are open for 250 days a year.
11 Volunteers including helping in the kitchen are paid expenses, usually £2 per morning or afternoon attendance (3 hours each). The part-time co-ordinators have indicated that they are keen to take on additional work.
12 Donations and service income for the new Centre will be equal in proportion to current ACCT.

Would you take the Council's offer? Cost the service. Pay particular attention as to how you would present your figures and arguments.

Suggested answer to Exercise – version 1

The new organization will be offering a 225-person facility – 75 in the former Council premises and 150 in ACCT.

There are management implications. On the assumption that the service will be jointly managed but also require additional staff there is the issue of overheads. Current management costs are:

	£
Director	25,000
Finance	20,000
Secretary	15,000
Catering	12,000
Office/admin	8,000
Total	80,000

The director's 10 per cent increase should probably also be paid to the finance officer/catering manager. On current total salaries of £57,000 × 10 per cent = £5,700. Revised management costs are £85,700 + £2,000 additional expenditure. This should be allocated on service level criteria of 225 places. Therefore 87,700/225 = £386.66 × 75 places = £29,000.

Trading income from catering at current 80 per cent usage –

Coffee 25p
Tea   25p
Lunch   100p
Total £1.50p per day × 60 persons (80 per cent of 75) × 250 days = £22,500 × 30 per cent = £6,750.

An initial income and expenditure budget can now be drawn up:

Income:	£
Direct:	
Grant	45,000
Catering	6,750
Donations (50%)	8,500
Insurance services (50%)	5,000
Total direct income	65,250
Expenditure:	
Direct costs:	
Manager	22,000
Catering assistant	10,000
Admin support	7,500
Activities/volunteer (50%)	10,000
Sessions (50%)	6,000
Volunteer expenses (50%)	2,000
Building (50%)	5,000
Total costs	62,500
Direct costs surplus/(Deficit)	2,750
Apportioned overheads	29,000
Total costs surplus/(Deficit)	(26,250)

At the direct cost level the service would seem to make sense but after allowing for management overhead costs of £29,000 it clearly does not. ACCT should therefore ask the Council for a grant of £71,250. Is this right?

Suggested answer to Exercise – version 2

Are there not savings for ACCT? Should this be recognized in assisting the trustees to make a decision? Has the management costs apportionment been correctly calculated? Surely the catering manager's, secretary's and director's time has a direct cost element to the county town (CT) premises before apportionment should take place? If we take out the direct costs of the catering manager's time as cook (£12,000), the director as manager (25,000) and the secretary as admin (10,000), this equals £47,000. The revised management overhead is therefore £87,700 − £47,000 = £40,700. This is the cost which should be allocated on a service level criteria/225 places. Therefore, costs are £180.88 (£40,700/225) per place. The new service should therefore have management costs of £13,567 (£180.88 × 75) and CT management costs are now £27,133. Adopting a cost centre approach for the new organization would give the following projected budget:

	Urban Centre £	County Town £	ACCT £
Income			
Council grant	45,000	80,000	125,000
Catering	6,750	13,500	20,250
Donations	8,500	17,000	25,500
Insurance/services	5,000	10,000	15,000
Investment income	0	5,600	5,600
Total income	65,250	126,100	191,350
Expenditure			
Direct costs	62,500	93,000(1)	153,500
Management	13,567	27,133	40,700
Total expenditure	76,067	120,133	196,200
Surplus (Deficit)	(10,817)	5,967	(4,850)

On this basis, ACCT could negotiate on seeking a grant, which it could justify at £55,817 but should not settle for less than £49,850. Other issues the trustees could use for negotiation are the catering service. Currently ACCT covers costs of the catering manager and even makes a small profit; the new facility does not have the capacity even at 100 per cent to cover its cost. The financial value of the contribution of volunteers is not shown. At the minimum wage rate (£3.60) the volunteer labour would equal (£4,000/£2 = 2,000 volunteer sessions × 3 hours per session = 6,000 hours × £3.60 per hour = £21,600 for CT and £10,800 for the new urban centre.

Note 1: County Town revised direct costs

Activities/volunteers staff	£20,000
Activity sessions	£12,000
Volunteers	£4,000
Building	£10,000
Director	£25,000
Catering	£12,000
Secretary	£10,000
Total	£93,000

8 Performance evaluation for voluntary organizations

Introduction

Commercial organizations have always been interested in efficiency in the narrow sense of profitability, because the rewards of the owners and the continuity of the business are dependent on profit. In the 1980s the Conservative Government introduced a Financial Management Initiative (FMI) to improve value for money measurement in the public sector. The FMI in turn created a number of efficiency studies, including one on Voluntary Sector funding (Home Office 1990) and the development of performance indicators in the public services.

The focus on performance measures for voluntary sector organizations has to be understood in both the social and the economic policy contexts we discussed in the first chapter, as well as in respect of developments in management study. The management perception of 'total quality management' is one of continuous improvement. It goes beyond the idea of providing a service to a static predetermined standard but recognizes that, in a competitive and changing world, successful organizations must continuously improve the value they give to their customers. This concept underpins the FMI and subsequent developments including the most recent – Best Value.

The House of Commons Treasury and Civil Service Committee in 1982 debated the issues of organization and management delegation when it sought to promote in each government department an organization and system in which managers at all levels have:

- a clear view of their objectives, and means to assess and wherever possible measure outputs and performance in relation to those objectives;
- well-defined responsibility for making the best use of their resources, including a critical scrutiny of output and value for money; and
- the information (particularly about costs), the training and the access to expert advice that they need to exercise their responsibilities effectively.

The Thatcher government, which launched the FMI, was responsible for taking many public sector bodies directly into the private market sector by way of privatization. Within the public sector, the 'Next Steps' programme, launched in 1988, set out to reorganize central government to take greater account of the needs of customers. Executive functions were increasingly transferred to agencies headed by chief executives with defined tasks and budgets. Reforms in the National Health Service were designed to separate the role of the customer and the provider, to allow negotiated contracts of service and to make managers responsible for performance against specified standards. The Treasury's Competing for Quality in the early 1990s continued the process of introducing service contracts and service level agreements which defined standards of performance and responsibility for achieving them; departments and executive agencies had to publish annual targets for market testing. Local authority compulsory competitive tendering (now abolished in Best Value) was extended and health authorities and trusts had to report on market-testing plans. This was within the context of John Major's Citizens Charter, which aimed to improve government services by greater customer focus and making public services more responsive to the wishes of their users (customers).

Public and voluntary sector organizations are not subject to the disciplines of the market, which usually ensure efficiency (Weston and Copeland 1988). Voluntary organizations do not have the same easily quantifiable measures of performance which companies have of profit and shareholder value measurement. This has therefore meant that voluntary organizations have to rely on other measurable performance monitors and goals. These issues also confront the public sector and the search for value for money has often been linked to what have been termed the three Es – these can be defined for voluntary organizations as:

1   Economic: not spending 95p to raise £1 – essentially minimizing waste.
2   Efficient: getting the best use out of what money is spent on – a high output to input ratio.
3   Effective: spending funds so as to achieve the organization's objectives – getting things done.

In a commercial organization, the main element is that of efficiency: the difference between cost inputs and revenue outputs, which represents profit, which is the principal aim. Profitability is both a measure of efficiency (profit output compared with capital input) but also an end in itself and thus a measure of effectiveness. Public services, however, even if required to break even or to earn a return on capital, usually have to place emphasis on effectiveness above efficiency, since they serve economic or social ends whose results are likely to take precedence over financial surplus. Even in the private sector, the profit maximization motive is increasingly having to account for wider community interests so three further Es have been introduced – Ethics, Environment and Equity.

Best value

More recently, in the public sector, the Local Government Act 1999 has introduced the concept of 'Best Value'. The government has defined Best Value as a duty to deliver services to clear standards, covering both cost and quality – by the most economic, efficient and effective means available. Best Value replaces Compulsory Competitive Tendering and will undoubtedly have an impact on voluntary organizations, particularly those who enter into contracts with local authorities. Best Value is concerned with continuous improvement fundamental performance reviews based on the four Cs:

1   Challenge – how services are being provided
2   Compare – service provision with others
3   Consult – local community on how services can be improved
4   Competition – as a means of securing efficient and effective services

A fifth C, Co-operation, can also be said to exist which is how the public, private and voluntary sectors can together improve service delivery. Best Value continues the move, which we discussed in Chapter 1, of the government's agenda to move local authorities away from provider of services to enabler.

To meet these requirements a Quality Standards Task group was established by NCVO in 1997 and recommended that the voluntary sector should:

*   Establish quality principles. These would describe an organization's fundamental beliefs that form the basis for its whole management ethos.
*   Commit to the concept and practice of continuous improvement. This would provide for the systematic and methodical enhancement of an organization's capabilities and performance.
*   Introduce the Excellence Model as the appropriate quality framework. This would facilitate the determination of the overall success of an organization, based upon an accepted set of management principles as well as values.

The Excellence Model was originally developed by the European Foundation for Quality Management and is promoted in the UK by the British Quality Foundation. They suggest that the following principles should be demonstrated by a quality voluntary organization (Bashir 1999):

*   Strives for continuous improvement in all it does.
*   Uses recognized standards or models as a means to continuous improvement and not an end.

- Agrees requirements with stakeholders and endeavours to meet or exceed these the first time and every time.
- Promotes equality of opportunity through its internal and external conduct.
- Is accountable to stakeholders.
- Adds value to its end users and beneficiaries.

Maximizing income

The theory of public company finance is based on the assumption that the objective of management is to maximize the market value of the company. Voluntary organizations do not share this aim, but it is vital that they maximize their resources to ensure the organization is delivering as effectively as possible on why it exists. For the finance manager this means focusing on two objectives:

- Smoothly financing current operations by making the most efficient use of current or liquid funds.
- Maximizing available and obtainable resources to enhance return on the resources or capital.

But before you can maximize them the question needs to be answered of where do voluntary organizations get their resources from?

The first authoritative financial statistics on the voluntary sector were not available until the mid-1990s. In 1995 the Government Central Statistical Office (now the Office for National Statistics) commissioned a consortium comprising the four national councils and a group of universities to determine the true income and expenditure of the sector. The consortium produced the UK Voluntary Sector Almanac (NCVO 1996, 1998, 2000). As part of this work the research team had to define the sources of income for the voluntary sector:

	Transaction type		
Sources of income	*Earned income/sales of goods and services*	*Voluntary income/ grants and donations*	*Return of investments*
General public	• Fees for goods and services (e.g. book/ product sales, residential home fees, concert tickets) • Membership subscriptions (with significant benefits)	• Street and door to door collections • Convenience and gift aid payments • Legacies • Membership subscriptions (no significant benefits)	–

continued over page

Government	• Local authority community care contracts	• Grants for core funding and project activities from central government and also the European Union	–
Voluntary organizations	• Services provided under contract	• Grants from charitable trusts	–
Business	• Sponsorship • Research services • Patent royalties	• Grants from businesses' community affairs departments	
Internally generated	–	• Covenanted profits from trading subsidiaries	• Equities • British Government Securities • Common Investment Funds

Income sources and risk

The risk of having just one source of funding means that if that source of funding is withdrawn, then the organization is likely to close. The growth of government funding to the voluntary sector has meant that some voluntary organizations have become totally dependent on that one government funder. However, it is not government funding that is the problem. The problem is the dependency on just one source, as the example of the Baring and Nuffield charitable trusts illustrates. All but £50 million of the Baring Foundation's assets were held in the shares of Baring Bank. The failure of the bank meant that the Baring Foundation lost most of its funds. Nuffield, reflecting its founder's fortune origins in the British Motor Industry, was equally overexposed with shares in car companies and suffered accordingly with the British Motor Corporation's decline in fortune in the 1960s. Voluntary organizations can determine their funding risk exposure, as Barnardo's illustrated. Following the Children and Young Person' Act in the late 1960s there was a growth in funding to the voluntary sector children organizations. The Board of Dr Barnardo's, responding to the opportunities, determined that in seeking government funds, such funding should be restricted to no more than 50 per cent of an individual project's cost.

Voluntary organizations should avoid being dependent on just one source, or if currently dependent should seek to diversify their sources of funding. Fund-raising is outside the remit of this book. Instead we are concerned with maximizing the use of these resources once they have been obtained.

Maximizing resources – strategic options

Forming alliances

Strategic alliances between voluntary organizations can be formed for a variety of reasons and take many different forms. The reasons for such alliances are also sometimes not financial. Alliance forms can include:

- Consortium arrangements, where a group of charities band together to have greater purchasing power – the charities consortium was formed in 1993. Taylor (1999) describes the activities of the current 23 members and their combined £1.2 billion of income as they seek to minimize the costs of goods, services and supplies with purchasing arrangements.
- Agency arrangements where one charity appoints another to carry out operations on its behalf.
- Joint ventures which as well as being between two charities, can also be between a commercial and a voluntary organization – for example financial services as offered by Age Concern.
- Mutual support where charities share information or lobby together.

Mergers

Mergers are common in the commercial sector but have, until recently, been less so in the voluntary sector. A merger is the joining of two organizations to form one organization. In the commercial world most interest in this activity occurs when the merger is not amicable but instead hostile, when it is referred to as a takeover or an acquisition. Given that voluntary organizations do not have shares and shareholders, it was believed that a hostile takeover could not happen. However, some charity mergers are not amicably agreed but have been forced by a funder, which threatens to stop funding one organization unless they merge with another. Charity mergers can also occur when there is a decline in support for a particular problem as, for example, the Terrence Higgins Trust and other HIV organizations.

The positive side of merger activity for voluntary organizations is the generation of significant cost savings and not wasting resources by competing with each other for funding.

Outsourcing

Outsourcing is the purchasing of services from third parties that were previously undertaken within the organization. Almost anything can be outsourced, from financial services to campaigning activity. Outsourcing is always worth considering if an external provider can perform that activity for less cost or to a higher standard.

Cash flow planning

It is essential for the survival of any organization to have an adequate inflow of cash. Cash flow planning as opposed to cash flow budgeting is a strategic level activity in which:

- The planning horizon is longer
- The uncertainties about future cash inflows and cash outflows are much greater
- The organization should be able to respond, if necessary, to an unexpected need for cash. Where could extra cash be obtained and in what amounts?
- A voluntary organization should have planned cash flows, which are consistent with:
  i its aims and objectives
  ii its reserve policy.

In Chapter 7, we demonstrated the opportunity cost of leaving funds in a bank account. We discuss reserves and developing a reserve policy in Chapter 9.

The importance of planning

Voluntary organizations must have cash in reserve for unforeseen circumstances. New organizations, in particular, need to have both a business plan and a budget for revenue surpluses in their early years until a sufficient level of cash is attained. As *The Good Financial Management Guide* states:

> the financially prudent organization plans from the very start to build working capital reserves equivalent to several months operating expenses.
>
> (Bashir 1999, p. 125)

Financial objectives will not be achieved unless the trustees and management know what they are trying to achieve and plan how to achieve those objectives. Quantified financial targets for the achievement of financial objectives should therefore be set out in a financial plan. The financial plan should cover a number of years – three, perhaps five, or possibly ten years or longer. The financial plan should be a part of the overall strategic plan of the organization.

With good financial planning a voluntary organization can assess in advance the need for (a) short-term cash flow, and (b) long-term finance. Devising a plan will mean the organization will focus on understanding:

- The management of its cash flow cycle; for example, the management of its debtors and creditors and therefore the efficiency of its accounting system.

- Whether it is likely to have surplus cash and what can be best done with the surplus cash when it arises. Alternatively, if there is a cash shortage the need to borrow funds and make a business case for them.
- Its income flows and whether it is possible to create reserves from them; for example, many government sources of finance will only allow a voluntary organization to 'break even'.
- A reserves policy and target.
- An investment strategy if funds are surplus to need and immediate cash requirements.
- A loan strategy if the organization is seeking to make long-term asset additions.

Investment planning

Once cash assets are accumulated beyond operational needs, consideration can be given to developing permanent investment plans. Statistics on the rate of return between funds left invested short term and funds invested long term since the 1960s have shown that long-term investments, such as company shares (equities) will always outperform short-term investments, i.e. money left in bank money market accounts.

Trustees have a duty to maximize the value of assets and to obtain the best rate of return but they must not risk investing in highly speculative investments. Equally, trustees must also balance the future needs of their charity against current needs. Charities need to decide how much to spend on current beneficiaries as opposed to future requirements.

According to Harrison (1994), there are four key parameters of investment policy which should be recognized in any statement of investment objectives:

- time horizon
- income needs
- legal powers
- non-financial criteria (i.e. ethical concerns).

Time horizon

As well as providing a dependable source of income, investments also provide a safety net for hard times. The issue for the charity is deciding how quickly the investment would be needed – how liquid is it. This is important because research on long-term investments have shown that they are linked to economic cycles. To really benefit you have to retain the investment through at least one cycle, normally a minimum of three and more likely five years.

Income needs

Investment is a trade off between immediate income and longer-term capital growth. The more income that is required, the less likely is the investment to grow.

Legal powers

The governing documents of the organization will determine the investment powers of the organization. For example, what percentage of funds may be invested in company shares, government bonds or cash. Previously, charities could be governed by the Trustees Investment Act 1961. This has now been replaced by the Trustees Act 2000, which, while not being so prescriptive in telling how to invest their funds, still places legal obligations on trustees (discussed in Chapter 9).

Non-financial criteria

Charities may wish to exclude investing in certain activities if they are in conflict with the charity's purpose; for example, alcohol rehabilitation charities and the brewing industry. Alternatively, but more rarely, it is possible that a charity's work may be directly relevant to an area of the economy. For example, BEN, the motor trades benevolent fund, may wish to support the British motor industry by investing in shares in car companies but if that industry was to have a recession, it would be in the dilemma of seeing its income falling as the need for its service increases. Trustees have to be aware that they must suspend their own personal beliefs and act in the best interests of the charity and its beneficiaries. The case brought by the Bishop of Oxford in 1991 (Harries 1993) confirmed that charity trustees had a legal duty to obtain the maximum financial returns on their funds. However, trustees can impose ethical constraints if they are satisfied that they would not lower returns or conflict with the aims of the charity.

The honorary treasurer of the Royal Society for the Protection of Birds (RSPB) describes how the RSPB monitors the charity's investment managers:

> We monitor our investment managers primarily on the basis of performance against the target returns agreed at the outset. However, we also consider performance against other fund managers and in terms of administrative efficiency.
>
> (Norrington 1999, p. 58)

Can maximizing returns be balanced with ethical issues? According to Jones (1998), the Finance Director of the World Wide Fund for Nature (WWF–UK), a 'real world' attitude to investment is required, which balances the objectives of maximizing returns with issues of ethics, and that certain investments could potentially impact adversely on the organization's objectives. WWF–UK has an environmental investment policy, which consists of three levels of test:

- Exclusion – companies failing the inherent sustainability test will be excluded.
- Extreme caution – companies having the potential to seriously damage environmental sustainability will be treated with extreme caution. Investment might, however, be made in those companies displaying very environmental credentials despite operating in difficult areas.
- Caution – companies with potential to undermine environmental sustainability would be treated with caution.

There are a number of organizations which provide an independent assessment of investment performance to assist charities. For example, the WM Company produces a number of tables on equity funds and fixed interest funds as well as Common Investment Funds, and these tables appear regularly in the magazines *Charity Finance* and *Charity Times*. For ethical investment there is the Ethical Investment Research and Information Service (EIRIS) which produces a free regular information bulletin as well as offering research assistance on companies.

Restricted funding and overhead costs

Charities have always had funds that contained restrictions on how they can be spent. Traditionally these funds came from charitable trusts or were donations where the donor imposed conditions. In recent years such restricted funding has come from statutory sources most often in the form of contracts. Restricted funding means that the voluntary organization is required to isolate the money. This means making sure that the accounting system can track such funds and prove the money has been spent on the purpose it has been given for. But the problem of restricted funds goes beyond financial accounting and auditing issues. Two major issues arise:

1 At a strategic level the amount of restricted funds can mean that a voluntary organization can find that its room for manoeuvre or independence is limited if restricted funds are much greater than its general funds which it has discretion to use.
2 Voluntary organizations must take great care in pricing a contract to make sure that all their costs are covered, otherwise they risk subsidizing statutory services with charity funds.

Voluntary organizations are not, however, powerless in this process. On appeals from the public, careful wording can mean that restrictions are not imposed. If an appeal was restricted, for example for a capital project, and excess funds were raised, the Charity Commission can give permission to divert the excess funds to similar work undertaken by the charity. For government contracts, the answer is to cost carefully and in particular make sure that projects cover, or make a contribution to, overheads. Sometimes funders object to overhead costs because they believe they have nothing to do with the particular activity they are funding. This is wrong. All organizations have overhead costs that are real administration costs and must be paid for. Many funders are resistant to paying overhead costs. *The Good Financial Management Guide* (Bashir 1999, p. 130) outlines three different scenarios and the strategy to overcome them:

1   The funder says it will not fund any overheads apportioned to a project. In this case, the funding application should include all costs that will be incurred as a direct result of undertaking the project. These may include additional telephone costs (on calls and rental of new line), recruitment costs and stationery costs, all included under the appropriate budget headings.
2   The funder queries the amount shown for overheads in the funding application. In this case, the voluntary organization should explain the rationale for allocating overheads: the staffing, management and premises, and how the organization works.
3   The funder has a policy of funding a fixed percentage for administration. In this case, the voluntary organization must be clear about the definition of administration costs and how the percentage is to be calculated. In most cases, this will be a fixed percentage of direct costs. If this is so, then it will be possible to include certain costs as direct – staff supervision, for example – that otherwise would have been treated as indirect.

Funds and reserves

There are various funds a charity can hold. These include:

- Unrestricted funds – these are held by the charity with no restriction placed on their use other than to be within the objects of the charity.
- Restricted funds – these are funds where the donor or the charity has placed some restrictions on their use.
- Designated funds – these are funds that the charity has designated for a specific project, for example a building fund. They can be undesignated by the charity if the purpose for which the funds are reserved is not required, as the funds are unrestricted.
- Endowment funds – these can be permanent or expendable. Often the charity can use the income generated from such funds but is unable to touch the fund itself.

The importance of having the right level of reserves cannot be overstated. As Hind states:

> The required reserve level is the basic building on which all other strategic plan assumptions are built.
>
> (Hind 1995, p. 158)

This is illustrated by the following case study example of St Dunstan's.

Case study – St Dunstan's

'St Dunstan's is a charity which was founded in 1915 to care for soldiers and sailors blinded during the First World War (1997 Annual Brochure). As the apparatus of warfare has expanded, and its consequences became apparent, so too has there been an expansion in the remit of the charity for those for whom it cares. And as blindness is for life, St Dunstan's commitment to care for servicemen and their widows is also for life (1996 Annual Brochure).

But war has not become a thing of the past, and services personnel are applying to become St Dunstaners from new conflicts each year. Also people who could cope with partial blindness in their younger years find that its progression in later years means that they need the special care the charity provides. And with the passing of the years, some of the elderly St Dunstaners now require intensive nursing care for other injuries sustained at the time they lost their sight, including loss of limbs, deafness or brain damage (1996 Annual Brochure), and despite the enormous costs involved, St Dunstan's has a commitment to care for men and women into the middle of the next century and beyond (Chairman's foreword to the 1997 Annual Report).

During the 1960s the Charity Commission advised St Dunstan's to stop fund-raising because they felt that there were sufficient funds for the foreseeable future. This has subsequently proved not to be the case. The biggest effect of this has been a fall from public consciousness with a corresponding loss of support for our St Dunstaners. After 82 years of caring for ex-service men and women, who were blinded in the service of their country, the majority of the public is unaware of the work of St Dunstan's (Chairman's foreword to the Annual Reports of the Charity, 1996 and 1997).'

The 1997 and 1998 Reports of the Council of St Dunstan's state:

> Council is of the opinion that, to meet its long-term commitment to . . . beneficiaries, the Reserves . . . are not currently sufficient. This view is supported by an actuarial valuation at 31 March 1996 (which) reported that, on current levels of expenditure and income expectations, St Dunstan's had a net present deficit of £3.1 million without any new admissions whatsoever. Council (also) believes that the Charity should continue to accept and care for new admissions (and) provide a lifelong

commitment . . . whereby a new admission could look for help or care up to eighty years or beyond.

Council therefore intends . . . not only to eliminate . . . the actual deficit . . . but . . . to establish a financial buffer against a future economic recession or charitable demands of an exceptional but short-term nature.

However, as the 1998 Annual Brochure points out, 'greater awareness of our organization has been achieved through our recent fundraising campaign (which) has led to an increase in enquiries . . . from people who can benefit from our services.'

Official guidance on reserves is now available from the Charity Commission (CC19) and is further discussed in Chapter 9.

Performance monitoring

In the commercial sector one helpful approach to accounts analysis is to ask the question – Should I invest my money in this company? Charities are not commercial organizations and do not have profit and loss accounts, which give a bottom line of how much profit has been made. In the absence of normal commercial criteria to analyse accounts, work has now been undertaken to develop measurements of performance especially for charities (Wise 1995). Some of the measurements reviewed are the same as for commercial organizations while others are adapted or are unique to charity organizations.

As an example, consider liquidity. Many small businesses often go bankrupt, not because they are not profitable but due to problems of cash flow, and therefore are unable to pay their bills. Many methods of analysis have been developed to assess commercial liquidity and some of these methods – called ratios – can be applied to charities, but with one important difference. Cash will have little or no restriction in a commercial organization. Is a charity different? Can we count restricted funds backed by cash as part of our cash available to pay bills?

Aims, inputs, outputs and outcomes

Before exploring techniques for analysing accounts, we consider recent management information developments, which, in the absence of the profit line, not-for-profit organizations have been developing. Instead of profit, charities have been encouraged to focus on aims and objectives. For example, the aim of an Age Concern organization may be to provide:

A service for older people which aims to enhance the quality of life by providing a safe, manageable and comfortable environment. Social stimulation and companionship thereby relieve loneliness and provide respite care for the carer.

Inputs is the term used to denote the resources used in the production of outputs. Inputs for the above services may include staff salaries, costs of activities, refreshments, etc. Inputs should be captured by the accounting system and will generally follow an accounting code classification according to the payment. Inputs will also include the income payments to finance the service whether it is a service charge or a grant.

For commercial consideration the respective inputs of income and expenditure would be added up and taken away from each other and either a surplus (profit) or deficit (loss) would be calculated. Internal management accounts drawn up as budgets in this traditional format should be prepared and monitored regularly by trustees.

For a commercial organization such reports would now end, and it is hoped that any profit would be distributed to owners. But is this sufficient for charity trustees? We would argue NO. The intention was to provide a day care service and the role of the trustees should be to establish whether the aims of the service were achieved. This is not found out from the simple budget against actual financial statement.

To ascertain these answers the term output has been used. Outputs are not readily expressed in financial value terms, as are the inputs. In the absence of money values to measure whether the service has been delivered, other methods have to be developed. Ideally these should be quantitative in nature as they allow for a degree of objectivity and can be easily measurable and understood and allow for comparison whether it is against an initial target, previous years or another similar service.

For example, a measurable output may be the number of people attending an Age Concern day care service. This can be compared with planned numbers and, over a period of time, whether the service is more or less used can be determined.

Outputs, however, are very different from outcomes. The outcome of the day care service mentioned would be to discover to what extent the quality of life was improved. This inevitably becomes a value judgement, but it is possible to seek information which can also be quantitative to in part answer this question, for example through questionnaires, and feedback from carers and relatives.

Ratio analysis

In analysing a set of published accounts it is useful to start by developing and then grouping questions into categories. In this way you can focus your attention on one aspect of the voluntary organization at a time. The categories suggested are:

1 Funds analysis
2 Liquidity
3 Management costs

4   Costs of generating funds
5   Resources arising (income)
6   Asset investment and performance.

These have been grouped on the basis of those considered most risky for trustees. The criteria of risk used are based upon potential personal financial penalties on trustees:

- Breach of trust;
- Wrongful trading – in this case continuing to operate the charity knowing it cannot meet its financial liabilities;
- Public accountability – how much is spent on administration, fund-raising;
- Performance measures for the charity.

Prior to analysing accounts under these categories there are three simple stages:

1 Put into simple numbers
Reduce the numbers down to a manageable size and then convert them into ratios. Reducing numbers is simply done by rounding down the numbers to three or four significant figures. The next stage is to turn the numbers into ratios. A ratio is a way of showing the size of a number relative to another number. For example when driving a car it is normal to keep an eye on the ratio of distance to time, that is miles per hour, in order to judge speed. Similarly, the ratio of distance to fuel used, that is miles per gallon gives us the principal indicator of how efficient our car is.

2 Compare
The only sensible way of drawing a conclusion about a statistic is to use it to make a comparison. For instance, it is pointless to say that we served 4,000 meals in our day centre unless it can be compared with how many were served in the previous year or what was the planned number of meals to serve.

3 Draw your own conclusions
The conclusion arrived at after following this process should be much better than the views at the start. Try and list your views before the process and compare them with your views after you have analysed the accounts.

Exercise

With the kind permission of the Charity Commission, a full set of SORP accounts is appendixed. Either use these or obtain a set of a charity's published accounts and work your way through these categories and answer the following questions.

Category 1 – *Funds analysis*

Questions

- Are restricted funds properly identified and explained?
- Are designated funds explained? Do you consider them definite commitments?
- How are these funds financed? Cash or cash equivalents? How realistic is the value of cash equivalents and how quickly can they be turned into cash?
- Ratio – what percentage against total funds do restricted and designated funds comprise. Has the charity a policy on what proportion of free-flow funds and restricted funds should comprise the total funds of the charity? This will also impact on what levels and type of reserves the charity should hold.

Category 2 – *Liquidity*

- Do current assets cover current liabilities?
- Can the charity pay all their creditors from bank balances?
- Ratios – the simple commercial ratio to use would be to divide current assets/current liabilities or liquid assets/current liabilities but do remember to consider the earlier point about restricted funds!

Category 3 – *Management costs*

The costs of administration are always a problem for charities. The public would like to think that charities have no administration costs, yet they also wish the charity to operate efficiently. We unfortunately are still a long way from the ideal scenario described by one former chief charity commissioner who publicly said he would not give to a charity which claimed it had no administration costs. For trustees, as strategic decision makers, the issue is to decide what they consider to be a reasonable level of administration expressed as a percentage of total income. For example, in determining this figure they will pay due attention to similar organizations as well as to accurate costing and the views of stakeholders.

Once an agreed percentage has been agreed – usually expressed as a range, say 10–12 per cent – it is important to ensure that our basic second process of comparison is adhered to. This means consistency is one of the basic rules of accounting. Consistency means treating items the same way year after year. Items which can be treated with discretion in the SORP, such as apportioning the chief officer's salary between direct charitable expenditure and management once determined, should be adhered to. Manipulating the figure by changing in different years different levels of percentages between the two defeat comparison and can lead to eventual financial problems as well as accountability issues. In essence, once a formula has been agreed, keep to it.

Calculating the ratio on administration costs as a percentage is quite easy and the issue is what benchmark you are taking – total income, total expenditure or as a percentage of charitable expenditure.

Category 4 – Cost of generating funds

Generating fund costs can be treated in the same way as management costs with some interesting additions. Fund generating costs can be viewed in the same way as the commercial ratio 'return on capital employed', one of the key ratios to determine profitability. How efficiently the charity uses its resources to raise funds should be a main monitoring issue for trustees. As with management costs the issues of comparison apply.

The simplest method of calculating the ratio would be to divide generating funds costs into total income. However, there may be problems with this approach in not reflecting accurately both the real costs of fund-raising and the real funds raised. Some costs of fund-raising may be capital items such as computer equipment, which is being depreciated. Has the computer equipment depreciation for fund-raising been allocated to fund-raising costs? Dividing into total income fund-raising costs may also be misleading. Have the fund-raisers been responsible for returns on investment, bank interest, etc.? Income, which has nothing to do with fund-raising, should be taken out of the calculation. In the SORP example, all the different costs are itemized. As with administrative costs, once a formula has been agreed as to what constitutes fund-raising costs, this must be kept to. Under Category 6 we look at how to evaluate fund-raising performance.

Category 5 – Resources arising (income)

This category begins with some fundamental observations:

- Has overall income increased since the previous year?
- Are there new sources of income?

You then need to set the answers against the previous plans for the year.

In addition, you will also look to see how the income of the charity is made up. For example, is there a dependency on one particular source of income? How secure is that income and what would happen if that income were to be withdrawn or reduced?

Category 6 – Asset investment and performance

Some fundamental questions need to be answered:

- Have significant amounts been spent on fixed assets?
- How have additions to fixed assets been funded?
- Prudent financial management maintains that long-term assets should be purchased from long-term income or specific capital appeals/grants.

Charities which have assets such as investments or properties should look at their assets and treat them to financial scrutiny. For example, cash which is surplus to current requirement should be worked hard and not left in current accounts. A simple method to calculate whether the cash has been working is to take the opening and closing balance sheet figures, add them together and then divide by 2 to give an average for the year. If current bank base rate is 6 per cent then the return should be around 4 per cent if the cash has been working. Although this is a relative crude indicator – for example, it makes a number of assumptions about levels of excess cash and interest rates – such analysis does open discussion with the staff/honorary treasurer as to what has been done with the excess cash during the year?

Using opportunity cost analysis enables a number of performance measurements to be developed on the accounts, which enable trustees to ask questions. It should be noted, as with the earlier cash question, that such analysis is not an end but only a beginning to seeking more authoritative answers. Fund-raising performance and use of freehold properties are operational issues and assets which respectively lend themselves to such interrogation by adopting a percentage of expected return and then comparing against actual return.

Limitations of ratio analysis – administration and fund-raising costs

Research on the public perception of charities has found that the costs of administration and fund-raising excite the greatest interest among the general public (Charity Commission 1999b). It is also an issue that causes great concern to charities (Paton 1999). The SORP, with its requirement for the disclosure of administration and fund-raising (now the cost of generating funds), allows, as we demonstrated, for the calculation of different ratios. Wise (1997) examined the administration costs in the voluntary sector and concluded that there were economies of scale which benefit larger charities, and therefore rationalization of the sector could be facilitated by merger activity which would bring benefits to donors and beneficiaries. The Directory of Social Change (1999) investigated fund-raising costs and criticized charities for not disclosing their fund-raising costs on a consistent and comparable basis. The report then highlighted and compared top charities spending more than £1 million per annum on fund-raising and those charities spending more than 40 per cent of donated income on fund-raising expenditure. Hyndman and McKillop (1999) looked at the efficiency of the 500 largest fund-raising charities and investigated the use of conversion ratios as indicators of scale efficiency. The authors critically questioned the assumptions made by practitioners of what should be acceptable and unacceptable ratio costs. Stressing that the different profile of charities – fundraiser or grant maker – and different types of fund-raising means that applying universal rules cannot be applied to all charities. Hyndman and

McKillop also raise the issue of definitions and accounting policies which makes comparisons between charities problematic. This theme was explored by Young (2001), who interviewed members of the SORP committee and asked how they defined administration costs, and concluded that despite the SORP definition, there is still considerable latitude in the allocation of costs. Breckell's (2001) research on fund-raising expenditure supports Hyndman and McKillop concerns that different factors may legitimately affect a charities cost income ratio and concludes that the relative performance of a charity's fund-raising should not be based on simple cost income ratios.

Project appraisal techniques

Investment appraisal techniques such as payback methods and the use of discounted cash flow are commonly used in the private sector and we believe these can be applied by voluntary organizations, particularly to evaluate whether to undertake a fund-raising project. Clearly such techniques cannot be used in isolation from other issues, such as ethical considerations and social objectives, but as voluntary organizations increasingly seek to maximize their fund-raising objective and appraise risk, quantitative appraisal can aid decision making.

The principal techniques and their application to charity project appraisal are the payback method and the average rate of return method, described below.

Payback method

Payback method takes the perspective that the commitment of funds to a project involves two things. The sacrificing of funds to other uses for the duration of the project and the risk that the money committed may be permanently lost. The principal determinant of payback is 'time' and how long management is willing to commit to that project before the initial investment is returned.

For example, a charity is considering setting up a trading subsidiary which will cost £5,000. The charity believes the trading subsidiary will make the following gift aid back to the charity:

Year	Gift Aid
	£
1	500
2	1,000
3	2,000
4	3,000
5	4,000

The trustees reviewing the proposal decide that they will approve the proposal if the initial cost is repaid within three years but not longer than that. Should the project proceed?

Answer:

Year	Cumulative return £
1	500
2	1,500
3	3,500
4	6,500

By year 4 the project more than repays the development costs and is making a positive return to the charity. However, it fails to meet the trustees' policy of payback in three years and should either not proceed or the trustees should be asked to reconsider their decision.

The payback method has the advantage that it is easy to understand, simple to apply and promotes a prudent approach to decision making, which is particularly important to trustees. The principal disadvantages are that it could reject a potentially lucrative project just because the initial outlay is high relative to the timed return. These disadvantages could prove damaging if, for example, this method was applied to a fixed-term fund-raising campaign. Using the above example, if this was a five-year project then the charity would have seen a gain in total over the five years of £10,500 (£6,500 + £4,000).

Average rate of return

To resolve the limitation of the payback technique, this method recognizes profitability and that it must relate to the amount of capital invested and to the period for which it is required. This requires trustees to determine a cost of capital from which they will evaluate a project. For trustees seeking to tie up medium-term funds (say five years), a useful cost of capital would be the yield on a government five-year stock (gilt). Let us assume this is currently 7 per cent.

Using the above example the method to calculate is as follows.

Determine the total cash inflow given by the project:

In our example this is	£10,500
Then deduct the amount of the original investment:	£5,000
Leaving:	£ 5,500

This is the amount the project earns over the five years of its life and is therefore equivalent to

£5,500/5 = £1,100 per annum

The amount invested in the project was initially £5,000. To calculate the return:

£1,100/£5,000 × 100 = 22 per cent

which easily exceeds the return from the gilt. In fact the return could be said to be double this rate – 44 per cent – as the amount invested at the end is nil. The project has both repaid the initial cost during the period and made a profit. We could therefore average the amount invested, which could reasonably be regarded as being half the initial outlay at £2,500.

However, the disadvantage of the average rate of return method is that it does not take into account when we will get our money back (the payback method) and the time value of money; it is also arbitrary – do you use return/average investment or return/total investment?

Discounted cash flow

Discounted cash flow (DCF) is a technique which takes into account issues concerning the time value of money and the problem of inflation (£1 today will be worth less than £1 in a year's time), the total return and the timing of cash flows to when we get our funds repaid. Recognizing the time value of money, discount tables (see the Appendix at end of this chapter) are used, which set out the factor to be used for any interest rate from one per cent upwards and from one year onwards. To illustrate, using the example and the 7 per cent rate of interest:

Year	Cash inflow £	Discount factor 7% from tables	Present value £
1	500	0.935	467
2	1,000	0.873	873
3	2,000	0.816	1,632
4	3,000	0.763	2,289
5	4,000	0.713	2,852
Total present value of project			8,113

The total present value of £8,113 means that if we were to have invested this sum we would at 7 per cent per annum cover our investment. As we have only had £5,000 requested then the margin in favour of the investment is £3,113 which is the net present value.

Allowing for risk

The conceptual superiority of DCF means that risk factors can also be factored into the equation. In our example we used gilts as representing a minimal risk for the charity with surplus funds. Any proposal that cannot meet at least the return from the same years as a gilt should not be considered. However, as risk with gilts is minimal then an allowance should be applied to allow for the greater risk element associated with the project. A risk premium discount factor can be applied, say 3 per cent in our example, and the project is then reappraised:

Year	Cash inflow	Discount factor 10%	Present value
1	500	0.909	454
2	1,000	0.826	826
3	2,000	0.751	1,502
4	3,000	0.683	2,049
5	4,000	0.621	2,484
			7,315

The present value of £7,315 less the £5,000 requested means the net present value is now £2,315 which means the project should still go ahead.

Cost benefit analysis and limitations of DCF applied to the voluntary sector

Cost benefit analysis (CBA) was developed in the public sector as a method of investment appraising which sought to place a monetary value on social benefits deriving from a project. Because of the judgement factor in determining an appropriate monetary value and unsuitable application of undertaking a numerical analysis to benefits, which are not readily quantifiable, its use has been limited. However, to the extent that benefits can be quantified it can assist in decision making, particularly between competing projects.

The following example illustrates the problems of using DCF in voluntary organizations when determining an appropriate cost of capital.

Illustrative exercise

The trustees of County Dial a Ride are assessing the aims of the organization which is to provide cheap or free transport to disadvantaged people for essential journeys. In particular, the issue of disabled peoples whose need the charity is not meeting is considered. Three options have been presented:

1   Install lift ramps to all of their minibuses. This would be a one-off capital cost of £1,500,000. Maintenance and repair costs would be absorbed in the current running budget.
2   Buy additional new minibuses with lift ramps and wheelchair space in the design. The initial cost would be £500,000 but additional operating costs including new drivers would be £180,000 per annum.

3   Provide vouchers to eligible passengers to use a local private taxi firm that has a number of specially adapted taxis for disabled passengers for a specified number of journeys per year. This would cost £250,000 per annum.

The life of the vehicles is five years and the trustees are presented with the following figures by the finance director with the cost of capital being 7 per cent. This has been based on the return on the reserve funds they have invested in government five-year stock, which will be the source of finance for the project.

	Cash inflow £	Discount factor 7%	Present value £
Option 1	1,500,000	0.713	1,069,500
Option 2	500,000	0.713	356,500
Year 1–5	180,000	4.100	738,000
			1,094,500
Option 3			
Year 1–5	250,000	4.100	1,025,000

Based on the present value, Option 3 would be the preferred choice but one trustee notes that this would mean that the organization would lose control while still having all the responsibility of the scheme. How do we know taxis will always attend and if they do not, will we get the blame? They also state that 'our drivers do more than just drive, they offer additional personal services and friendship.' They point out that the charity also has funds invested in a common investment fund, which currently returns 10 per cent. Why not use that as the cost of capital?

Revised option at 10 per cent cost of capital

	Cash inflow £	Discount factor 10%	Present value £
Option 1	1,500,000	0.621	931,500
Option 2		0.621	310,500
Year 1–5	500,000	3.790	682,200
			992,700
Option 3			
Year 1–5	250,000	3.790	947,500

At 10% cost of capital the options are reversed with Option 1 now being the cheapest.

This example illustrates the problems for voluntary organizations using DCF. First, what should be the appropriate discount rate to choose? Second, quantitative techniques do not take into account social benefits. Does this mean that DCF has no value to voluntary organizations? We think not. Evaluating different fund-raising projects by seeking the best return is important and should not be left to arbitrary decision making. We deliberately chose government stocks and common investment funds to illustrate a method of determining an appropriate rate of return to evaluate fund-raising projects. These rates provide voluntary organizations with an independent benchmark to evaluate fund-raising projects.

Deciding between different projects or methods should also be subject to evaluation using objective assessment methods. The problem of how to incorporate different social benefit issues can to an extent be resolved by applying a weighting in the same way we demonstrated with risk. However, it must be noted that at this point the choice of the internal discount factor and the weightings can be subjective and clearly should be applied rationally and fairly.

Social accounting and audit

Social accounting and audit developed in response to the recognition by some corporations that their responsibilities go beyond simple profit maximization and has been defined as

> The process of selecting firm-level social performance variables, measures, and measurement procedures, systematically developing information useful for evaluating the firm's social performance; and communicating such information to concerned social groups, both with and outside the firm.
>
> (Ramanathan 1976, p. 434)

Social accounts concentrate on non-financial operations and measure performance against set criteria of mission, objectives and other targets. As was illustrated with the WWF–UK investment policy, however, these do impact and interrelate to financial objectives, policies and procedures. Camelot, the lottery operator and not a charity, have undergone the process of producing a social report, which was independently audited by a commercial subsidiary of the New Economics Foundation. The report runs to forty-five pages and covers Camelot's responsibilities to its deemed stakeholders – the public, employees, community retailers, suppliers' pressure groups, subsidiaries and shareholders. Under each heading a series' targets and how they are achieved, including quantified performance measures, are used. For example:

Success factor:	*Trust in Camelot*
Issue:	Belief that Camelot is responsible and trustworthy
Policy:	Tracker study
Measures (and targets):	% of adults agreeing
Achievement:	43% of adults believe Camelot is responsible
	47% of adults believe Camelot is trustworthy

How many voluntary organizations know what their trust profile is with their stakeholders?

Critics of social accounting focus primarily on the methodology problems, particularly as only recently a standard for social accounting has been developed. In 1999, the Institute of Social and Ethical Accountability (ISEA) issued AA1000, which states:

> AA1000 is a contribution to the further clarification of what constitutes good practice in accountability and performance management. It has been designed as a 'foundation standard' and offers a common currency of principles and processes that underpin and therefore provide reassurance about specialist standards. AA1000 is also designed to function as a stand-alone quality system and process. The suite of applications that make up the AA1000 Framework provides the basis for professional training and for specialist application of the core standard.
>
> (http://www.AccountAbility.org.uk)

While this is a welcome start, the experience with accounting standards shows that there are major conceptual and practical problems (Underdown and Taylor 1985; Belkaoui 1992; Kam 1990) in standard setting. In addition, there is a relative lack of interest in social accounting by the accounting profession and auditors (Wilson and Gatward 1998). We currently have no information as to the use of social accounting and audit by voluntary organizations but reports in the charity press indicate a mixed response to social auditing by voluntary organizations. Bubb (2000) reports on the initiative of the Association of Chief Executives of Voluntary Organisations (ACEVO) in which thirteen voluntary organizations carried out social audits as part of a project to raise awareness about social auditing. However, Falush (2000), reporting on the Consumers Association accreditation scheme for charities, found that only two charities had submitted to external checks. A case study on social auditing for voluntary organizations has been published featuring material on Traidcraft Exchange, a UK charity that is linked to Traidcraft plc, a company that sells products from the Third World (Redfern 1998).

The methodological approach of Traidcraft to social accounting features six steps:

1   Identify the social objectives and ethical values of the organization.
2   Define who the stakeholders are.
3   Establish a comprehensive set of social performance indicators.
4   Measure performance, keep records and prepare a set of accounts.
5   Submit accounts to an independent audit.
6   Report the results publicly.

And the following philosophy based on quality not quantity:

Social accounts are more difficult to audit than their financial equivalents. Many of the measures and indicators of social performance are qualitative statements rather than quantifiable values. Social accounting requires the organisation to recognise its duty of accountability to all its stakeholders. Different stakeholders may 'see' events differently, and therefore assign different values to the organisation's performance. Financial accountants are generally not required to deal with 'polyvocal' accounts of performance. In addition, there can be no social 'balance sheet' or 'profit statement'. Social responsibility cannot be summarised with financial measures of costs and benefit. Neither does social accounting allow poor performance in one area to be offset against good performance in a different area. It does, however, attempt to measure improvements over time against the organisation's own targets, external benchmarks and the expectations of its stakeholders.

(Redfern 1998, p. 143)

The philosophy underpinning social accounting and that of the voluntary sector should be complimentary. Whether the new requirement in the Charity SORP requiring trustees to make a risk assessment will see a greater interest in social accounting remains to be seen.

Conclusion

Performance evaluation in the voluntary sector is relatively unsophisticated. Even in the most commercial of areas voluntary organizations seem reluctant to use appraisal techniques. Research for the NCVO's Almanac on the performance of trading subsidiaries found performance evaluation fairly crude and based mainly on the amount of surplus. The following table from the research illustrates the methods of evaluating sales performance:

Evaluation method	Charities	
	Number	Per cent
Volume of gross income	100	55
Size of profit/surplus	78	43
Growth in income	74	41
Profit/Surplus as per cent of turnover	68	38
Amount covenanted to parent charity	36	20
Other	25	14
Profit/Surplus as return on investment	21	12
None	21	12

Source: Palmer *et al.* 1998, p. 18

Note: The analyses under 'other' were of a wide variety, mostly specific to the operations of the charity concerned (such as attendance at performances, donations received with cards sold, attendance at specific meetings, subsidy per passenger journey, training qualifications awarded, pence per head, etc.) and also more commonly applicable measures (such as numbers of clients helped, quality of service, budget comparison, market penetration, occupancy, etc.).

The absence of profit should mean that voluntary organizations should be focusing on other methods to evaluate performance. Applying commercial techniques, for example, on ratios is fraught with difficulties and findings need to be treated with caution. Appropriate performance measures for the voluntary sector in the absence of its own specialist techniques are currently a mixture of private and public sector applications.

Exercises

Discussion exercise on funding

A voluntary organization funding goes through periods of growth, stagnation and decline. What strategies can a voluntary organization take to avoid stagnation and decline in its funding sources?

Project Appraisal Exercise

The fund-raising director of a hospice presents two different direct mail schemes to boost legacy income. Both schemes will require an investment of £80,000 and will last for five years. Scheme 1 is projected to produce the following income:

Year	Income
	£
1	15,000
2	25,000
3	30,000
4	40,000
5	40,000
Total	150,000

The income for Scheme 2 is projected:

Year	Income
	£
1	40,000
2	40,000
3	30,000
4	25,000
5	5,000
Total	140,000

The trustees are advised that they have surplus funds currently in a deposit account paying 7 per cent. Assess the merits of the schemes.

1 Payback method

	Scheme 1		Scheme 2
Year	Amount repaid £	Year	Amount repaid £
1	15,000	1	40,000
2	40,000	2	80,000
3	70,000	3	
4	110,000		

The second scheme repays the investment in two years, the first scheme does not do so until year 4.

2 Average rate of return

	Scheme 1	Scheme 2
Total cash inflow	£150,000	140,000
Investment	80,000	80,000
Surplus	70,000	60,000
Divided by life of project – 5 years	14,000	12,000
Rate of return	17.5%	15%

Both schemes produce a better rate of return than the deposit account.

3 Using DCF but no allowance for risk

Scheme 1

Year	Cash inflow	Discount factor 7%	Present value
1	15,000	0.935	14,025
2	25,000	0.873	21,825
3	30,000	0.816	24,480
4	40,000	0.763	30,520
5	40,000	0.713	28,520
Total present value of Scheme 1			119,370

Scheme 2

Year	Cash inflow	Discount factor 7%	Present value
1	40,000	0.935	37,400
2	40,000	0.873	34,920
3	30,000	0.816	24,480
4	25,000	0.763	19,075
5	5,000	0.713	3,565
Total present value of Scheme 2			119,440

Although on the average rate of return and in total cash the first scheme makes a better return, the second scheme is less risky with a shorter payback. Scheme 2 under DCF has a slightly better net present value.

Appendix – discounted cash flow (DCF) tables

Rate of discount (%)

Year	1	2	3	4	5	6	7	8	9	10
1	0.990	0.980	0.971	0.962	0.952	0.943	0.935	0.926	0.917	0.909
2	0.980	0.961	0.943	0.925	0.907	0.890	0.873	0.857	0.842	0.826
3	0.971	0.942	0.915	0.889	0.864	0.840	0.816	0.794	0.772	0.751
4	0.961	0.924	0.888	0.855	0.823	0.792	0.763	0.735	0.708	0.683
5	0.951	0.906	0.863	0.822	0.784	0.747	0.713	0.681	0.650	0.621
6	0.942	0.888	0.837	0.790	0.746	0.705	0.666	0.630	0.596	0.564
7	0.933	0.871	0.813	0.760	0.711	0.665	0.623	0.583	0.547	0.513
8	0.923	0.853	0.789	0.731	0.677	0.627	0.582	0.540	0.502	0.467
9	0.914	0.837	0.766	0.703	0.645	0.592	0.544	0.500	0.460	0.424
10	0.905	0.820	0.744	0.676	0.614	0.558	0.508	0.463	0.422	0.386
11	0.896	0.804	0.722	0.650	0.585	0.527	0.475	0.429	0.388	0.350
12	0.887	0.788	0.701	0.625	0.557	0.497	0.444	0.397	0.356	0.319
13	0.879	0.773	0.681	0.601	0.530	0.469	0.415	0.368	0.326	0.290
14	0.870	0.758	0.661	0.577	0.505	0.442	0.388	0.340	0.299	0.263
15	0.861	0.743	0.642	0.555	0.481	0.417	0.362	0.315	0.275	0.239
16	0.853	0.728	0.623	0.534	0.458	0.394	0.339	0.292	0.252	0.218
17	0.844	0.714	0.605	0.513	0.436	0.371	0.317	0.270	0.231	0.198
18	0.836	0.700	0.587	0.494	0.416	0.350	0.296	0.250	0.212	0.180
19	0.828	0.686	0.570	0.475	0.396	0.331	0.277	0.232	0.194	0.164
20	0.820	0.673	0.554	0.456	0.377	0.312	0.258	0.215	0.178	0.149
21	0.811	0.660	0.538	0.439	0.359	0.294	0.242	0.199	0.164	0.135
22	0.803	0.647	0.522	0.422	0.342	0.278	0.226	0.184	0.150	0.123
23	0.795	0.634	0.507	0.406	0.326	0.262	0.211	0.170	0.138	0.112
24	0.788	0.622	0.492	0.390	0.310	0.247	0.197	0.158	0.126	0.102
25	0.780	0.610	0.478	0.375	0.295	0.233	0.184	0.146	0.116	0.092

Rate of discount (%)

Year	11	12	13	14	15	16	17	18	19	20
1	0.901	0.893	0.885	0.877	0.870	0.862	0.855	0.847	0.840	0.833
2	0.812	0.797	0.783	0.769	0.756	0.743	0.731	0.718	0.706	0.694
3	0.731	0.712	0.693	0.675	0.658	0.641	0.624	0.609	0.593	0.579
4	0.659	0.636	0.613	0.592	0.572	0.552	0.534	0.516	0.499	0.482
5	0.593	0.567	0.543	0.519	0.497	0.476	0.456	0.437	0.419	0.402
6	0.535	0.507	0.480	0.456	0.432	0.410	0.390	0.370	0.352	0.335
7	0.482	0.454	0.425	0.400	0.376	0.354	0.333	0.314	0.296	0.279
8	0.434	0.404	0.376	0.351	0.327	0.305	0.285	0.266	0.249	0.233
9	0.391	0.361	0.333	0.308	0.284	0.263	0.243	0.225	0.209	0.194
10	0.352	0.322	0.295	0.270	0.247	0.227	0.208	0.191	0.176	0.162
11	0.317	0.287	0.261	0.237	0.215	0.195	0.178	0.162	0.148	0.135
12	0.286	0.257	0.231	0.208	0.187	0.168	0.152	0.137	0.124	0.112
13	0.258	0.229	0.204	0.182	0.163	0.145	0.130	0.116	0.104	0.093
14	0.232	0.205	0.181	0.160	0.141	0.125	0.111	0.099	0.088	0.078
15	0.209	0.183	0.160	0.140	0.123	0.108	0.095	0.084	0.074	0.065
16	0.188	0.163	0.141	0.123	0.107	0.093	0.081	0.071	0.062	0.054

17	0.170	0.146	0.125	0.108	0.093	0.080	0.069	0.060	0.052	0.045
18	0.153	0.130	0.111	0.095	0.081	0.069	0.059	0.051	0.044	0.038
19	0.138	0.116	0.098	0.083	0.070	0.060	0.051	0.043	0.037	0.031
20	0.124	0.104	0.087	0.073	0.061	0.051	0.043	0.037	0.031	0.026
21	0.112	0.093	0.077	0.064	0.053	0.044	0.037	0.031	0.026	0.022
22	0.101	0.083	0.068	0.056	0.046	0.038	0.032	0.026	0.022	0.018
23	0.091	0.074	0.060	0.049	0.040	0.033	0.027	0.022	0.018	0.015
24	0.082	0.066	0.053	0.043	0.035	0.028	0.023	0.019	0.015	0.013
25	0.074	0.059	0.047	0.038	0.030	0.024	0.020	0.016	0.013	0.010

Rate of discount (%)

Year	21	22	23	24	25	26	27	28	29	30
1	0.826	0.820	0.813	0.806	0.800	0.794	0.787	0.781	0.775	0.769
2	0.683	0.672	0.661	0.650	0.640	0.630	0.620	0.610	0.601	0.592
3	0.564	0.551	0.537	0.524	0.512	0.500	0.488	0.477	0.466	0.455
4	0.467	0.451	0.437	0.423	0.410	0.397	0.384	0.373	0.361	0.350
5	0.386	0.370	0.355	0.341	0.328	0.315	0.303	0.292	0.280	0.269
6	0.319	0.303	0.289	0.275	0.262	0.250	0.238	0.227	0.217	0.207
7	0.263	0.249	0.235	0.222	0.210	0.198	0.188	0.178	0.168	0.159
8	0.218	0.204	0.191	0.179	0.168	0.157	0.148	0.139	0.130	0.123
9	0.180	0.167	0.155	0.144	0.134	0.125	0.116	0.108	0.101	0.094
10	0.149	0.137	0.126	0.116	0.107	0.099	0.092	0.085	0.078	0.073
11	0.123	0.112	0.103	0.094	0.086	0.079	0.072	0.066	0.061	0.056
12	0.102	0.092	0.083	0.076	0.069	0.062	0.057	0.052	0.047	0.043
13	0.084	0.075	0.068	0.061	0.055	0.050	0.045	0.040	0.037	0.033
14	0.069	0.062	0.055	0.049	0.044	0.039	0.035	0.032	0.028	0.025
15	0.057	0.051	0.045	0.040	0.035	0.031	0.028	0.025	0.022	0.020
16	0.047	0.042	0.036	0.032	0.028	0.025	0.022	0.019	0.017	0.015
17	0.039	0.034	0.030	0.026	0.023	0.020	0.017	0.015	0.013	0.012
18	0.032	0.028	0.024	0.021	0.018	0.016	0.014	0.012	0.010	0.009
19	0.027	0.023	0.020	0.017	0.014	0.012	0.011	0.009	0.008	0.007
20	0.022	0.019	0.016	0.014	0.012	0.010	0.008	0.007	0.006	0.005
21	0.018	0.015	0.013	0.011	0.009	0.008	0.007	0.006	0.005	0.004
22	0.015	0.013	0.011	0.009	0.007	0.006	0.005	0.004	0.003	0.003
23	0.012	0.010	0.009	0.007	0.006	0.005	0.004	0.003	0.003	0.002
24	0.010	0.008	0.007	0.006	0.005	0.004	0.003	0.003	0.002	0.002
25	0.009	0.007	0.006	0.005	0.004	0.003	0.003	0.002	0.002	0.001

9 Banking and investment

Introduction

Not every voluntary organization will have investments although most of the larger ones today do. However, before we look at the banking and investment policies and procedures within charities, we first examine the subject of reserves. This is for two major reasons. First, without reserves a charity will have nothing to bank or invest, and second, the level of charity reserves has for some time created problems within the charity sector and with its dealings with the Charity Commission.

Reserves – the legal questions

Introduction

Concern has continued to grow about the level of reserves that some charities hold and how these reserves were built up. Currently the legal position on reserves is still not exactly clear. However, it is true that the law does impose some restrictions on the retention of income.

Whilst the Charity Commission appreciates that reserves are necessary for a variety of legal and operational reasons, their main area of concern seems to centre on the level of 'free reserves'. These are described as unrestricted reserves after taking account of operational needs, such as the charity's working capital commitments, the need to maintain a fund-raising base and in certain cases redundancy, maternity and similar contingencies.

The index to the 1995 SORP did not mention the word 'reserves' but did have quite a few references to 'funds' in conjunction with words like 'capital', 'earmarked', 'designation', 'restrictions', etc. (see further 1995 Charities SORP paras 36–44). SORP 2000, published in October 2000, does make several references to reserves and we will return to these in the conclusion.

Priorities

The Charity Commission's priorities in drawing up guidelines for charity reserves are to produce a document, which provides:

- a clear understanding within the charitable sector and between the Charity Commission and the sector on acceptable reasons for reserves;
- recognition that it is the needs of charity beneficiaries which should dictate charities' policies on the application of income;
- common standards in charities' fund-raising appeals and other public statements; and
- assurance that charity trustees are making proper use of their charities' funds.

The Charity Commission publication *Charities' Reserves* (CC19) issued in May 1997 provided guidelines that were drawn up after consultation with bodies such as the Charity Finance Directors' Group. CC19 has recognized that not all charities are the same and therefore it was impossible to come up with one hard and fast rule that would fit every charity's situation.

There are four fundamental questions that need to be answered in relation to reserves in charity accounting.

What are reserves?

One dictionary definition of reserves is 'something kept back or set aside for future use or contingency'. The words 'future use' and 'contingency' are a recurring theme. This definition is certainly one that was used at the Cancer Research Campaign (CRC) to cover that put aside for what was described, perhaps too loosely, as 'the rainy day'. As a grant-making charity, CRC in the early 1990s felt the need to refine this approach as it was essential to provide cover for future commitments, both legal and moral.

In CC19, reserves are defined as:

> Income which becomes available to the charity and is to be expended at the trustees' discretion in furtherance of any of the charity's objects (sometimes referred to as 'general purpose' income); but which
>
> - is not yet spent, committed or designated (i.e. it is 'free').

Our definition therefore excludes

- permanent endowment;
- expendable endowment;
- restricted funds;
- designated funds; and
- income funds which could only be realised by disposing of fixed assets held for charity use.

As the document goes on:

> There is an argument for saying that two of these types of funds –
> expendable endowment and designated funds – ought to be counted as
> reserves. The argument is that in each case the trustees are free to regard
> the funds, if they so choose, as available for general purpose expenditure.

This is probably a dangerous argument. Although they go on:

> We acknowledge that there are no legal restrictions preventing trustees
> treating these two types of funds as free, general purpose funds. But
> there are practical reasons, explained below, why the funds should not
> normally be regarded as free (though there are exceptions).

Is there a need for a sector-wide policy?

Having defined reserves we now need to move on to consider whether it is
possible or even feasible to have a sector-wide policy. Whilst all charities
should have given thought to having a reserves policy, because charities are
so different it is almost impossible to come up with one simple straightforward rule which will be fair and right for all charities. For example, charities without permanent endowment may need far greater reserves than
those with such endowment because their future income may be less secure
so it would appear sensible that no sector-wide policy is feasible or desirable.

Why should charities have a reserves policy?

The strategic planning process should throw up the answer to this question.
To be effective a charity needs to plan because, unfortunately, at some time
contingencies do arise. It is essential that a charity provides cover for its
commitments, both legal and moral. To ensure, wherever possible, a balanced budget, the planning process should be based on a careful assessment
of future needs, uses for funds and probable income. The process must naturally assess the risks involved and the reserves policy set-up must take
account of all these factors.

The need for and uses of the reserves should be clearly explained, both in
the accounts and by the trustees in the annual report. Raising the profile of
this issue is beneficial not only to the large, grant-making charities but also
to the smaller, grant-funded charities. The raising of this issue must help
convince statutory grant funders that some reserves, for example working
capital, are necessary and essential to ensure the continuity of the charity
and to maintain the level of service that it gives.

At the end of the day there will also be the possible threat of that
awkward media probe. It is the need to explain the reason for holding
reserves that is essential. The charity world has done itself no favours in its

failure to be proactive on this issue. Too frequently it has been put on the defensive by the media who have attacked charities on the level of their reserves. Reserves policy issues must be thought through and declared.

As the Charity Commission leaflet CC19 referred to earlier puts it:

> If a charity retains income as a reserve, rather than spending it, the charity needs to justify its action.

Justifying reserves – which is a central theme of the guidance – does not mean excusing or being defensive about reserves. It means being able to demonstrate, by reference to a charity's current position and future prospects, why holding a particular level of reserves is right for the charity at that time.

How does a charity establish a reserves policy?

It can be a somewhat lengthy process and one during which the charity needs to consider carefully an assessment of the risks. This is never an easy thing to do. It will be essential to look at projected income streams and determine how dependable donations, legacies, grants, fees, sales, and so on, are. What are the risk factors that could affect them? Dividend yields and interest rates also need to be assessed.

What does the charity know about its forward expenditure – fixed versus variable – recurring versus non-recurring – revenue versus capital – short- and long-term commitments? It may have to consider legal versus moral issues or whether there are high priority initiatives requiring extra expenditure. Every charity must reflect on its own position, make decisions and will need, effectively, to do some very concentrated 'navel gazing'! What is important to one charity may be considerably less so to another. Unfortunately, no hard and fast rules can be laid down.

Once a charity has agreed its reserves policy, and it will need to take this through its usual committee structure, it should make sure that 'it tells it like it is'. This may vary from a very brief note in the trustees' report to something much longer.

A charity should have a reserves policy based on a realistic assessment of its reserves needs. In some cases the policy is proposed by senior employees or by a subcommittee of the trustee body, but it should be formally agreed by the trustees acting as a board and needs to be recorded in writing. The policy should cover as a minimum:

- the reasons why the charity needs reserves;
- what level of reserves the trustees believe the charity needs;
- what steps the charity is going to take to establish or maintain reserves at the agreed level;
- arrangements for monitoring and reviewing their policy.

Reserves and the SORP

As we have seen, the Charity Commission published in May 1997 its long-awaited document on the subject of reserves. It is to be hoped that this will finally resolve all and certainly most of the outstanding questions on this emotive subject. This guidance makes it absolutely clear that the underlying principle in relation to reserves has to be justified and explained. As the leaflet puts it:

> The giving public are not generally concerned with the legal and accounting technicalities. But they are entitled to be reassured that a charity with reserves has good reasons for keeping funds in reserve, and to know what those reasons are.
>
> Justifying reserves – a central theme of this guidance – does not mean excusing or being defensive about reserves. It means being able to demonstrate, by reference to a charity's current position and future prospects, why holding a particular level of reserves is right for the charity at that time.

Paragraph 28 of the 1995 SORP, as we have seen, lists the narrative information which trustees should include in their annual report. As CC19 puts it:

> Information about a charity's reserves should be included as part of the narrative prepared under paragraph 28. We believe that trustees should:
>
> - state whether or not they hold reserves;
> - explain why they hold or do not hold reserves and, if they do, in respect of what future needs, opportunities, contingencies or risks; and
> - give the level of reserves at the last day of the financial year to which the report relates.

SORP 2000, unlike its predecessor, makes several references to the topic of reserves. Specifically, it makes it clear when talking about the narrative information to be included in the trustees' annual report that there must be a statement of the charity's policy on reserves stating the level of reserves held and why they are held. Additionally, the Appendix to the SORP seeks to define what is meant by reserves:

> In this SORP we use the term 'reserves' (unless otherwise indicated) to describe that part of a charity's income funds that is freely available for its general purposes. 'Reserves' are therefore the resources that the charity has or can make available to spend for any or all of the charity's

purposes once it has met its commitments and covered its other planned expenditure.

(Charity Commission SORP 2000)

The SORP then goes on to expand further the points made in CC19 in relation to expendable endowment and designated funds going further than that document to make it clear that:

A charity will not be justified in creating, or transferring resources to, a designated fund where the main purpose of doing this is to allow the charity to show a reduced level of reserves.

(Charity Commission SORP 2000)

The Appendix completes its look at reserves by making the point that in no circumstances can restricted funds ever be regarded as general purpose funds. As it says quite clearly:

Restricted income funds do not fall within the scope of reserves as the term is used in this SORP. Nevertheless, the legal principles on the retention of income apply to restricted income funds, as do the principles of justifying and explaining any retention. For the purpose of applying the principles in this SORP it is suggested that the trustees treat each restricted income fund as if it were a separate charity. Thus, each material restricted income fund would have its own 'reserve', which should be justified and (if practicable) explained in its own right.

(Charity Commission SORP 2000)

Reserves – a case study – Cancer Research Campaign (CRC)

Introduction

Influenced by depressed stock markets, ever-increasing unsatisfied scientific demand and a growing investment in shops, the CRC finance committee, in November 1990, initiated a fundamental review of the appropriate level of reserves.

The last such review had been carried out in 1984 when it was concluded that 'taking account of all the factors and bearing in mind that funds for research projects are committed on an annual basis, reserves should be in the range of 10–14 months' future total expenditure.'

Financial background

Data table 1 — reserve ratio

As at 31 December	1986	1987	1988	1989	1990
Reserves (£'000)					
Free	32,957	33,835	37,097	40,253	31,926
Total	34,923	35,153	39,246	45,000	38,944
Year ended 31 December	1987	1988	1989	1990	1991 budget
Expenditure (£'000)					
Main objects	24,636	28,556	35,537	39,314	44,397
Appeals and administration	2,921	3,568	3,875	4,563	5,413
Total	27,557	32,124	39,412	43,877	49,810
As at 31 December	1986	1987	1988	1989	1990
Ratio: reserves as future Total expenditure (months)					
Free	14.4	12.6	11.3	11.0	7.7
Total	15.2	13.1	12.0	12.3	9.4

It was essential that CRC's finances were administered in an efficient and responsible way, neither building up too large a reserve, nor allowing it to fall to too low a level. In 1990 there had been four years of rapid growth with income up 70 per cent over the period from £25.7m to £43.6m and therefore CRC carried out a review of its reserves policy.

The finance committee proposed that it should be the appropriate level of free reserves which would be considered, i.e. excluding those reserves represented by fixed assets which are likely to prove difficult or impractical to liquidate in time of need.

It is worth pointing out that although these reviews took place well before the issuing by the Charity Commission of CC19 *Charities' Reserves* in May 1997, CRC had no endowment funds, permanent or expendable, no restricted funds and no designated funds. Effectively, therefore, free reserves as defined in the Charity Commission booklet is exactly the same as the free reserves as defined by CRC and set out in the previous paragraph.

The need for reserves

It remained clearly essential that the finances of CRC should be administered in an efficient and responsible manner with adequate provision for realistic eventualities. This, however, had to be balanced against CRC's *raison d'être* of spending via grants the maximum amount possible on its main objects and thus avoiding holding an unnecessarily high level of reserves.

As carried out previously, this reserves policy took account of all the risks that were seen to be facing CRC, encompassed a full SWOT (strengths, weaknesses, opportunities and threats) analysis, before arriving at the final revised policy.

In this context the main purpose of reserves was seen as enabling:

- research to continue at an appropriate level with adjustment to be made in an orderly manner should CRC be faced with a serious reduction in income;
- unexpected research initiatives of a high priority to be met.

Reserves also generated a reliable income stream, dealt with the equalization of cash flows, and provided funds for capital expenditure.

Income

Data table 2 – historical performance – two-year income bands

	1981/2 £'000	1983/4 £'000	1985/6 £'000	1987/8 £'000	1989/90 £'000
Donations	9,648	12,011	13,767	15,575	19,730
Legacies	18,347	25,909	29,231	39,885	52,670
Investment and other income	3,220	3,024	4,445	5,498	6,341
Total	31,215	40,944	47,443	60,958	78,741
% mix					
Donations	31	29	29	26	25
Legacies	59	63	62	65	67
Investment and other income	10	8	9	9	8

In assessing the appropriate level of reserves, a distinction needed to be made between normal fluctuations in voluntary income and a serious fall caused, perhaps, by some sort of 'scandal', recovery from which could prove difficult. To deal with the former (and also fluctuations in investment values) the concept of a range in terms of months' future total expenditure, expressed as minimum/desirable levels, was endorsed.

Although it was extraordinarily difficult to assess the likely scale of any such scenario, a number of points could be made:

1   although public dismay might manifest itself in an immediate drop in donation income, a consequent fall in legacies was likely to take considerably longer to filter through;
2   investment income would not be affected;
3   although there would be some impact on shops, it would not be substantial.

Data table 3 – 40 per cent income reduction

	1991 budget £'000	1991 revised £'000	1991 + 4 estimate £'000
Donations	11,350	6,810	6,810
Legacies	32,450	32,450	19,470
	43,800	39,260	26,280
Investment and other income	4,324	4,324	4,324
Total	48,124	43,584	30,604
Reduction		4,540	17,520

The table illustrates the impact of a 40 per cent reduction in donation income followed four years later by an equal percentage reduction in legacy income, with total income then stabilizing at these levels, i.e. probably a worst case scenario (all figures in 1991 £s).

Tackling this situation

In the very short term, significant savings on appeals and administration costs could be difficult to achieve. However, a rigorous review of those costs would need to be conducted and for the purposes of the case study a phased reduction from £5.4m in 1991 + 1 to a level of £3.5m in 1991 + 4 was assumed.

The scientific appendix (not reproduced here) detailed broadly how a drop in income of this magnitude could be addressed by a planned reduction in expenditure. Inevitably, without indiscriminate cutting, which in some areas would render the research cost ineffective, there would have needed to be some use of reserves.

The impact on reserves of the 40 per cent reduction in voluntary income partly offset by the savings on expenditure might follow the pattern set out in the next table.

Data table 4

	1991 budget £'000	1991 revised £'000	+1 £'000	+2 £'000	+3 £'000	+4 £'000	+5 £'000
Income							
Voluntary	43,800	39,260	39,260	39,260	39,260	26,280	26,280
Investment and other	4,324	4,324	4,000	3,900	3,800	3,800	3,800
Total	48,124	43,584	43,260	43,160	43,060	30,080	30,080

Expenditure

Main objects	44,397	42,050	39,760	39,570	36,800	35,060	26,580
Appeals and Administration	5,413	5,413	4,870	4,410	3,950	3,500	3,500
Total	49,810	47,463	44,630	43,980	40,750	38,560	30,080
Change in reserves	(1,686)	(3,879)	(1,370)	(820)	2,310	(8,480)	–
Year-end free reserves	29,345	27,152	25,782	24,962	27,272	18,792	18,792
Ratio (months)	7.9	7.3	7.0	7.4	8.5	7.5	

To move, in the above manner and in 1991 terms, to a base level of main objects expenditure of £26.5m with other costs at £3.5m would therefore have required a draw-down on reserves of some £11m.

Reserves policy

At the end of 1990, with planned expenditure of £49.8m in 1991, free reserves stood at £31.9m, which represented 7.7 months future total expenditure. As a result of stock market improvements during 1991, this ratio had risen to 8.2 months.

The Imperial Cancer Research Fund had, over the previous 3 years, reduced its free reserves from £56m to £35m with a resultant fall in their reserves ratio from 15 to 8 months. This had occurred as it had liquidated reserves to provide more funds for research and to finance expansion into shops.

Against this background, a case could be made for a minimum reserve level of some £25m and a target level of £30m–£35m. In terms of 1991 budgeted total expenditure this gave a range of 7 to 8–10 months.

The decision therefore of the finance committee was to recommend that CRC's reserves policy should be amended to maintaining free reserves in the range of 6–9 months' total expenditure, where 6 months is the minimum and 8 months the desirable level. CRC had for some time referred in its literature to its reserves policy. This varied from the very brief note similar to that which appeared in the Director General's review and ended with a comment like:

> the position is closely monitored and plans are in place to ensure that expenditure on research and other items is restrained should there be any risk of our free reserves falling below the minimum.
>
> (Cancer Research Campaign 1991)

to a fuller explanation. For example, in the particular year following this significant review the subject was covered more fully, setting out precisely the reserves policy and explaining how it had been reached.

As the actual free reserves were, when the decision was taken, above the desired level the forward planning for 1991/92/93 was set to reduce the level of reserves by going in for planned deficit budgeting. The proposal was to increase research expenditure above voluntary income for a number of years but eventually to return to a neutral budget once reserves were down to within the approved level. Effectively the additional grants were of a one-off nature rather than recurring.

The story since then

However, the years 1991 to 1993 saw increases in income which were not in any way nearly as high as those experienced in the previous four years. Indeed in 1991 there was a very small reduction but this position was fortunately reversed in 1992 when income returned to the 1990 level followed by a 10 per cent increase in 1993.

However, CRC's research expenditure during that same period increased, as planned, at a much faster rate and by the end of 1993 it was 26 per cent higher than it had been in 1990. Thus, increasingly, CRC to support its research expenditure incurred deficits which were effectively being funded from reserves. However, if the deficit had not been planned within a defined reserves policy, this situation would have given considerably more cause for concern than it did.

In 1993 CRC was able, because of the depth of its reserves, to spend more on research than it had raised from voluntary income. Quite clearly, expenditure could not exceed income indefinitely, even given a reserves policy. CRC's advantage was that having a reserves policy it reached a definitive point when the situation had to be reviewed. As the minimum level of reserves was approached, measures were taken as part of a strategic planning process in the reserves policy to increase reserves to the top end of the desired range.

Budgets for 1994/95/96 were set so as to reduce research expenditure below the level of income so that the reserves were once more increased. Once this position was achieved, CRC had then returned to a balanced neutral budget. Therefore, the reserves policy allowed for a gradual phased approach rather than dramatic swings. Without a reserves policy CRC would not have been in a position to take the very hard decisions then facing it.

Conclusion

Unfortunately there is no ready answer to the questions on reserves. However, quite obviously, if no thought is given to the what/why/how questions then the reserves policy would certainly be wrong and therefore need attention. Worse still, of course, is the total lack of a reserves policy. While having a reserves policy would not provide the solution to all the problems, it would certainly make life considerably easier.

Reserves – trustees' report

Introduction

As we have seen earlier, the revised 2000 Charities SORP has specified information that needs to be contained in the trustees' annual report. The Charity Commission has published a booklet (November 2000 – CC66) of *Example Reports and Accounts*. This contains some very useful guidance in relation to reserves as well as all the other various topics covered by the SORP.

Example

One of the seven *Example Reports and Accounts* illustrates clearly the Charity Commission's view on reporting on reserves policy.

Arts Theatre Trust Limited

In this example the following appears in relation to reserves policy.

> In 1999 the Trustees carried out a detailed review of the charities' activities and produced a comprehensive strategic plan setting out the major opportunities available to the charity and the risks to which it is exposed. The trustees monitor progress against the strategic objectives set out in the plan at each quarterly meeting and a comprehensive review of the plan is carried out annually. As part of this process, the trustees have implemented a risk management strategy that comprises:
>
> - An annual review of the risks that the charity may face;
> - The establishment of systems and procedures to mitigate those risks identified in the plan; and
> - The implementation of procedures designed to minimise any potential impact on the charity should any of those risks materialise.
>
> The strategic plan focused the trustees on the need to refurbish and develop our ATC Park site further, resulting in the application for funding mentioned previously. A successful outcome is dependent on the charity meeting the challenges such a major project presents and managing our finances prudently.
>
> The trustees have forecast the level of free reserves (that is those funds not tied up in fixed assets, and designated and restricted funds). The charity will require to sustain its operations over the period when it is anticipated that some of the income generating activities may be curtailed temporarily whilst the anticipated project will be carried out. The trustees consider that the most appropriate level of free reserves at

31 March 2001 would be £475,000 reducing to £325,000 at 31 March 2002. The actual free reserves at 31 March 2001 were £381,000 which is £94,000 short of our target figure. Whilst the current level of reserves may prove sufficient, it is the trustees' view that it is prudent to ensure that there are sufficient free reserves to provide financial flexibility over the course of the forthcoming challenges.

The trustees have therefore planned a new fund-raising strategy concentrating on raising funds from our existing audiences and customers of our wholly-owned trading subsidiary, HTC Limited, with a view to increasing our free reserves to the appropriate level. The trustees will closely monitor this initiative against the budgets that have been set. As part of the feasibility study we have shared our plans with our bankers, Cruffs Bank Plc, which has indicated that it will provide support in order to see our planned development come to fruition.

Investments

Introduction

The recommendation in the 1995 SORP, retained in SORP 2000, that long-term investments, including property, should be included at market value in charity accounts has proved to be one of the most controversial of the proposals. However, it is consistent with the SORP's underlying theme of making charity accounts more comparable. The initial adverse reaction to the proposal was probably caused not only by concerns about the cost of revaluation but also by the view that it could have a great effect on some charities' accounts. It will undoubtedly further increase the pressure on charities to state clearly their policies on investments and reserves.

Fixed assets

The treatment of investment assets in SORP 2000 reads:

> Investment assets (including investment and investment properties (Appendix 1: Glossary) and cash held for investment purposes) should be classified as a separate category within fixed assets, except where the intention is to realise the asset without reinvestment of the sale proceeds. In such a case it should be reallocated as a current asset (para 231). The reason for this is that investment assets are generally held with the overall intention of retaining them long-term (i.e. as fixed assets) for the continuing benefit of the charity in the form of income and capital appreciation.

> (Charity Commission SORP 2000)

In the original 1988 SORP unincorporated charities had the option to include investments in a separate category between fixed assets and current assets. This treatment, however, was not available to incorporated charities and in line with the prescriptive style of the 1995 SORP this alternative option has been removed. Obviously as the charity's trustees should be clear about whether they are holding investments for the long term or short term, a decision stemming from the particular needs of the charity, the removal of this alternative accounting treatment was regarded as an improvement.

Property

The Glossary of SORP 2000 defines investment property as

> an interest in land and/or buildings which is held primarily for the purpose of producing an income for the charity, any rental income being negotiated at arm's length.

It does not, therefore, include land or buildings acquired with a view to resale at a profit or, more importantly, property which is owned and used by the charity for carrying out its purposes.

This definition was of assistance to those charities who were concerned that their administration buildings and buildings used for their charitable objectives, such as an old people's home, research laboratory, etc., would need to be shown in the accounts at market value. Thus only property which is a genuine investment earning a return will be caught by this definition.

Valuation

SORP 2000, like its predecessor, recommends that all fixed asset investments be valued at market value at the balance sheet date, or at 'the trustees' best estimate of market value'. The addition of this phrase might be seen by some as an appeasement of the general concern about the costs of professional valuation. In fact it is entirely consistent with current commercial accounting practice where directors can estimate values of investments in-between obtaining a regular professional valuation.

The Glossary of the SORP comes up with a helpful definition for market value as:

> The price at which an asset could be, or could be expected to be, sold for or acquired in a public market between a willing buyer and a willing seller.

The definition then goes on to explain that one should use the mid-point of the quotation for shares listed on the Stock Exchange whilst for other assets one would use a trustees' or valuers' best estimate.

Where a charity as a result of this method has effectively carried out a revaluation, then the SORP recommends following closely existing company law requirements. This means that it will be necessary to show in the notes to the accounts the fact that the investments have been revalued, the date and the basis of each revaluation. If, for example, the Stock Exchange Daily Official List has not been used, then the name and qualification of the person responsible for making the valuation should also be disclosed. In cases where that individual is an employee or trustee of the charity that fact should be stated.

The SORP offers guidance on the reasonable approach to be taken when there is no readily identifiable market price available for shares and goes on to suggest that for assets other than shares, valuations should be carried out at least every five years. This has been criticized by some because of the possible costs involved. However, whilst cost is a legitimate concern this must be weighed against the reason for showing investments at market value in the accounts.

The SORP argues, quite strongly, that market value best represents a true and fair value of the worth of those assets to the charity at the balance sheet date. This value is important because the trustees are under a legal duty to manage surplus funds for the best interest of the charity. This means that they must obtain the best investment return without incurring undue risk on those funds. Not only will the inclusion of market value in the balance sheet and its consequent effect on reserves make the trustees more aware of the resources under their control but through the published accounts it will also make the trustees more accountable to donors, beneficiaries and the general public.

There has been some concern expressed that the use of market value for investment can be misleading. This stems from the often temporary nature of market movements. Another major crash on the Stock Exchange could have a devastating but potentially misleading effect on a charity's balance sheet if share prices subsequently recovered. This could be a serious problem but, if the fluctuations are of a very short-term nature, disclosure of this fact can be made in the accounts. If they represent a permanent reduction in value or if the fall is of an unknown duration then it is prudent to reflect the situation in the accounts and plan accordingly.

Another area of concern is the effect that the revaluation of investments will have on reported reserves. In recent years the popular press and others have attacked charities which appear to have large reserves. Frequently there are very good reasons why a charity needs such large reserves and it may be a sign of prudent management rather than something that deserves criticism. It is really a question of explaining the reserves policy in the accounts and educating the reader, which must be paramount, rather than not disclosing the true resources available to the charity.

Current asset position

Investments that do not fall within the definition of fixed asset investments will be current assets and will be valued at the lower of cost and net realizable value. The decision to classify certain investments as current assets will be partially determined by trustee intentions. It would be unwise for trustees to try to avoid the need to revalue investments by regarding them as current assets! The classification and treatment in the balance sheet should reflect the needs of the charity. For instance, funds raised as emergency appeal funds should not be tied up in long-term investments and would therefore be regarded as current assets. However, funds which are built up for long-term projects should be invested in an appropriate long-term investment to ensure a suitable return is made. Artificial manipulation of classification might seriously distort the accounts and, in extreme cases, the trustees might be asked to justify their management of those assets.

Analysis

The SORP suggests, at paragraph 238, that in the notes to the accounts an analysis of the investment assets should be provided. It sets out as a minimum the following categories:

a   Investment properties;
b   Investments listed on a recognized Stock Exchange, or ones valued by reference to such investments, such as unit trusts and common investment funds;
c   Investments in subsidiary or associated companies, or in companies which are connected persons;
d   Other unlisted securities;
e   Cash and settlements pending held as part of the investment portfolio;
f   Any other investments.

It is further suggested that a geographical split should be shown distinguishing those investments that are in the UK and those which are outside. Details of heavy concentration in any investment, for example over 5 per cent by value of the portfolio, should also be shown.

Gains and losses

Obviously the inclusion of investments at market value means that charities are making unrealized as well as realized gains and losses. The 1995 SORP drew attention to the differing nature of realized and unrealized gains by requiring charities to disclose the extent to which their funds are unrealized. In other words a note of caution, while market value may provide a true and fair view of the charity's worth it does not necessarily reflect the value which would be available in the future because market values change.

Choosing an investment manager

Introduction

The 1993 Charities Act came into force in a number of stages. The first tranche included the two dreaded sections relating to the statutory powers of investment by charity trustees. The first section enabled the Home Secretary to relax the restriction on wider-range investments imposed by the Trustees Investment Act (TIA) 1961, whilst the second section allowed the Secretary of State to make regulations authorizing trustees of charities to invest in a range of prescribed property in addition to investments authorized by the Act.

Charities found that with the relaxation of rules and winding down of the functions of the Official Custodian for Charities (OCC) they were required to take a more active role in the management of their investment portfolios. Many charities were in fact already doing this as the OCC did not manage portfolios, only administered them. Now, of course, the Trustee Act 2000 has widened the scope further.

How does one set about choosing an investment manager? Is it better to opt for one of the larger houses or a smaller one? Are there investment managers who provide specific services for charities?

To answer these questions one needs to cast the net far and wide, collecting information on a good range of firms in order to draw up a short-list of candidates. It is worthwhile visiting the firms one has short-listed to see them at work, meet the people involved and thoroughly research their track record. Do not make the list overlong as it will become an impossible task to select the most suitable candidate. One could of course, cynically, always choose a firm known to the chairman of the trustees!

What to look for when choosing an investment manager

Assuming that the charity is already large enough to require independent external investment management, an important question the charity needs to ask itself is: Is the minimum fee being charged worth it, bearing in mind the value of our portfolio?

As is the norm, fees tend to be based on a sliding scale with a minimum fee. Thus the lower the sum invested, the higher percentage that fee will represent. With many investment managers charging minimum fees of £10,000, portfolios need to be of some significance in order for payment of this level of fee to be worthwhile. A point to remember is that all fees quoted will be subject to VAT and that in this particular case VAT is not recoverable by the charity.

There are number of other criteria, besides the question of cash, which need to be considered when selecting an investment manager.

The first thing that one should look for is empathy: the investment manager must be someone who can understand and get behind what the charity is doing. One must not be just another name to slot into the firm's expanding client list. The manager must at least have sympathy with one's objectives, even if he does not actively support them.

Second, whilst not vital for the investment managers to have a specialist department dealing with charities, it is certainly helpful.

Third, consistency in the investment management team should be sought. As in all these things personal relationships are vital, and to have to continually rebuild them is a nuisance and will not make for good performance.

Fourth, one needs to look at the size and reputation of the investment house bearing in mind that size does not necessarily provide security. What one is looking for here is the quality of the investment approach and previous performance track record. Be warned, however, history does not always repeat itself, particularly in the investment field, and this year's winners are not necessarily next year's.

Product versus service

So in choosing an investment manager the charity itself needs to be clear what it wants from the service. How frequently should the manager report to the charity? Is the investment manager required to carry out all of the investment function, or just the administration of the charity's portfolio? Whether or not the charity delegates the administration, it needs to look closely at the efficiency of that administration in making up its mind and choosing.

Trustees of a charity can choose a standard off-the-shelf product such as a collective investment scheme, an exempt unit trust or a pooled fund. They can equally well choose to turn to an investment manager capable of providing an identifiable individual portfolio service for each client, be they large or small. It is a simple matter of product versus service. For the smaller charity with limited investment funds looking for a simple risk-free approach then pooled fund or collective investment schemes probably provide the best way ahead. Where, however, there are larger sums to be invested and the trustees can set out their requirements, a service approach is probably the best one.

The question of costs

Charities should be no exception to the rule when it comes to fees. That is to say, fees should be negotiated as though the charity were a normal commercial client and services were not provided as a special favour. However, of course smaller charities should be treated differently from larger charities, but it could be argued no differently from the way in which investment managers should treat small pension funds. That is to say, fees for smaller pension funds are always at a lower rate than would be charged for the larger pension fund, or at least they should be.

Much use is now being made of consulting actuaries to assist a charity and its managers and trustees in choosing investment managers. Several firms who have specialized in the process of assisting pension funds select and monitor the performance of their investment managers have become involved in the charity field. They can provide independent advice in a very professional manner but obviously there will be fees involved.

The charity world is looking for a good efficient service from professional investment managers who must have some knowledge of charity business and those, in the charity world, must be prepared to pay properly for this.

Pulling all this together there is a need for the charity world to make absolutely clear to the investment managers what it is that is required. Thus a clear and precise definition of one's objectives is necessary.

So when selecting an investment manager there are several key questions that the charity, as well as the investment manager, need to ask:

- What are the long-term objectives?
- What return is it reasonable to expect from investments?
- What degree of risk is acceptable in achieving the desired return?

In assessing one's adviser always go back to first principles and revisit the initial brief. How responsive has the manager been to one's wishes? If service is important, then continuity will be even more important. For many charity finance directors good administration is essential and, in this respect, the investment manager must be involved. Track record, as we have seen, does not guarantee continued excellent performance and so some measurement against indices is important.

Fraud – the urgent case for investor protection

We are now living in a much more materialistic world and one unfortunate aspect of this has been an increase in the general level of dishonesty. It is rare for churches to be unlocked today and likewise charities are no longer immune, if they ever were, from the fraudster, therefore a much greater vigilance is now required. The fraud attack can come from without and, unfortunately, ever increasingly from within. There is, however, often a very thin dividing line between what is maladministration and what is out and out fraud. So protection is vital to safeguard a charity's funds.

The problem

The problem of fraud often arises because the internal control systems operating within the charity are poor or even non-existent. Whilst these may not in themselves always be detrimental, as many charities with poor/non-existent internal control systems have not suffered from fraud, the lack of adequate controls are a godsend to the dishonest. The moral is that if you are sure that you have honest staff then you can have poor internal control systems – but who in the charity world should take that risk? Poor administration can too often become maladministration which may then lead to fraud.

Internal controls

The various types of fraud perpetrated on charities have become more and more ingenious, and therefore the systems that need to be put in place to prevent them have to be as good and as watertight as possible. However, perhaps this is going too far, as many frauds do not start out as such but develop often by accident. 'I just borrowed some of the day's takings and intended to pay them back the next day before banking' to quote from an internal audit report of one large charity's shop chain. It is developments such as the sale of donated goods by charities through charity shops that have unfortunately led to an increase in fraud, albeit often of a minor nature. It is so easy to help oneself to cash when the internal controls are weak, thinking that one will repay it, and then of course finding that you can't, or more often that it is so easy to help oneself without being found out that you go on doing it.

In many respects, it is far easier to perpetrate a fraud on a charity than in the general business world because so frequently there is a lack of paperwork. When, for example, one buys on credit from a large departmental store one will receive an invoice and possibly pay by cheque sent through the post to the store or credit card company concerned. Life in the charity world is very different, most transactions with charity shops will be in cash with no invoices and often no receipts issued. So cash controls are imperative.

Publicity

Does all this matter? Fraud is of course far more important to a charity than to a normal business. Why is this? Put simply, as an example, if one was employed in, say, the chemical industry and disappeared to Brazil with £5m of the firm's funds it would not have affected their reputation and probably would not have damaged their future sales. It would certainly not have affected their competitors or the chemical distribution industry generally.

However, if, say, the finance director of the Cancer Research Campaign (CRC) departed to Brazil with £5m, or even a somewhat smaller sum, of CRC's investment funds then the effect would certainly have been felt by CRC and the charity world generally. The CRC's reputation as a trusted charity would have been damaged, the press would have had a field day and yet again *all* charities' reputations would have been openly questioned and debated. Quite frequently in cases of this nature the income of the charity in question suffers and there are attacks from all and sundry on the taxable and other benefits currently allowed to charities. Investor protection therefore becomes an issue.

Increase in cases

Fraud is unfortunately on the increase, of that there is no doubt at all. An article as long ago as 1993 in *Accountancy* entitled 'Fraud Prevention and the Accountant', whilst looking specifically at commercial concerns, made some very telling points that were and still are just as equally relevant to charities.

- About 90 per cent of companies see themselves as potential victims of fraud.
- One of the frequent aspects of fraud within companies is that its perpetrators are often people who are generally regarded as honest.
- Most fraud is opportunistic. The person sees a weakness in a system and takes advantage of it. It is normally done by employees who have been there for a very long time.

As that article tellingly put it, once fraud is discovered it will be the accountants who are the most under pressure. First, of course, they will probably be prime suspects themselves, and second, if not, they may well be blamed because of the lack of adequate internal control systems. Where not accused it is undoubtedly certain that they or the internal audit department, where there is one, will end up with the problem of sorting out the mess.

Charity frauds

What of externally perpetrated frauds on charities, which unfortunately are seen more and more as 'soft touches' by the conman? Where once it would have been unheard of for fraud to happen, it is certainly not so today. In a society where churches have to be closed to avoid theft, it is not surprising that charities are also under attack from external fraudsters; for example, the attempt by Nigerian fraudsters to swindle CAFOD and Christian Aid and the investment scam against the Salvation Army.

The first case was undoubtedly an extension of a wave of fraud from the back streets of Lagos that fooled over one hundred small UK businesses. CAFOD was contacted by fraudsters towards the end of 1993 advising them that they had been left the beneficiary of a will of a devout Catholic married to a Nigerian. After considerable correspondence between the UK and Nigeria, CAFOD received a cheque for £150,000 drawn on The Central Bank of Nigeria but were advised by their Nigerian contact that they needed £6,000 within eight days to pay death duties. As the request had arrived just before Christmas CAFOD asked for an extension. Following the Christmas break and having not at that stage banked the cheque from Nigeria, a member of staff in CAFOD's accounts department noticed that the sort code was wrong. After talking to their own bank CAFOD was warned about increases of Nigerian perpetrated fraud and declined to remit anything to Nigeria. Not surprisingly, their Nigerian contact made no further attempt to get in touch with them. As CAFOD's assistant director, Robert Miller, was quoted at the time: 'This fraud almost convinced us. They are obviously very skilled.'

The second case highlights the ever-increasing risk to charities as they build up investment portfolios. The Salvation Army was the victim of a very sophisticated fraud perpetrated by an unscrupulous businessman based in the UK with an overseas partner. The problem was yet again not fraudulent employees but weak internal controls. In addition, what controls there were could be easily overcome by autocratic leadership; this though not crooked was certainly misguided in the case of one senior employee.

The major problems were therefore twofold. First, too much power was vested internally in one individual and, second, too much dependence was placed on a very small untried firm of investment advisers who turned out to be 'conmen'. It is worth bearing in mind the maxim 'beware of advisers promising fantastically high returns well above the market average'.

Another investment fraud

Another example where the case for investor protection was needed, was the 'fraud' perpetrated against the Universities Superannuation Scheme (USS). Here the investment manager of USS, an employee, had too much power and internal controls were again weak. It appears from a reading of the case that he acted foolishly, although possibly not fraudulently, by investing a very large proportion of the USS funds in a non-quoted company ('makers/distributors of toys'). It later transpired, when the company got into difficulties, that there was a very close relationship between the managing director of the company and the USS employee. It turned out that the investment management had been persuaded, by various means, to invest a considerable percentage of USS funds in the company and effectively held the majority of the shares.

Lessons for charities

All these examples illustrate an unfortunate weakness of many large charities. Although they are big organizations they tend to see themselves as being different from equally large businesses run for profit even as far as administrative matters are concerned. To some extent this is inevitable. Charities depend, as we have seen, on trust much more than businesses do. Charities frequently have voluntary part-time staff both in the field and at headquarters; and of course all trustees are voluntary.

Are these cases the tip of the iceberg or is fraud relating to charity investment an infrequent occurrence? The answer is probably the latter although undoubtedly some cases of fraud certainly go unreported or worse still unnoticed!

What is true, however, is that the number of cases of fraud and the size of losses is likely to go on rising. Therefore, there is most certainly a strong argument for introducing some form of investor protection. Auditors have wide responsibilities that include trying to catch fraud. Under an auditing standard on fraud and error issued by the Auditing Practices Board, auditors must design audits to vet companies' defences against fraud that might risk accounts being materially wrong.

The standard, whilst emphasizing that auditors are not responsible for detecting fraud, states that they will have to assess the risks in each company they audit, including risks that management itself might commit fraud. Risk factors include the presence of dominant individuals beyond board control and needlessly complex financial structures. The standard suggests warning signs, such as high turnover of staff in the finance department and unusual deals just before the year end.

Other factors to look for, many of them often prevalent in charities, include:

- Holiday entitlement not taken up
- Understaffing in the accounts department
- Incomplete files or altered accounts
- Evasive replies to auditor questions.

Insurance

Exposure to fraud can be reduced by improving internal financial controls, segregation of activities and by the charity establishing their own in-house internal audit function. However, even the best systems and the most stringent controls can fail and to protect the assets of the charity, the trustees should consider arranging some form of fidelity insurance. This can often be taken out as a specific insurance or it can be included under one or other of the trustees' liability insurance policies that are now available.

Liability as a charity trustee is almost unlimited, although one can now insure using the Directors' and Officers' type insurance which the Charity Commission, after representation from various bodies including the Charity Finance Directors' Group, agreed to allow. Previously, the Charity Commission had felt that payments for premiums on this type of insurance were a benefit in kind to the charity trustees and were therefore not allowable. However, following negotiations, they agreed to a suitable wording for this type of cover and to accept that the premium is a legitimate charity business expense. Before taking out this type of insurance, charities must check their governing instrument to ensure that they have the power to do so and if not they will of course have to amend their governing instrument accordingly.

Conclusion

As the range of investments that a charity can be involved in has widened, the need to protect investments will increase. As the Charity Commission has made clear:

> The extension of investment powers in a scheme will almost invariably be subject to the appointment of a professional investment manager.

But:

> The trustees must remember that they retain overall responsibility for supervising the actions of the investment manager and are entitled to cancel the appointment of the investment manager if the services falls short of the trustees' requirements.

In making the case for charity investor protection we must not create situations where the fraudster is protected. Whilst there appears to be no generally available statistics relating specifically to charity fraud, it is accepted that most frauds generally are under £150,000 so the Salvation Army case could be said to have been exceptional; apparently something like only 10 per cent of frauds are for sums in excess of £100,000. Thus some of the frauds perpetrated recently in the charity world most certainly qualify as exceptional.

Quite clearly, charities need to become much more vigilant both to the threat from within and to that from without. Unfortunately, no-one is immune.

Exercise – responsibility and the New Trustees Act 2000

This exercise can be used/answered either as a written essay or in a group discussion.

> All that can be required of a trustee to invest, is, that he shall conduct himself faithfully and exercise a sound discretion. He is to observe how men of prudence, discretion and intelligence manage their own affairs, not in regard to speculation, but in regard to the permanent disposition

of their funds, considering the probable income, as well as the probable safety of the capital to be invested.

(Harvard College v. Ampry 1830)

Required:

a   Outline the constraints imposed on charity investments by the Trustees Act 2000.
b   Discuss the notion that this rule formulated in the 1800s (given above) is relevant to the investment policy of charities in the twenty-first century.

Answer to exercise

(a) Trustee Act 2000:

The old prescriptive investment provisions of the Trustee Investment Act 1961 have been abolished and there will no longer be any obligation to divide investments into Narrower and Wider ranges or confine investments to eligible securities.

Trustees will now be able to invest freely within the UK and overseas. In addition, there will be no need for the company to have a five-year dividend history. The Act does not define what constitutes an investment. The Charity Commission has indicated that they will use the Law Commission definition of an investment, which is expected to produce an income or a capital return (Brown 2001).

While this may offer charities the opportunities to invest in hedge and private equity funds, the status of derivatives is still ambiguous. The Charity Commission would need to be convinced if a charity wished to so invest.

In this respect, while the prescriptive aspects of the 1961 Act have gone, the prudent and risk criteria – the so-called 'standard investment criteria' – remains. Trustees therefore need to appraise the suitability of each investment and the diversification among their investments.

Certain investment vehicles are considered to be particularly low risk, mainly Common Investment Funds.

(b) The quotation is still relevant today – though the language may be different!

A charity still has to observe the following:

•   maximize investment income
•   maximize capital growth of its investments.

It should be noted that these objectives pull the portfolio in opposite directions.

- Trustees have a duty of care imposed on them to act as a prudent person of business.
- Charities no longer have to follow the constraints of the TIA but do have a duty to take advice and the Charity Commission outlines the form this advice should take.
- Trustees must always ensure they invest in accordance within the charity's objects and powers.
- Trustees act as custodians for the beneficiaries.
- Trustees cannot speculate with investments.
- Delegation to an investment manager must be strictly within the charity's objects.
- Trustees in absence of delegation are responsible for:
    i   safeguarding investments
    ii   ensuring all income received
    iii ensuring assets and stock mix is correct.

10 Charity tax

Introduction

This chapter outlines the tax exemptions, looks at how charities can organize their trading activities tax efficiently, examines the tax consequences of the various methods of giving to charity, sets out the role of the charity dealing with employee taxation and reviews some of the VAT effects. It is not intended to be comprehensive, and advice should always be taken before acting upon the contents.

Charities benefit from extensive tax exemptions, and can claim repayment of tax paid by their donors on some types of gifts made out of donors' taxed income. However, it is essential that they keep within the tax rules for their activities and expenditure, and follow the set procedures (see further the Inland Revenue publication IR75 – *Tax Reliefs for Charities*).

The main exemptions – income, gains and inheritance tax

A charity benefits from exemptions from income or corporation tax on most of its income, provided that the income is spent only for its own charitable purposes. Using income for other than the charity's purposes is a breach of trust. This may trigger an investigation by the Charity Commission, and the use of its statutory powers to remedy maladministration, which may jeopardize the charity's registration. The Inland Revenue has the power to inform the Commissioners where it suspects that a charity is using its funds for purposes outside its own charitable ones.

Charities are also exempt from capital gains tax and a charitable trust is not subject to inheritance tax. These issues are discussed later in this chapter. While there is no general exemption from value added tax (VAT) for charities (a charity has to pay VAT like anyone else on many goods and services that it buys), there are some special VAT rules to help charities, covered later in this chapter.

Income tax

Charities are exempt from income tax on all income, except trading income and some income assessable under Case VI of Schedule D. The exemption therefore extends to interest, rents received, income from property abroad, profits from discounting transactions, donations under Gift Aid, and grants from other charities, provided that the income is spent or invested only for the charity's purposes (ICTA 1988 Section 506). Some income is received after tax has been deducted, for example donations under Gift Aid. In such cases, the charity can ask the Inland Revenue for repayment of this tax.

In 1997 the first Labour Budget for 18 years included an announcement which effectively meant the abolition of payments of tax credits for pension schemes and UK companies on dividends paid on, or after, 2 July 1997. However, charities were not affected by these changes until 6 April 1999 and they are effectively receiving compensation through public expenditure for a five-year transitional period. This compensation takes the form of a payment to a charity of a percentage of the dividend it receives. The percentages arc will be:

	Net %	*Gross %*
2000–2001	17	14.5
2001–2002	13	11.5
2002–2003	8	7.4
2003–2004	4	3.8

For comparison, in 1998/1999, the tax system represented 25 per cent of the net (after tax) dividend. By way of example, the tax credit on an £800 dividend was £200, meaning that the gross income was £1,000. The same £800 in 2000/2001 had an associated tax credit of £136, giving the charity a gross income of £936. By 2003/2004 the same dividend will yield the charity a gross income of £832 and of course in 2004/2005 it will be only £800, i.e. gross = net.

Whilst the Chancellor has recognized the special position of charities, by phasing the present system effectively over seven years, there is no denying its eventual effect. According to the figures published by the Inland Revenue in their Press Release, the payments of tax credits in 1997/1998 was estimated at about £350m for charities and non-profit organizations.

Profits from trading by a charity are exempt in two cases provided that the profits are always used for the charity's purposes:

• Where the trade carries out a primary purpose of the charity, for example where a medical relief charity runs a hospital.
• Where the trade is carried out mainly by beneficiaries of the charity, for example a workshop for the disabled run by a charity set up to provide work for disabled people.

In addition, lotteries may be run by charities without them suffering tax on the resulting profits.

Other trading profits are not exempt from tax, even in cases where the profits can be used only for the purposes of the charity, although some fund-raising activities are exempt. More details of trading by charities are covered later in this chapter.

Corporation tax

The exemptions from income tax and capital gains tax apply to corporation tax in exactly the same way. Charities that are formed as limited companies or unincorporated associations are otherwise liable to corporation tax (ICTA 1988 Section 6).

Capital gains tax

Where a charity makes a capital profit, for example from selling investments, it is exempt from capital gains tax provided that the profit is used for its charitable purposes.

Under the Taxation of Chargeable Gains Act 1992 Section 256, a capital gain is not chargeable to capital gains tax, if it accrues to a charity and is used for charitable purposes. Charities are therefore exempt from tax on profits on the realization of investments or other property. This exception can, however, be lost where the charity has incurred non-qualifying expenditure.

A gift to charity of property, on which capital gains tax would normally be charged, is exempt from the tax. The donor is not charged capital gains tax on property such as land and buildings, shares, antiques, paintings or other valuables given to charity.

However, there may be a capital gains tax charge where property held by a charity ceases to be so held otherwise than by being applied for charitable purposes. The property is treated as having been sold by the trustees at its market value. Any gain is calculated under the normal capital gains tax rules and the trustees are charged with the tax. The tax charge is extended to any gains on the sale of property that the trust held earlier, if the money received from the earlier sale was used to buy the property now leaving the charity. This rule is designed to stop the misuse of the capital gains tax exemption by a donor making a temporary gift to charity.

Capital sums received from developing land are caught by the income tax net and the exemption of ICTA 1988 Section 505 in respect of the rents and profits of any lands does not cover development profits. A charity which finds itself holding land no longer needed for the use of the charity, and wishing to dispose of it, is obliged to get the best price obtainable. What may be appropriate in any particular circumstances is a matter for professional advice.

The attraction of keeping some or all of the development capital profit for the charity brings with it tax problems. This is an extremely complex area and charities can fall foul of the ICTA 1988 Section 776 trap. Unless, therefore, a charity is regularly concerned with the disposal of development land, advice from professional tax advisers should always be sought.

Restriction of the exemptions

The exemptions from income, corporation and capital gains taxes are restricted in most cases where a charity uses its income for non-charitable purposes. However, this restriction does not apply to charities with income and gains of less than £10,000 in a 12-month period, unless the charity is acting with one or more other charities for the purpose of trying to avoid tax. It should be understood that there is also a risk that the charity will, by making non-charitable purpose payments, be acting *ultra vires*.

Where the restriction operates

The restriction operates where a charity has:

- relevant income and gains of more than its qualifying expenditure; and
- non-qualifying expenditure.

Where these occur, the charity is taxable on the excess of its relevant income and gains over its qualifying expenditure, or the amount of the non-qualifying expenditure, whichever is the lower. The charity can choose which of its income is to be taxed. Thus, for example, it can keep Gift Aid donations exempt so that donors do not lose their higher rate tax relief.

In some circumstances, non-qualifying expenditure is treated as non-qualifying expenditure of an earlier period, resulting in income of that period becoming taxable.

Relevant income and gains

Relevant income and gains means all the charity's income and gains, whether or not it would be exempt apart from the restriction. It does not include gifts that are not income, but does include gifts made under Gift Aid, which are treated as income.

Qualifying expenditure

Qualifying expenditure is expenditure incurred for charitable purposes only. Where the charity makes a payment to an organization outside the UK, it is qualifying expenditure if the overseas organization uses the money for charitable purposes. However, the Inland Revenue may require evidence of this.

Non-qualifying expenditure

Non-qualifying expenditure is expenditure other than qualifying expenditure, qualifying investments or qualifying loans.

- Qualifying investments are most investments available on the open market, such as bank and building society accounts, government loans, and shares and securities of quoted companies, as well as investment in land. Other investments qualify where the Inland Revenue is satisfied that they are for the benefit of the charity and not for tax avoidance purposes (by the charity or anyone else).
- Qualifying loans are loans to other charities, loans to beneficiaries of a charity made in the course of carrying out the charity's purposes, money held in a bank current account and other loans, provided that they are for the benefit of the charity and not for tax avoidance purposes. The Inland Revenue will look closely at such a loan made to a company owned by the charity to finance its trading activities. They will examine such things as interest rate, security, provision for repayment, cash flow forecasts and business plans before accepting that it is a qualifying loan for those purposes.

Repayment of loans

Repayment, by a charity, of money it has borrowed is treated as neither qualifying nor non-qualifying expenditure.

Inheritance tax

All outright gifts to charities, whether by will or during a lifetime, are exempt without limit from inheritance tax. The main value of this exemption is for gifts made by a will, as all gifts made during a lifetime are in any case exempt provided that the donor lives for seven years after the gift.

A charity that takes the form of a trust is exempt from the ten-yearly charge to inheritance tax that can arise for other trusts, provided that the property is held for charitable purposes only. However, inheritance tax is payable where property is held on a temporary charitable trust in the following circumstances:

- Where the property stops being held for charitable purposes, unless the reason for it leaving the trust is because it is being applied for a charitable purpose elsewhere.
- Where the trustees do something that reduces the value of the property held by the trust, except making a gift for charitable purposes.

However, there are several instances in the circumstances shown above in which no tax arises. The main ones are where the value of trust property is reduced because of the payment of costs or expenses connected with the property, or where no gratuitous benefit to anyone else is intended.

Where a charge to inheritance tax does arise, the amount payable is a variable percentage of the amount by which the value of the property within the trust has been reduced as a result of the event referred to above. If the trust itself pays the inheritance tax (rather than the recipient of the property), then the amount of tax must be added to the reduction in the value of the trust's property. For example, if the value of property in the trust is reduced by £20,000 before inheritance tax is paid and the rate of tax is 20 per cent, then if the trust pays the tax its liability will be £5,000 (20 per cent of £25,000).

The rate of tax depends on how long the property has been held on charitable trust, and is a maximum of 30 per cent where the property has been held for 50 years or more. Charities formed as limited companies or unincorporated associations cannot be charged inheritance tax.

Trading activities

The trading income of charities is not normally exempt, by statute, from tax unless it falls into one of two narrow categories. Most fund-raising activities are exempt, provided that they meet certain conditions. Any other trading activities in which a charity wants to engage should normally be carried on by a separate company owned by the charity. Provided that the funds of the charity are invested in such a company, in accordance with the Charity Commission guidelines and those of the Inland Revenue, the charity's tax exemptions should not be restricted.

The Inland Revenue published in April 1995 a very useful booklet in its Charities Series CS2 entitled *Trading by Charities*. This offers some extremely good guidelines on the tax treatment of trades carried on by charities and should be read thoroughly by any charity that is considering trading.

A charity is liable to tax on trading profits that fall outside the exempt categories. One example of this historically has been underwriting commission, where a charity has underwritten a new issue of shares and for the risk of so doing, has received a small commission without necessarily buying any of the shares. The commission less appropriate expenses, i.e. the profit, is liable to tax.

The Inland Revenue effectively regards any profits derived from underwriting carried out by a charity as taxable. This is because either they are deemed to fall within Schedule D Case I as trading, i.e. where it is done on a regular basis, or where it is not trading income then the profits are chargeable under Schedule D Case VI.

Selling donated goods is not considered to be a trade and so a charity may run a shop without setting up a separate company, provided that the shop does not buy in any goods for sale. However, this is often too restrictive and so charity shops are frequently run through a separate company.

Fund-raising activities

In discussing the meaning of trading it is clear that many of the traditional and now generally accepted ways of charity fund-raising could be classed as trading. The Inland Revenue has recognized that considerable problems could result if it attempted to enforce tax conditions on certain activities.

The Finance Act 1995 Section 138 amended ICTA 1988 Section 505, specifically to remove the taxation of profits made from running a charity lottery. Effectively the amendment exempts from tax, under Schedule D, profits accruing to a charity from a lottery provided that the lottery is promoted and conducted in accordance with the Lotteries and Amusements Act 1976 Section 3 or 5, or the Betting, Gaming, Lotteries and Amusements (Northern Ireland) Order 1985 Article 133 or 135. In addition, of course, the profits have to be applied solely for the charity's purposes.

Therefore, the profit generated from fund-raising activities, such as jumble sales, bazaars, carnivals, fireworks displays and similar events, although they are strictly speaking a form of trading (ICTA 1988 Section 832), are exempt from tax provided that both the following conditions are satisfied:

• The event is of a kind which falls within the exemption from VAT under Group 12 of Schedule 9 to the VAT Act 1994.
• The profits are given to charity or used for charitable purposes.

The rules relating to fund-raising events and the various tax exemptions were consolidated as a result of the 2000 Budget, so that an event that qualifies for exemption from VAT will also be exempt from income and corporation tax. This is to tidy up an anomaly that existed between the rules on one-off fund-raising events in relation to the VAT exemption, and the Inland Revenue Extra Statutory Concession (ESC C4).

From 1 April 2000, where fund-raising events, including participative events and events on the Internet, are run by a charity or by a voluntary organization to raise funds for a charity, any profits from the events will be exempt from income and corporation tax, provided the events qualify for exemption from VAT. Additionally, the number of events allowed in any one year in any one location has been increased to 15 of each type or kind of event. For small-scale events the exemption will apply to any number of events, provided the gross weekly income from those events does not exceed £1,000.

On 31 March 2000 the Inland Revenue published the revised Extra Statutory Concession exempting the profits from more fund-raising events from income and corporation tax. Charities and their advisers will no longer have to deal separately with the Inland Revenue and HM Customs and Excise to determine whether a fund-raising event qualifies for exemption.

Small-scale trading

Currently, where a charity carries on a trade as part of its charitable purpose then the profits are normally exempt from tax. However, where the trade is purely for the purpose of raising funds, for example the sale of Christmas cards, then the profits generated will not usually be exempt from tax. From April 2000 a tax exemption was introduced to cover the profits of certain small-scale trading activities carried on by charities that were not otherwise already exempt from tax. This may mean for many charities there will no longer be the need to set up a trading company to carry on these activities.

This exemption will apply provided the total turnover from all of the activities does not exceed the annual turnover limit, or if it does then the charity must have had a reasonable expectation that it would not do so and all the profits must be used solely for the purposes of the charity. The annual turnover limit is £5,000, or if the turnover is greater than this then 25 per cent of the charity's total gross incoming resources is subject to a maximum limit of £50,000. Incoming resources are defined using the rules set out under charity accounting regulations and include the total receipts of the charity from all sources, e.g. grants, donations, legacies, investment income, income from trading activities, etc.

As an example, if a charity is selling Christmas cards as a fund-raising trading activity and the total sales revenue is £4,500 (where this is the only taxable fund-raising trading activity), then the profits will be exempt from tax because the turnover does not exceed £5,000. However, if the turnover from the sale of Christmas cards was £45,000, which is less than the overall limit of £50,000, then to qualify for the tax relief the total gross incoming resources of the charity would need to be greater than £180,000 (£180,000 at 25 per cent = £45,000).

If the total turnover of the taxable fund-raising trading activity for a tax year exceeds the annual turnover limit then the profits will still be exempt from tax, provided the charity can show that at the start of the tax year it had a reasonable expectation that the turnover would not exceed the limit. The Inland Revenue Guidance Notes published with the Budget in March 2000 gave some examples of why this might be, for example the charity expected the turnover to be lower than it turned out to be, or the charities incoming resources were lower than originally expected.

Companies owned by charities

The use of a trading company can be of great assistance to any charity. The Charity Commission welcome this approach and have said 'where a charity wishes to benefit substantially from permanent trading for the purposes of fund-raising we advise that it does so through a separate non-charitable trading company, so that its charitable status is not endangered.'

However, four important steps have to be considered, as follows.

1 Funding the trading company

The funding of the trading company needs to be looked at very carefully. The charity should, if possible, avoid investing its own funds in the trading company; this form of investment is risky and trust law requires funds to be invested with the minimum of risk. Investment in trading companies may also be non-qualifying expenditure and result in a restriction of the charity's tax relief. The charity should avoid making loans to the trading company because such loans may not be for charitable purposes and could put at risk its charitable and tax exemptions. Any essential loan must be made on strictly commercial terms, i.e. interest must be charged and actually paid.

2 Establishing the trading company

If in setting up the trading company it is done by investing the charity's funds in shares to be held by the charity, either directly or through nominees, then it will be necessary to ascertain that the charity's governing document permits such investment.

3 Asset transfer

Where the company's trade is carried on from owned or rented premises, then these should be retained or put into the ownership and name of the charity. This is to retain capital gains tax exemptions and maintain the rate relief available to the charity, which is not applicable to the trading company. However, the trading company must pay the charity for the use of such premises and any other services provided to it.

4 Distribution of profits

It is necessary to ensure that the memorandum and articles of the trading company allow it to distribute profits and make similar annual payments.

Profit retention

From 1 April 2000 companies with taxable profits of up to £10,000 suffer a corporation tax rate of only 10 per cent. Charities with such trading subsidiaries are therefore able to retain profit without facing a significant tax bill in order to build up the working capital of the trading subsidiary. This may be a cheaper alternative to funding the subsidiary with the retained profits, rather than borrowing from external sources or using the charity's own funds.

In order to ease the climb from 10 per cent corporation tax to the 20 per cent rate for profit above £350,000, there is tapering relief at the rate of one-fortieth applicable to profits between £10,001 and £50,000. Companies with profits between £50,001 and £300,000 will continue to pay tax at 20 per cent. The full rate of corporation tax remains at 30 per cent.

Profit transfer

A trading company owned by a charity is liable to corporation tax on its profits, like any other trading company (ICTA 1988 Section 338). However, there were three ways in which it could pass its income to its parent charity and at the same time claim relief against its corporation tax liability. These were by covenant, dividend or Gift Aid.

The 2000 Budget changed all that, and now the profit is paid over to the parent charity gross, i.e. without deduction of tax. The gross amount of the donation is allowed as a charge on income against the trading income (and capital gains) of the trading company in the accounting period in which it is incurred.

Companies owned by charities have nine months after the end of the financial year for the trading subsidiary to pay over the donated profit.

Giving to charity

Depending on its type, a gift made to charity may qualify for tax relief or exemption which the donor can claim and/or entitle the charity to claim a tax repayment. Use of the available tax exemptions can bring considerable benefit to the charity, both by increasing the value of gifts where tax repayments are claimed and by encouraging people to make gifts in cases where the donor benefits from the exemption.

The Inland Revenue publishes very useful leaflets, which are currently being revised, on giving to charity, and setting out how businesses and individuals can get tax relief. Following the 2000 Budget, the Inland Revenue published a very useful guidance note for charities – *Getting Britain Giving* (21 March 2000).

Deed of covenant

A deed of covenant is a legal document placing an obligation on the donor to make regular payments to a charity (ICTA 1988 Section 347A(7)). To be tax effective, it must have been capable of running for a period that exceeded three years and have been incapable of earlier termination. The deed had to be in the correct legal form and include the word 'deed'.

Tax treatment

Payments under a deed of covenant were treated for tax purposes as made net of basic rate tax. The charity could recover the tax from the Inland Revenue, increasing the value of the gift. Individuals who are liable to tax at the higher rate (40 per cent) could also receive higher rate tax relief on their payments. For example, a payment of £78 would allow the charity to claim £22 from the Inland Revenue and reduce the tax bill of the higher rate taxpayer by £18. Claims for repayment were made annually, or more often by completing the official single sheet form R68 accompanied by a schedule or schedules of income included in the claim.

2000 Budget changes

Covenant payments falling due on or after 6 April 2000 are covered by the new Gift Aid measures as the tax relief for covenants has been withdrawn. However, where a covenanted payment, which fell due before 6 April 2000, was made on or after that date the new Gift Aid measures did not apply to the payment; instead the existing rules for Deeds of Covenant continued to apply.

In particular, the rule entitling a charity to reclaim tax at the basic rate in force when the covenanted payment fell due, rather than when it is made, continues to apply. This means that if a charity receives a covenanted payment after 6 April 2000, which had legally fallen due before that date, it will not be disadvantaged by the reduction in the basic rate from 23 to 22 per cent that came into force with effect from 6 April 2000.

Charities do not have to get a Gift Aid declaration in respect of payments made under Deeds of Covenant that were already in existence and still remained in force at 6 April 2000. Effectively the Deed of Covenant will stand in place of the Gift Aid declaration. Notwithstanding this, any declarations made outside the terms of the deed or after the expiry of the deed must be covered by a Gift Aid declaration. Likewise, quite clearly a new Deed of Covenant introduced on or after 6 April 2000 must be covered by a Gift Aid declaration.

Gift Aid

The Finance Act 1990 introduced the concept of a new relief for single gifts by individuals made on or after 1 October 1990.

General rules prior to 5 April 2000

One-off donations are called Gift Aid. They are treated as net of tax and a tax repayment can be claimed in a similar way to donations under a covenant. Gift Aid required a minimum donation of £250 until 5 April 2000 since 16 March 1993 – prior to this it was £400 with effect from 1 July 1992 – at introduction it was £600. The maximum limit of £5 million was removed in the 1991 Budget, although it is accepted that this has had little or no effect on giving.

The donor had to be a UK resident and the gift had to be made out of taxed income and could not be due under a deed of covenant or under a payroll deduction scheme. Any benefit received by the donor could not exceed 2.5 per cent of any gift up to a maximum of £250 in any one year.

The gift had to be in cash with no conditions attached. Clearly, fund-raising collections that are not a gift out of one individual's taxable income did not qualify, nor did the writing off of a loan to a charity or several small taxable gifts amounting to £250 in total; each gift had to be for at least £250 net of basic rate tax.

A donor who paid higher rate tax could claim further tax relief. Companies could also make gifts under Gift Aid and in this case there was no minimum except for close companies, as defined by ICTA 1988 Section 414 where the minimum of £250 still applied.

2000 Budget changes

Considerable improvement was made and undoubtedly a change to the way in which individuals and companies give to charity:

- No minimum limit
- Giving by Internet or telephone
- Higher tax relief against income or capital gains tax
- Companies giving gross.

The new measures came into force for individual donations made on or after 6 April 2000 and company donations made on or after 1 April 2000.

Forms

Gift Aid declarations are the new forms that replaced the old Gift Aid certificates.

The way in which the system operates does appear to be more flexible. Donors are able to provide a declaration in advance of their donation, at the time they make the donation or at any time after the donation, subject of course to the normal time limit within which a charity can reclaim tax. The declaration is also able to cover one donation or any number of donations and can be made in writing or orally.

Charities are able to design their own Gift Aid written declaration form, but it must satisfy all of the following requirements and contain:

- The charity's name
- The donor's name
- The donor's address
- A description of the donation(s) to which the declaration relates

- A declaration that the donation(s) is/are to be treated as Gift Aid donation(s)
- A note explaining that the donor must pay an amount of income tax or capital gains tax equal to the tax deducted from his or her donation(s).

Donors are able to make gifts orally and the legislation allows for this. Information collected over the telephone and which then needs to be sent to the donor in writing includes:

- All the details provided by the donor in his or her oral declaration
- A note explaining that the donor must pay an amount of income tax or capital gains tax equal to the tax deducted from his or her donation(s)
- A note explaining the donor's entitlement to cancel the declaration retrospectively
- The date on which the charity sent the written record to the donor.

This procedure should be carried out to ensure that the charity can reclaim the tax in respect of the donation. All these records need to be kept as part of an audit trail should there be a subsequent Inland Revenue audit.

Benefits

The rules relating to the benefits that a donor can receive from a charity following a gift to it were amended to combine the old differing rules for covenants and Gift Aid, producing a very complex set of rules. There are two tests for the value of the benefits that a donor or a person connected with the donor may receive.

Relevant value test

Amount of donation	Value of benefits
£0–100	25% of total donations
£101–1,000	£25
£1,001+	2.5% of total donations

Aggregate value test

The value of the benefits plus the value of any benefits received in consequence of any Gift Aid donations made by the same donor to the same charity earlier in the same tax year exceeds £250.

If the value of the benefits received exceeds either of these tests, the donation will not qualify as a Gift Aid donation. The existing rule that disregards the benefit of right of admission to the premises of a heritage or wild-life conservation charity, which applied only to the Deed of Covenant scheme, has been extended to the revised Gift Aid scheme. This relaxation covers only the donor or any member of his/her family and does not include non-family guests of the donor or any benefit other than the admission price.

Record keeping

Charities need to keep records to show that their tax reclaims are accurate. In other words, there must be an audit trail linking each donation to an identifiable donor who has given a valid Gift Aid declaration and all the other conditions for recovering tax must have been satisfied.

These records do not have to be kept on paper and may be held on the hard drive of a computer, on a floppy disk, CD ROM or stored on microfiche. However, signed declarations should always be kept in a form that preserves the signature, e.g. microfilm or electronically scanned in.

Where adequate records are not kept, then the charity may be required to repay the Inland Revenue any tax that it has reclaimed. In addition, there will be interest to pay on the tax and the charity may also be liable to a penalty. Effectively this is no change from the pre-2000 Budget situation.

The form of records to be kept is not prescribed in any detail in the legislation and does not appear to have changed significantly as a result of these new Gift Aid measures. Therefore, what this means in practice will depend on the size of the charity, the number of donations it has and the kind of systems in use.

The suggested length of time for keeping records for a charitable trust is confusing. Thus, records must be kept until:

> The 31 January next but one after the end of the tax year to which your tax reclaim relates (for example, if you make a tax reclaim for the tax year 2000/2001, until 31 January 2003), or
> one year after you make your tax reclaim, rounded to the end of the next quarter (for example, if you make a tax reclaim on 25 May 2002, until 30 June 2003), or FICO completes any audit it has commenced whichever is the later.

If the charity is a company, records have to be kept for six years after the end of the accounting period to which the tax claim relates.

Audit

In the event that the Inland Revenue carries out an audit of a charity's tax reclaim, the auditor will usually ask to see the following information:

- Any written Gift Aid declarations
- In the case of oral Gift Aid declarations, a copy of the written records sent to the donor

- Any correspondence to or from the donors which relates to their Gift Aid donations
- Cash book recording receipt of cash donations
- Bank statements
- Credit card companies' statements
- Any other records kept relating to donations.

Reclaims

As far as reclaiming tax on donations is concerned, a revised, simpler claim form with accompanying schedules is available.

Just before the 2000 Budget the Inland Revenue issued a letter to charities which gave details of:

- New automated repayment services using BACS
- The authorized signatory form.

A copy of the form was attached to this letter which needed to be completed and returned to the Inland Revenue with the first repayment claim made on or after 6 April 2000. Since that date, the Inland Revenue will only repay claims if an official of the charity, who has been authorized on the form, signs them.

Marketing

Where an individual wants to give a valuable asset to charity a good fund-raising strategy is to get the individual to sell the item and Gift Aid the proceeds. Because of the tax effect under Gift Aid this increases the sum received by the charity above what it would have received if it had taken the asset and sold it. One does, however, need to consider very carefully the capital gains and income tax position of the individual concerned and ensure that all the usual other conditions are met.

It is possible to combine the inheritance tax exemption and Gift Aid. The donor's will should make a gift of money to a trusted individual and express a wish that the money should be given to charity. Where the individual makes the gift to charity within two years of the death, inheritance tax exemption is given to the estate and the charity can claim repayment of tax under the Gift Aid scheme. A gift made this way gives rise to tax reliefs of up to 93 per cent of the amount of the gift. This scheme may be challenged by the Inland Revenue in the courts.

Payroll giving (Give as You Earn)

With the agreement of the employer, it has always been possible for an employee to arrange for the employer to make donations from after-tax pay to a chosen charity.

The Finance Act 1986 introduced a scheme whereby, again with the agreement of the employer, an employee could have deductions made from pre-tax pay, and passed over to an 'agency' charity which in turn would pass on the money to a charity or charities nominated by the employee. Employers who wish to set up such a scheme must make the necessary contractual arrangements with an agency charity approved by the Inland Revenue such as the Charities Aid Foundation.

Limits

The table below shows the maximum amount per year, and per month (in brackets), that an individual has been able to give since Payroll Giving was introduced up until the 2000 Budget.

1987	£120	(£10)
1988	£240	(£20)
1989	£480	(£40)
1990	£600	(£50)
1993	£900	(£75)
1996	£1,200	(£100)

There is no minimum sum.

Relief

A charity cannot claim any tax repayment on donations under a Payroll Giving scheme. The employee receives tax relief instead via the PAYE system. Thus, the net cost to an individual of making the maximum gift of £1,200 per year in this way in 1999/2000 was £924 for the basic rate taxpayer and £720 for the higher rate taxpayer. In both cases the charity received £1,200.

2000 Budget changes

As part of the government campaign to 'Getting Britain Giving', there is a 10 per cent supplement on all donations made under the Payroll Giving scheme in the period 6 April 2000–5 April 2003. This supplement is being paid by the government and will be distributed to charities via the agencies currently running the scheme, and those agencies will do so without any deduction for administration fees.

The Charitable Deductions (approved Schemes) (Amendment) Regulations 2000 came into force on 6 April 2000. Agencies that distribute Payroll Giving donations to charities have to distribute them to the chosen charity within 60 days. If an agency fails to distribute the donations within the time limit, it will have to inform the Inland Revenue and explain why it has not done so.

Additionally, with effect from 6 April 2000, the £1,200 per year maximum limit on the amount that an employee can give under this scheme was abolished.

Marketing

Using Payroll Giving by getting a group of employees to join together and give, can engender a great sense of belonging. Marketing is important and visits by personnel from the charity concerned to address employees are important to get these schemes going and keep them operational. As the charity will need to get the company involved before Payroll Giving can take place, another way of increasing the charity's income would be to persuade the company to make a matching payment under Gift Aid to that of its employees.

Company giving

This part examines company giving. Businesses, whether they are in the form of limited companies, partnerships or self-employed individuals, can help charities in several ways.

Deeds of covenant and Gift Aid

Prior to 1 April 2000 limited companies could make donations by deed of covenant or Gift Aid in the same way as individuals. The charity's right to claim tax repayment was the same as for individuals, except that different forms were used, but the company's tax position was different. The company had to make the payment to the charity net of basic rate tax in the same way as an individual, but had to pay the basic rate tax to the Inland Revenue, or set it off against the basic rate tax deducted on any payments that it received net of tax (such as interest received other than from a bank).

The company received tax relief for the net payments plus relief against its corporation tax. This meant that for a company paying corporation tax at the small companies' rate (20 per cent), a covenanted or Gift Aid payment to charity resulted in the charity receiving, for example, a total of £100 at a cost to the company of £80. For a company paying corporation tax at the full rate (30 per cent) the cost to the company was £70.

This has effectively changed following the 2000 Budget.

Gifts of services and in kind

A business can help a charity by providing the services of an employee free or at a reduced rate. A special tax relief allows the salary and other costs of such an employee to be a tax deductible trading expense of the business, even though the employee is not working for the business (ICTA 1988 Section 86). The secondment should be on a basis which is expressed and intended to be of a temporary nature. What is temporary is not precisely defined, but most secondments to charity (which are rarely for more than two years and often for a year or less) would qualify. There is no VAT charge on the value of the employee's services.

If a company makes a gift of stock or equipment to a charity there are various ways in which this can be handled, each with different tax implications. Gifts to charity are allowable for tax purposes where made wholly and exclusively for the purposes of the trade of the company or where they can be justified as so being made (ICTA 1988 Section 577 (9)). Small gifts to local bodies, which are not charities, are similarly allowable under ESC B7 (see later section on Other gifts by businesses).

Sponsorship

A common means by which businesses help charities is by sponsoring the charity or, more usually, one of its events. This can take several forms, including payment of a set sum of money, the provision of facilities or goods, or the payment of a percentage of sales of certain goods sold by the company.

There are no special tax reliefs to allow the business to claim a tax deduction for the amount it spends on sponsorship. However, under the general tax rules for business expenses, the business can claim a tax deduction if the money was spent 'wholly and exclusively' for the purpose of trade. Where sponsorship involves a measure of publicity for the sponsor, as is usual, this condition should be met, as the sponsorship will, in effect, form part of the business's advertising and promotion budget.

Where a business receives such consideration for its sponsorship payments, the payments are not pure gifts and may be regarded as trading income of the charity. The charity may be liable to VAT on the sponsorship payment if the sponsor receives publicity or other facilities in return.

Payments received from affinity credit cards are regarded as trading income, although by special exemption only 20 per cent of the income is treated as VAT-able (see VAT Notice 701/1/95 p. 15). This concession negotiated by the Charities' Tax Reform Group means that the income from such credit cards is split into income relating to payment for services supplied by the charity and a donation or annual payment for which the charity provides no consideration.

HM Customs and Excise guidance is that only one-fifth of the initial payment is standard rated income, the rest being a donation and outside the scope of VAT. The Inland Revenue advise that if, instead of a single contract between the charity and the donor, the contract is split between the charity and its trading subsidiary it is possible for the part received by the charity to be exempt from tax as an annual payment.

Other gifts by businesses

Other gifts to charity are tax deductible by Inland Revenue concession (ESC B7), provided that:

- The gift is reasonably small in relation to the donor's business activities.
- The charity is local to the business.
- The charity is not only for the benefit of people connected with the business.
- The gift is 'wholly and exclusively' for the purpose of the trade (which means broadly that the business must gain some benefit from the gift).

The business is liable to VAT on the value of goods it gives to charity unless the goods cost £15 or less or are of a type that are zero rated or exempt. However, if it makes a small charge for the goods, the business will pay VAT only on the amount that it charges.

Loans by businesses

This is yet a further example of anti-avoidance legislation being relaxed by concession in favour of donors to charities. Under existing Inland Revenue practice, it is understood that an interest-free loan to a charity does not result in adverse tax consequences for the lender. The requirements that need to be met are:

- The loan is in cash.
- There is no arrangement as to its application, that is it must be for the general purposes of the charity and cannot be restricted for a specific purpose.
- The loan will be repaid in cash.
- The loan is not part of a larger arrangement.

Since the relief is concessionary, charities are advised to establish the Inland Revenue's approval of the arrangements in advance, especially where large sums are involved.

2000 Budget changes

Gifts to charities by companies are now made gross, and the company will receive tax relief on the full amount of its donation. Companies, including those owned by charities, will no longer have to deduct tax from their Gift Aid donations or provide a Gift Aid declaration form. Therefore, charities should not reclaim tax on any donations they receive from a company. However, if a company incorrectly deducts tax from its donation then the charity will have to advise the company accordingly about the new rule and ask it to pay over the sum it has incorrectly deducted.

Other tax efficient giving to charity

There were two further significant aids to giving to charity which were announced in the 2000 Budget.

1 Gift of shares

Tax relief is now granted to the donor where listed shares and securities, units in authorized unit trusts, shares in open-ended investment companies, holdings in foreign collective investment schemes and unlisted shares and securities dealt in on a recognized Stock Exchange (such as shares traded on the Alternative Investment Market), are given to charity. This is in addition to the existing relief for gifts of shares, securities and other assets to charity. When calculating capital gains, it will be set off as a deduction against the individual or company's income or profit for tax purposes. This new relief came into effect from 1 April 2000 for companies, and 6 April 2000 for individuals.

Donors are able to claim this deduction in the tax year in which the disposal takes place. The amount that they can deduct will be the market value of the shares or securities on the date of disposal plus any incidental costs of disposing of the shares less any consideration given in return for disposing of the shares and the value of any other benefits received by the donor in consequence of disposing of the shares.

Charities will not be in a position to reclaim any tax on the donations of shares which they receive, as the donors can claim the tax relief at their top rate of tax on their Self-Assessment or Corporation Tax return.

2 Gifts of certain trusts

A relaxation of the income tax provisions affecting people who settle property on UK-resident trusts and remain beneficiaries was introduced where the beneficiaries also include a charity.

These provisions ensure broadly that settlor-interested possession trusts and settlor-interested trusts are taken outside the provisions of the tax act, to the extent that income arising to the trustees in the year is given to a charity. The provisions do not apply to bare trusts – that is trusts in which the beneficiaries have an indefeasibly vested interest in the capital and income of the trust – and in such a case, any payment by the trustees to a charity would be treated as a payment by the beneficiary and potentially qualify under the Gift Aid provisions.

Settlors affected by these changes will no longer need to include on their self-assessment returns income which the new provisions take outside the charge to tax. A revised version of the self-assessment helpsheet is available which explains the changes and helps settlors calculate the amounts of taxable income.

The charity as an employer

Charities, except the very smallest, often employ staff and therefore need to comply with the rules for deducting tax and national insurance on their employees' pay. Charities enjoy no special privileges or exemptions as far as this aspect of taxation is concerned, and charities can therefore be charged interest or penalties where they do not comply with their tax obligations as employers. The rules of pay as you earn (PAYE), returns of expenses and benefits in kind provided for employees (P11Ds) are exactly the same as those for non-charitable organizations.

The introduction of self-assessment means that for many charity employees, a fully detailed tax return is required and in addition the tax liability may also have to be self-calculated. An entry in the expenses and benefits section of the employee's return shown as 'per P11D' will no longer be accepted, nor will the P11D provide the necessary information. As employees cannot complete their tax returns correctly or on time without accurate timely information, it is essential that charity employers make certain that they get all the returns off by the due dates.

The 1998 Budget abolished the foreign earnings deduction, retaining it solely for seafarers. This clearly had implications for charities with UK staff working overseas, as previously charities had been able to claim a 100 per cent deduction for earnings from employment carried out wholly or partly abroad during a qualifying period of 365 days or more. Charities should have taken advice in respect of their overseas employees, as tax exemptions may still be claimed in cases where non-UK residence status can be claimed for tax purposes.

Value Added Tax

VAT is a veritable nightmare, unless one has an understanding of the basic principles of the tax, its pitfalls and penalties, and even then, problems will remain. It is not necessary to have a profit motive to be within the scope of VAT. The fact that an activity being carried out by a charity is not trading for corporation or income tax purposes does not necessarily mean it is not a business supply for VAT purposes.

There is no general VAT exemption and charities have to pay VAT on most goods and services that they buy. A charity which is not carrying on a business cannot register for VAT, which would allow it to reclaim VAT on its purchases. However, fund-raising activities where goods and services are supplied for payment are businesses, and a charity, or its trading company, must register for VAT where the annual value of such supplies is more than the VAT registration threshold.

It is possible to register voluntarily for VAT purposes when the annual turnover is below the threshold. Once registered, a charity is able to reclaim VAT paid on relevant inputs, that is to say any items purchased which have

VAT charged on them. However, the charity will have to charge VAT on all its taxable supplies and will have to make VAT returns.

Any voluntary registration application cannot be backdated by more than three years. This is to bring the voluntary registration rules into line with the refund capping rules for businesses already registered. The three-year cap will not apply in the case of obligatory registrations.

A very useful source of information for charities when looking at VAT is provided by HM Customs and Excise in their VAT Notice 701/1/95 issued on 1 January 1995 and Update No. 1 issued in February 1997, both of which are entitled Charities, which give some very helpful definitions including:

- Outside scope – supplies not covered by VAT, for example non-business supplies or those made outside the European Union.
- Exempt – within the scope of VAT, but no VAT is charged when making these supplies – an individual or organization that makes only exempt supplies cannot register and cannot recover VAT incurred on purchases.
- Zero rate – rate of VAT which is nil – i.e. no VAT charged on taxable supply but the supplier can register and recover VAT on purchases.

The definition of business and its application to charitable activities is dealt with in paragraphs 4 to 12 inclusive on pages 5 to 16 of this Notice and should be read thoroughly. It is essential to understand this definition if a charity undertakes these activities because of the considerable effect on a charity's affairs if it is not clearly understood and rigorously applied.

Although the definitions given above have the effect of meaning that no VAT is charged on the supply, they do not amount to the same thing! Where a charity makes a zero-rated supply, for example the sale of donated goods, it is effectively charging VAT at zero per cent and can then recover any tax paid on input.

However, where the supplies are exempt, e.g. dividends, then no VAT is charged by the supplier and it is not possible to recover any tax paid on inputs. Similarly, no recovery may be made where the supply can be said to be outside the scope, e.g. legacy income. In these two cases there would effectively be a VAT cost to the charity as it would be unable to recover any VAT incurred on inputs relating to outputs outside the scope of VAT and cannot recover all of that relating to exempt activities.

Zero-rating on inputs for charities is very important as it helps to keep costs down and allows much more to be spent on the charitable objectives. However, not all goods and services that charities have to purchase are zero-rated, as already mentioned, and this leaves most charities with the additional cost of what is called irrecoverable VAT.

Therefore, charities, unlike most businesses, cannot recover all the VAT charged to them on goods and services. This is primarily because charities are involved in fund-raising and similar activities, most of which are outside the scope of VAT. Therefore, the VAT on the costs involved in carrying out these activities cannot be reclaimed so there is irrecoverable VAT.

Some businesses, and this includes many charities, have a mixture of outputs in all three categories. Effectively if they therefore register in order to be in a position to recover VAT on costs incurred in making the VATable supplies, they will be partially exempt because of course some of their supplies are exempt and some are not. Partial exemption will be looked at in some detail later.

An important distinction must be made between donations, which are outside the scope of VAT (i.e. non-business), and sponsorship payments, which may be. If the donor receives more than an insubstantial benefit, for example by way of publicity or facilities provided by the charity, the payment may be taxable because a supply is being made. Lotteries and raffles (where prizes are won by pure chance) are exempt from VAT, but most entry fees for competitions (where winning needs some skill) must include standard rated VAT, unless the organizer is below the VAT registration threshold and is not registered for VAT.

For a list of items that are zero-rated specifically for charities or the full detailed conditions applying to that list, reference should be made to VAT Notice 701/1/95 pages 19 to 28. The list of zero-rated inputs (purchases) for charities in the UK is longer than that of any other country in the EU. When charities have particular problems they should obtain and read the appropriate leaflets, take professional advice and obtain clearance from their local VAT office where necessary.

Special VAT relief for charities

Some of the main sources of VAT relief are:

1 Outside scope (i.e. non-business)

- Donations to charity.
- Supplies by charity of goods and services below cost for the relief of distress. These supplies must be made at least 15 per cent below cost and effectively funded by the charity's own resources.
- Membership subscriptions to a charity that give no personal benefit.

2 Exempt

- One-off fund-raising events.
- The supply of welfare services by a charity except for profit.
- Sales from hospital trolleys.
- Provision of care or medical treatment and goods in connection thereof made by an approved hospital.

3 Zero-rated

- The sale of goods donated for sale, for example in a charity shop or at a jumble sale.
- Advertising by a charity for educational or fund-raising purposes.
- Certain building works (relevant charitable purposes).
- Supplies of some goods to charities for the blind, particularly talking books.
- Supplies of aids for the handicapped to a charity for the use of handicapped people.
- Donation by a charity of specified medical and scientific equipment to a health authority, hospital or charitable institution which provides medical care or treatment.

One-off fund-raising events

Charities often organize special events for both fund-raising and public relations. A 'one-off' fund-raising event exemption applies to all admission charges, the sale of commemorative brochures, the sale of advertising space in those brochures and sponsorship in connection with fund-raising events which are separate from, and do not form, any part of a series or regular run of like or similar events. The 2000 Budget brought many changes and HM Customs and Excise published a very useful notice on this topic (701/59).

There are a number of matters to consider:

- What events qualify?
- How often can they be carried out?
- What about the location and geographical proximity to other events?
- What about national events?
- How about joint events?
- Which events do not qualify?
- Must the exemption be used?

A fund-raising event is one organized and promoted exclusively to raise money for the benefit of the charity or qualifying body. Social events which incidentally make a profit do not fall within the exemption. People attending or participating in the event must be aware of its primary fund-raising purpose. An event is an incident with an outcome or a result: activities of a semi-regular or continuous nature such as the frequent operation of a shop or bar cannot therefore be an event.

The list below, which is not exhaustive, sets out HM Customs and Excise's views as to the different kinds of events which may be held for fund-raising purposes.

- Ball, a dinner dance, disco or barn dance
- Performance; for example concerts, stage productions, and other events which have a paying audience

- Film show
- Fête, fair or festival
- Horticultural show
- Exhibition – including art, history, science, etc.
- Bazaar, jumble sale
- Sporting participation (including spectators)
- Sporting performance
- Games of skills/contests/quiz
- Endurance participation
- Fireworks displays
- Dinner, lunch, barbecue
- Auction
- Raffle, lottery

Eligible events are restricted to no more than 15 events of a similar type in a year at any one location. Where a concert is repeated on successive evenings, each performance is a separate event and counts towards the maximum number of 15 events allowed within the exemption. These restrictions are to prevent distortion of competition with other suppliers of similar events that do not benefit from tax exemption.

Additionally, there is a special rule for small-scale fund-raising events (e.g. coffee mornings). They will not count towards the 15 event limit, provided total gross takings do not exceed £1,000 in any one week. Location is the geographical area within which the fund-raising activity takes place. Similar kinds of events held in different locations would qualify for exemption provided all other conditions were met. For example, several balls held by a national charity in different cities on the same day would qualify for relief. Clearly, events which need to be held in special premises, such as sports grounds, swimming pools or theatres, are easy to define. Each of these will be accepted as a location. However, an event held in multi-use premises, such as a village hall, will need to be held in different villages or town boroughs in order to qualify.

An event organized by two or more charities or two or more qualifying bodies qualifies for exemption only if all the charities (including their trading subsidiaries) and qualifying bodies have organized, whether individually or with others, less than 15 exempt events, of that type, in that location, in the year. A joint event organized by a charity and a qualifying body is exempt only if the charity (including its trading subsidiaries) and the qualifying body have organized, whether individually or with others, less than 15 similar events in the year. However, a joint event organized by a charity or qualifying body and anyone else cannot be an exempt fund-raising event as only events organized exclusively by charities, their trading subsidiaries and qualifying bodies may be exempt fund-raising events.

Events that do not qualify for exemption include:

- Each event which counts towards 16 or more of the same kind held at the same location during the financial year.
- An event that takes over £1,000 will not qualify as a small-scale event (but it will count towards the 15-event allowance).
- Events which only form part of a social calendar for members.

Asking the public for donations through street collections, flag days, etc., are not events for the purpose of this relief. The selling of goods does not itself constitute an 'event' unless it is an organized bazaar or similar. Therefore, the sale of goods through retail outlets is not eligible for relief under these provisions, even where all the proceeds are received by a charity.

Every event in a programme of 16 or more events will be taxable at the standard rate. The exemption applies only up to 15 events of the same kind at a location. To exempt the first 15 events in a longer sequence risks distortion of competition as far as HM Customs and Excise are concerned. VAT exemption is mandatory for any event that fulfils all the conditions. An event which does not meet one or more of the conditions will not qualify for exemption as a fund-raising event.

Events arranged by a professional fund-raiser may qualify for exemption if the charity, trading subsidiary or qualifying body is the principal in making the supply. However, if the agent charges or retains any part of the gross receipts, then this is consideration for agency services and will be subject to VAT. This applies even if the amount is less than or equal to the cost of arranging the event.

A VAT-registered agent can recover the VAT on their own administration costs. However, any VAT the charity or qualifying body incurs in connection with the event will not be recoverable, as would be the case if the charity or qualifying body had made all the arrangements for the event itself.

The fact that a fund-raising activity is exempt from VAT and any profit will not be taxed does not mean that charities can undertake it directly. In many cases the charity's governing document may mean the charity lacks the necessary powers. When the charity has the powers, charity trustees nevertheless need to carefully consider the risks to the charity's property. The charity's assets have been given for its charitable purposes and should not be exposed to any serious or substantial risk of loss from fund-raising activities. Risks which might be acceptable commercially will not necessarily be acceptable for a charity to undertake directly.

The Charity Commission strongly advises trustees to take professional advice before doing anything to expand the charity's direct fund-raising activities in any way that falls outside the tax and VAT exemptions. It will normally be appropriate for all larger-scale activities to be conducted by a trading subsidiary rather than the charity itself.

Large-scale events such as celebrity concerts, sporting events, etc., can be an important way of raising funds. However, experience shows that they also carry a high degree of risk and charity trustees should not normally undertake such activities within the charity. Instead they could be carried out by a trading subsidiary of the charity thereby protecting the charity from the risk of loss. In order for charities to take full advantage of the new tax regime, a wholly-owned trading subsidiary of the charity that passes all its profits to charity, and will be subject to VAT in the same way as a charity, can be set up.

However, the weakness of this particular exemption remains that any VAT incurred on the cost of putting on the one-off fund-raising event is not recoverable. However, as these events should be producing a profit or surplus the exemption from charging VAT normally outweighs this irrecoverable cost.

Donated goods

The sale of donated goods is a business activity and therefore a VATable supply is being made. However, such sales to the general public are regarded as non-trading by the Inland Revenue and remain zero-rated for VAT purposes, provided that they are made by a charity or taxable organization which passes the profit to charity. Probably the greatest advantage of the zero-rating of the sale of donated goods is that as a result, all the VAT incurred on the costs of disposing of the donated goods is fully recoverable.

However, where a charity sells bought-in goods, for example Christmas cards, then it must remember that these may well be standard rated. Again, therefore, if there is to be a mixture of donated and bought-in goods sold through a charity shop it could be advisable, particularly where the bought-in goods are a VATable item, to set up a trading subsidiary to carry out these activities.

In November 1996 there was an attempt to change zero-rating for donated goods so that it only covered those sold by a charity or an organization which covenants the profit to charity where the goods were exported, sold from charity shops or sold through charity auctions or similar events. Following lobbying by the Charities' Tax Reform Group, this proposal was amended. Effectively, goods donated to charities which the charity cannot sell for ethical, safety or quality reasons and which are subsequently sold direct to the rag trade, for example, will still qualify for the zero-rate relief.

Additionally, as a result of the 2000 Budget zero-rating was extended to include goods made available exclusively for

- disabled persons
- those persons receiving means-tested benefits
- hire.

Advertising

In addition to the general rules for the zero-rating of printed matter, there are special rules for charities. Advertising which is either for fund-raising purposes or for making known the charity's aims and objectives is zero-rated.

This means that the supplier should not charge a charity VAT when it uses printed material to:

- seek donations;
- publicize fund-raising events; or
- give information about the charity.

As a result of the 2000 Budget, HM Customs and Excise issued a notice dealing with 'Charity Advertising and goods connected with collecting donations'. This replaces paragraph 16(A)–(E) of Notice 711/1/95.

Following the imposition of VAT on general newspaper advertising in 1984, charities successfully campaigned for the retention of a zero rate for certain advertisements. Over the years the scope of the relief has widened to include broadcasting of advertisements as well as printed media advertisements. Concessionary zero-rating of certain types of printed matter have variously been allowed from time to time.

Charities can advertise very broadly and this covers television, cinema, billboards, the sides of buses and other vehicles, newspapers and printed publications. In each case the space must be owned by a third party and so space on someone else's Internet site will also be covered by the relief. If space is sold to a charity for advertising on other items, such as beer mats or the reverse of till rolls, this will also be covered by the zero rate. However, the sale of the items themselves cannot be relieved of VAT, unless they are relieved under other provisions.

Certain methods of advertising are excluded from this relief, where they are not the supply of someone else's advertising time or space, or in the form of marketing and promotion. Therefore, the following are specifically excluded:

- marketing and advertising addressed to selected individuals or groups. This includes telesales and direct mail by post or e-mail. In practice this will mean that items delivered by post (direct mail packages) will not be covered, although there may be relief for individual elements of the package under the provisions for printed matter and concessions, e.g. appeal letters;
- advertising in, on or through a charity's own website whether or not the website is owned, rented or loaned to the charity. For the same reason adverts in a charity's own magazine, notices, calendar, diary or shop window, etc., do not qualify for relief;

- the design and preparation of a charity's own website;
- supplies connected with adverts that a charity produces itself.

The preparation of an advertisement will qualify for relief provided it is intended that the advertisement will be placed in purchased advertising time, material or space. The services covered here are, for example, the design of a poster or the filming or recording of an advertisement to be broadcast.

The law states that the goods and services must be closely linked to the design or production of the advertisement to qualify. This includes, for example:

- A finished article like a film or sound track, or an element to be incorporated like a photograph or picture or a script or a sound track.
- The conversion from one format to another more suitable format.
- Alternative versions of an advertisement produced to see which works best, for example, will all qualify for relief even if it is the intention that only one version will be used.

HM Customs and Excise also continues to allow the zero-rating of the following items which are directly used in fund-raising campaigns. This is in line with the original intention to facilitate charitable fund-raising activities.

- Collecting boxes.
- Some stationery.
- Lapel stickers/badges.

The concession extends to all kinds of boxes and receptacles for money. All collecting 'boxes' may be zero-rated provided they comply with the following conditions:

- they must be tamper proof, that is capable of being sealed, and
- they must bear the name of the charity either by indelible printing or embossing or having raised letters.

Examples of the types of boxes which might be made to comply with the above are:

- pre-printed card collecting boxes,
- moulded plastic collecting boxes,
- hollow wood or plaster models, whether table-top or floor standing or for wall mounting, and
- wood and glass receptacles.

However, general purpose buckets are not covered by the concession, but specially designed tamper-proof bucket lids which are used to seal buckets making them suitable for charity donation are included in the relief. Additionally, bucket-shaped boxes, which cannot be used for anything except collecting donations of money, will also come within the scope of the relief.

Elaborate boxes, which have an additional purpose, such as gaming or quiz machines, or have some form of mechanical entertainment, will not come within the concession. However, boxes where a simple balance mechanism moves the money from one level to another or the weight of a coin causes it to roll helter-skelter fashion into the box are included in the relief.

General stationery supplied to charities is not covered by the relief. However, the concession allows the following supplies of printed matter to be zero-rated when supplied to a charity:

- collecting envelopes which ask for donations of money, and similar envelopes used by religious organizations in their planned giving schemes,
- pre-printed letters appealing solely for money for the charity,
- envelopes used in conjunction with appeal letters and for forward donations provided they are overprinted with an appeal request related to that contained in the letter.

The concession also means that lapel stickers, emblems and badges which are to be given free as an acknowledgement to donors of money, and have a nominal value, can be purchased free of VAT by charities. This relief is restricted to small items designed to be worn on clothing and includes paper stickers, ribbons, artificial flowers (if these are used as a symbol of the charity) and metal pins and badges. Large items for decorating buildings, vehicles, monuments, etc., will not be eligible for relief even if these are just bigger versions of a lapel badge.

Those emblems given in return for an anticipated donation of £1 or less are considered to be of nominal value. In practice this would mean that the cost to the charity would be considerably less than £1 per unit. Where a charity makes lapel badges itself then it cannot have relief for goods bought to make them nor can other tokens to be given away be zero-rated.

Property

The VAT position on property has changed considerably in the past 17 years or so with significant effect on charities. As a result of the Finance Act 1984, alterations became standard rated (except for some special work on protected buildings) where previously they had been zero-rated. Then in 1989, to comply with the decision reached in the European Court of Justice on 21 June 1988, the government of the UK was forced to extend the scope of

VAT at the standard rate, and to include the supply of non-residential buildings and associated construction services.

The effect of these changes to the VAT regulations was that zero-rating became confined to sales of the freehold or the grant of a long lease by the person or persons constructing dwellings, some other residential buildings, e.g. old people's homes, and certain properties for non-business charitable use and to construction services relating to these buildings.

VAT Notice 742A on property development points out that the first supply of a new building will be zero-rated if:

- the building qualifies,
- the relevant certificate from the purchaser or lessee has been supplied,
- the supplier grants a major interest in all or part of the building or its site, and
- the building is new or a self-contained annexe.

All these conditions have to be met, and if only part of the building is eligible for zero-rating, then it will be necessary to apportion the consideration received when it is disposed of (see page 22 VAT Notice 701/1/95).

Effectively three types of building qualify for zero-rating which includes those used for a relevant charitable purpose as well as those used for a relevant residential purpose and domestic dwellings.

Therefore, the VAT legislation allows supplies made in the course of construction of a building, intended for use solely for a relevant charitable purpose, to be zero-rated. Services of architects, surveyors or any other persons acting as a consultant or in a supervisory capacity do not qualify for zero-rating and these services are standard rated. However, as a planning point, it is possible for the contractor to agree a design and build contract which would allow these services supplied under the contract to be zero-rated as the service is then all inclusive.

In addition, supplies of materials, builders hardware, sanitary ware and other articles of a kind ordinarily installed by builders as fixtures may also be zero-rated provided they are supplied by the person supplying the construction services. Again, this is a case of an all-inclusive service.

As far as alterations are concerned these are generally standard rated although there are two main exceptions to this rule which are zero-rated:

- Approved alterations to residential or charitable protected buildings.
- Certain alterations supplied to handicapped persons or to a residential charity providing facilities for the handicapped.

These will include:

- provision of toilet and bathroom facilities;
- installation of lifts;

- construction of ramps or widening of doors or passages to facilitate entry or movement.

The 2000 Budget extended the existing VAT relief on bathrooms to cover adaptations or extensions in day-care centres where 20 per cent of the users are disabled. Also now covered is the provision, adaptation or extension of bathrooms for disabled people in sheltered flats and houses where the landlord is a charity.

One of the peculiarities in VAT law is the charging of VAT on rents. Many charities find themselves in rented property either as a landlord or tenant. Normally the grant of any lease and the premiums and rents payable are exempt supplies for VAT purposes. However, changes in 1989 already referred to, brought in a provision whereby certain supplies, which would have otherwise been exempt, could from that date be treated as standard rated. Owners and landlords have been able to elect to waive the requirement to exempt from VAT certain supplies of buildings and land. Thus, the owner or landlord decides whether or not to charge VAT on the rent.

This facility is commonly referred to as 'the option to tax' and has the effect of allowing owners and landlords to apply the standard rate of VAT to certain sales of freeholds, grants of leases and other interest in land which would otherwise have been exempt. Once an election has been made, it cannot be revoked for a period of twenty years and it will apply to a whole building and cannot be split so that where the building has one or more tenants then they will either all be charged VAT or none of them will be.

These changes may have had a significant impact on charities. The option to tax is that of the landlord and the tenant has no role in the decision. Therefore, charities that are wholly or partly exempt will suffer an irrecoverable VAT cost in renting an opted property. However, the option cannot be exercised in respect of any building intended solely for qualifying residential or charitable use and therefore a charity can avoid VAT on the rent on such buildings if they are so used for non-business purposes.

In this complex area of property, charities are well advised to read fully VAT Notice 742 on land and property and consult their VAT advisers.

Partial exemption

There is a particularly thorny problem which many charities have been faced with since its introduction following the Partial Exemption VAT Act 1983. Effectively partial exemption is the result of a business making taxable and non-taxable supplies, from the point of view of VAT. Any VAT incurred, on costs, relating directly to exempt outputs is not recoverable. Only input tax related directly to taxable outputs is recoverable. However, this is where the complications set in, as VAT on items such as administration costs which are not directly attributable either to the taxable or the exempt outputs may in part be recovered. Many charities therefore fall into the category of businesses that are partially exempt.

Unfortunately, business for VAT purposes is not defined, nor have the decided cases produced any general principles. So, deciding what is business and what is non-business is always problematical. In most charities some activity is likely to be non-business. If so, agreement will be needed with HM Customs and Excise to apportion such overheads on a fair and reasonable basis, in order to identify the disallowable input tax before attribution (if applicable) of the remaining input between taxable and exempt supplies. Various methods can be used and as the amounts involved can be considerable, the challenge is to calculate a method in the charity's best interest but which is still acceptable to HM Customs and Excise.

It is suggested that there should be regular reviews of the items that can be classed as business, and experiments carried out on the apportionment of the residue based on the previous year's accounts. It would be helpful and sensible to discuss the results with a VAT adviser, provided of course they understand and know your business. In agreeing the relevant method with HM Customs and Excise there may well be a possibility of recovering input tax for previous periods. This is particularly relevant where you have previously been operating to an agreed method.

Once the business/non-business split is sorted, there are a number of other problem issues. Undoubtedly some of the charity's business supplies will most probably be exempt. Subject to some fairly inadequate *de minimis* levels, a charity with exempt supplies will be struck by the partial exemption clause.

The restrictions on partial exemption only apply if there is a significant amount of input VAT relating to exempt activity. If this activity is below certain limits, then it is possible to recover all the input VAT ignoring the fact that the charity has some exempt supplies. In these cases the charity will be defined as fully taxable. Where it can be shown that in the normal accounting period the exempt input tax is £625 or less per month on average, then all such input tax in that period will be treated as attributable to taxable supplies.

If a charity makes exempt supplies only, it has no right to register for VAT and consequently would not be able to recover any VAT on expenditure. If a charity makes taxable and exempt supplies, it can register for VAT. The current *de minimis* requirements are that all VAT can be recovered by a charity which makes both exempt and taxable supplies provided the VAT on expenses attributable to exempt activities is less than £625 per month on average and 50 per cent of total input tax incurred. This means that a charity which makes relatively few taxable supplies gets very little VAT back. If the *de minimis* limit is exceeded, all 'exempt' VAT is disallowed and not just the amount in excess of the limit. Most, if not all, charities have non-business income, e.g. grants and donations. Any VAT on costs attributable to this income is irrecoverable regardless of the amounts involved.

In addition, charities are able to ignore exempt input VAT relating to investment income and incidental rental income. If these sources of income are the charity's only exempt supplies then the charity will not have to check whether it is within the *de minimis* limits.

Further reading on this subject and reference should be made to the VAT Notice 706, Partial Exemption.

Sponsorship

As charity fund-raisers come up with more and more new ideas for raising money, it can come as a nasty shock to find out that seven forty-sevenths of the income might go to HM Customs and Excise instead. Sponsorship can create all sorts of problems and it often means different things to different people. Sponsorship income may result from a genuine donation, a trading transaction or a mixture of the two. Put simply, if anything is supplied or deemed to have been supplied in return for financial support or sponsorship, then a taxable supply has been made as far as HM Customs and Excise is concerned and VAT is payable. HM Customs and Excise do, like the Inland Revenue, accept that a payment where only an acknowledgement has been given can be classed as a donation and therefore non-VATable as outside the scope.

If the contribution is made on the condition that a company's name or trading style is advertised or promoted, then it is advertising which is of course a VATable supply. Furthermore, if the company receives some benefit in return, e.g. tickets to a gala concert, then this too is a VATable supply and it will be in both cases standard rated.

In essence, if the charity is providing anything in return for money received, VAT will become an issue. It is important, therefore, to think through agreements fully in advance. Care must also be taken in considering the VAT treatment of the provision of a charity's name and logo. In most circumstances this would be viewed as a supply, giving rise to standard-rated publicity services. It may well be that the sponsor concerned will agree to pay VAT on top of the payment they were going to make, particularly where they can recover the VAT within their own trading operation. Where a company takes an advertisement in your annual report or charity programme, that payment will be standard rated because a supply has been made to the company, even if the company regards the payment as a donation.

Mixed deals, that is those where there is an element of both VATable and non-VATable supply taking place, should, if possible, be split with the VATable supply put through the trading subsidiary, and the non-VATable supply put through the charity. In other words the donation goes to charity and the revenue from the trading activity goes to the trading subsidiary. Obviously this will not always be possible and where this is the case, then it is certainly advisable to put the complete transaction through the trading subsidiary.

One area particularly hard hit through the addition of VAT was that of affinity credit card schemes, where charities entered into agreement with banks, building societies and similar financial institutions. The cards, often reflecting the logo or objectives of the charity, led to the commercial body making a donation to the charity involved in respect of each card issued and for each occasion when the card was used. However, this 'donation' has been decreed by HM Customs and Excise to be a payment in respect of promotional/advertising activities and as such is a VATable supply.

By concession, negotiated by the Charities' Tax Reform Group, the income from such affinity cards is split into that part relating to a payment for services supplied by the charity, e.g. use of the logo, mailing list, etc., and a donation for which the charity provides nothing in return. HM Customs and Excise had argued that the whole of the initial payment, often £5, and a percentage of turnover paid by the bank or similar institution to the charity was taxable because it was paid for services provided by the charity. The Charities' Tax Reform Group was instrumental in bringing HM Customs and Excise together and it was agreed that for new contracts set up on the correct basis, there can in effect be two separate legal agreements. The first would be for 20 per cent of the initial payment which would then be taxable as payment for services received, with the second agreement for the remainder which would be outside the scope and treated as a donation, therefore neither VATable nor subject to corporation tax.

Unless a contract specifies that a sum payable is exclusive of VAT then the law assumes that it is inclusive whenever VAT is due. See further VAT leaflet 701/41 entitled Sponsorship, which is a general leaflet not specifically aimed at charities.

Conclusion

Charities benefit from a wide range of tax and VAT exemptions and their proper use can maximize income and reduce costs. A charity can often use the exemptions given to donors to persuade the donor to give more. Charity administrators and trustees should make sure they are correctly informed and updated in respect of tax and charity law, and keep detailed records of all income and expenditure.

11 Future directions

This final chapter is divided into two parts. First we explore some particular themes and issues directly relevant to financial management and the role of the finance director. We then conclude with a discussion of the wider environment and the future for the sector.

Regulation and the Charity Commission

The Charity Commission is increasingly becoming a more proactive organization in delivering what has always been its role: 'giving the public confidence in the integrity of charity'. The monitoring of charity accounts and ensuring returns are made are seen as key priorities and are welcomed. The failure in the past of the Commission to ensure the filing of accounts reflected badly on both the Commission and the sector as a whole. The Commission, we have suggested, has a difficult role as regulator in that its 'customers' are primarily volunteers. We recognize that problem but we do not believe it is an excuse to condone absent or late filing of accounts and annual returns. The responsibilities of charity trusteeship, as the Commission's own advice leaflets state, are onerous and should not be taken on lightly. Making such a statement and then excusing trustees, however, does not give the public confidence. If the number of trustees is in decline due to a pro-active model (Palmer and Harrow 1994) then so be it. In our opinion, it would be preferable to have a smaller active group of trustees rather than many inactive persons. The Commission has started to send accounts back to trustees that do not comply with the regulations. We welcome this initiative and hope that trustees will subject their auditors to increased scrutiny and ensure they are receiving value for money.

The regulated voluntary sector and voluntary organizations seeking funds from government will therefore see further pressure exerted on them to demonstrate their accountability and effectiveness. The unregulated sector does not exist in a vacuum and we believe it will feel the 'ripple' effect of these interactions. Radical thought on charity law and the absolution of the Charity Commission have been raised (NCVO 2000). This could lead to there being one 'voluntary sector', though quite how this would be defined and regulated has yet to be determined.

Charity trusteeship and organizational accountability

We need to understand more about the motivations of trustees. There is now an abundance of 'how to do it' literature and the NCVO and Charity Commission publications in this area provide sound advice. So why is it that trustees, many top business people, get it wrong? Charity trustees and management committee members will increasingly find themselves having to disclose more and more information about themselves personally and their decision making. Organizations will face calls for accountability from a variety of stakeholders including, increasingly, service users. We believe there will be a greater use of social accounting and other measures that go beyond the financial audit. Charities will also focus more on ethical investments. All this will mean that trustees will have to think strategically as well as focusing on the internal working of the organization. The finance director in many charities could have a key role in being the 'risk assessment and compliance officer'. All this will have a cost that will mean administrative cost ratios will rise.

Professionalism and human resources

The trend in voluntary organizations to professionalism will continue. The current half a million full-time staff will increase as more statutory service funding flows into the sector. Voluntary organizations will have to establish professional human resource functions to meet increasing legislation, have competitive conditions of service and staff development programmes. This will involve an increase in administrative costs. Voluntary organizations will also need to have a greater understanding of the human resources, both paid and unpaid, to ensure it is properly managed. The successful charity finance director will have to undertake a variety of roles, which go beyond the current training of an accountant. They will need to have a strategic vision, be able to understand policy, fund-raising and be sensitive to change. They will need communication skills both technological and verbal to inter-relate with colleagues and trustees.

SORP and auditors

We have covered the revised SORP in detail. If the radical changes involving fund accounting were going to be changed, which would see a return to the pre-1995 situation, then this would have happened at the SORP review. We would not expect a subsequent review for many years. It is therefore now a matter of ensuring that charities fully understand and are complying with the regulations. We cited research showing a general improvement in accounting by charities but there are still too many examples of non-SORP compliance. Isaacs (2000) is highly critical of the role of auditors in this process – auditors who allow charities not to follow or are just ignorant of the SORP.

A phenomenon in the world of charity audit in the 1990s has been the growth in second-tier firms with specialist charity units. The number of charity accounting and audit specialists has grown, and we hope this will help to continue to improve the quality of charity accounting and financial reporting. It also means that charities, as they seek to obtain the best value from their professional advisers, have a competitive market from which to select their auditors. This can only be good for the sector, which should regularly, either by review or by tender, actively monitor the services they are receiving.

Performance – making the most from cash and banking services

Pharoah (1997) identified major problems with the capability and capacity of charity finance functions. Despite the initiatives by the Charity Finance Directors' Group to improve the profile of senior finance staff, many are still seen as little more than bookkeepers. One way to improve this image can be done by charity finance directors taking the initiative in improving returns on the very large cash funds – £7.5 billion amounting to 11 per cent of total assets (NCVO 2000) – held by charities.

We illustrated in Chapter 7 the opportunity cost of leaving funds in current bank accounts. Moving the funds to deposit accounts or the bank's internal money operation can improve returns. But is this enough? We believe not. Milton (1999) undertook research which reviewed the rates of high-street banks against rates obtained by directly accessing the money markets through a broker. In a series of case studies, which illustrated different cash deposits, he found that the money market consistently offered higher rates than high-street banks. An example is described below.

A grant-making trust places their surplus cash on an overnight basis. The comparison in the table shows its bank's overnight rate against the money market's call rate:

	Bank[a]	*Money market*[b]	*Actual difference*	*Percentage difference*
1993	5.12	5.74	0.62	12.11
1994	4.24	4.96	0.72	16.98
1995	5.52	6.18	0.66	12.11
1996	5.19	5.80	0.61	11.96
1997	5.79	6.38	0.59	10.19
1998	6.50	7.02	0.52	8.00

a Source: The charity and the average rate then calculated for each year.
b Source: Martin Brokers (UK) plc. Rates are those quoted at 7.30a.m. each working day and averaged throughout the year.

The interest rate differences amounted to a loss on interest received, in excess of £25,000 over the period on the charity's average deposit of £700,000. Additionally, during the analysis it emerged that the bank balance never fell below £500,000 – yet they persisted in placing money solely on an overnight basis!

Why then are charities not improving their performance? Milton (1999) suggests that the perception of complexity and risk, not borne out in practice, was the major problem. In particular, he cited trustee behaviour as a major problem, as trustees either did not understand the money market or were resistant to giving freedom to their finance directors to explore money market returns.

Another area where charities could improve their performance is by pooled banking arrangements. Jackson (1999) identifies the following advantages to charities with a group/branch structure:

- better return on funds, improved negotiating position with bank;
- improved knowledge about the banking of the organization;
- groups/branches may be more closely monitored by Head Office;
- identify branches in trouble;
- daily picture of the overall financial position;
- regular analysis by the finance director – trends, activity levels of individual branches;
- identify sudden changes – dormant branch activity becomes active without notice – possible fraud;
- ability of the finance director to assist branches, guide and advise;
- improved audit procedure resulting in cost savings, SORP compliance;
- easier consolidation;
- ability to offset debit balances against overall 'group' picture.

Jackson, however, also identified major obstacles to improved procedures including the attitude of trustees. Jackson also cited charity culture and the fear of the 'Head Office' taking over. Jackson believed that if the finance director was proactive in promoting pooled activity they could overcome these barriers. In particular, the finance director needed to demonstrate that it was a fair process which involved:

- engagement – giving a say at local level and taking views into account
- explanation – disclosing the reason behind decisions and seeking feedback
- expectation – avoiding uncertainty and defining individual roles.

The Unity Trust Bank, which originated in the Trade Union movement, has successfully organized pooled arrangements for Trade Union branches. Discussions are now under way with a number of membership-based charities to offer the same services (Davies 2001).

New equity finance – trusts or borrowing

As well as there being a record number of new charities each year there have also been created in our society a record number of millionaires. The charitable trust was originally created to be a mechanism through which wealthy individuals could transfer their fortune and leave it in perpetuity. The millionaires of the twenty-first century do not seem to have followed their predecessors in creating charitable trusts, as with some notable exceptions most new charities are fund-raising with no permanent endowment. We do not believe that the charitable trust will see a renascence with 'dotcom' or 'lottery millionaires' choosing such vehicles if they decide to give money to charity. It is easier and involves no public scrutiny or accountability to simply Gift Aid such donations.

In the absence of new charitable trusts, which could be viewed as being the equity of the sector, where else would voluntary organizations be able to seek finance from to build their asset base? Certainly not from government sources and unlikely from business who are both keen on seeing immediate return for their investments. From the Almanac (NCVO 2000) we know that charity assets are valued at £65.1 billion with liabilities of £4.4 billion. Liabilities therefore only make up 7 per cent of the sector's total assets of which loans and other liabilities account for just 11.7 per cent, some £514 million. Andrew Cunnell, Head of Corporate Finance of the Unity Trust Bank, has observed that the sector is low geared with little use made of loan finance, and comments, 'The comparison with the use of debt by the "for profit commercial sector" is striking.' In a series of focus groups we organized for the Unity Bank with charity trustees and staff, the reasons for the low gearing of the sector were discussed. Suggestions included:

- Trustee aversion to risk.
- Management capabilities.
- The sector paradigm, which includes the ethos that spending on projects should be funded by grants and donations, and that projects will not be undertaken until the funding is in place.
- Costs.

These reasons are diverse and complex and include cultural and managerial factors, which go beyond understanding loan finance and require further investigation. This is potentially another area for the charity finance director to take a lead and enjoy a role similar to their commercial counterpart. Housing Associations have for many years successfully built their asset base on the strength of a mixture of public and private finance. The rest of the voluntary sector needs to follow in exploiting what is a relatively untapped source of finance.

Mergers and co-operation

We expect to see an increase in merger activity in the charity sector. Financial reasons for merger in the voluntary sector are usually to meet a decline in funding as was seen by the Terrence Higgins/Lighthouse merger; or merging to become more efficient in delivering services, raising funds and improving their administration. The Charity Commission has played a minor but important role in assisting groups of smaller charities to merge where they were out of date or just too small to be effective. The research report by the University of Liverpool Charity Law Unit on 'Legal Issues in Charity Mergers' (Morris 2001) provides a comprehensive framework and series of recommendations to the very complex issues involved in charity mergers. A complication also recognized by the Commission (Stoker 2001) who we expect to see playing a facilitation role, but will also take a higher profile in encouraging co-operation between charities.

We have outlined the work of the Charities Consortium on joint purchasing power and discussed pooled banking arrangements for charities with branches. One area which lends itself for co-operative arrangements is internal audit. As we discussed previously, internal audit is relatively undeveloped in charities. In part this may reflect concerns about administrative costs, but also preferences by finance directors for a management accountant rather than an internal auditor (Palmer 1996). Shared or consortium internal audit arrangements have been used in the Health Service and Housing Associations. These are models charities should be exploring – perhaps a role for the Charity Commission? – and should appeal to medium-sized charities who are too small to have an internal audit function but are large and complex enough to benefit from regular review and risk assessment.

Smaller voluntary organizations

Through research studies, networking organizations and the Charity Commission we now have a large amount of information about the very large charities. Through the NCVO and academic research programmes we are also beginning to understand a lot more about medium-sized charities with incomes between £1 million and £10 million.

Smaller charities, and particularly small voluntary organizations with incomes of less than £250,000, we still know very little about. There is a perception that they are badly run and underfunded with poor financial practices. Some exploratory research studies (Vincent *et al*. 1998; Harrow *et al*. 1999) found examples of excellent practice. Our lack of precise knowledge of the issues and problems of the very small voluntary organization is found in some of the prescriptive solutions offered by management consultants, for example on trustee and management committee training based on the small business literature and experience. However, how similar are voluntary organizations to small businesses and do they need the same advice?

Smaller voluntary organizations have, as their very reason for existence, activity that will see them either becoming a large charity SCOPE, staying small or disappearing after the initial enthusiasm and energy fades.

We need to know a lot more about the smaller organization subsector. We do know, through our participation at the Community Accountancy Conference over the past few years, that there are particular issues and problems ranging from financial planning, relationships with funders and audit. To improve knowledge and service to the sector we would hope that community accountancy projects will grow in number. At present, like many of their clients, they are short-term project funded.

The wider environment – into the twenty-first century or back to the nineteenth?

The Times comment article by the Chancellor of the Exchequer Gordon Brown (2001) can have a number of interpretations. One perspective is of Labour finally abandoning its commitment, articulated by the Webb's in the late nineteenth century, of government intervention as being the principal method of ensuring social justice. Alternatively, it continues the process of Labour as a party of social reform and is merely a change in strategy – a perspective which recognizes that statutory services are not the only method of delivery which dominated much of the Labour Party thinking in the twentieth century. Brown is also following the pragmatic path of former Labour ministers from Lord Longford in the 1940s, Crossman in the 1960s and Ennals in the 1970s, of acknowledging the role of the voluntary sector.

We do not believe the Brown perspective is a return to the nineteenth century. Contained in the Brown article was the announcement of £300 million to support innovation and volunteering and the role of government as an enabling State. This is the important philosophical difference. Unlike its nineteenth century predecessors, which shared a commitment to 'laissez-faire' doctrines, New Labour is committed to intervention – a perspective that is also shared by the other political parties. While the style and commitment may differ, the all-important philosophical perspective remains the same. If we have returned to 'anything', it is to the consensus the political parties had reached in the 1950s over the Welfare State. Despite calls from its right wing to reverse the reforms of the previous Labour government and dismantle the Welfare State, the Conservative governments ignored such pressure. As indeed New Labour did to its own left wing in 1997 on privatization and municipilization (Atkinson and Wilks-Heeg 2000).

On this basis, we believe that for at least the next five years there will be a political consensus to the voluntary sector, which will see a continued real growth in resources from statutory sources. We are less certain whether we will see a 'new giving age'. The term 'civil society' means exactly what? As O'Connell comments:

> The more the term civil society has been used in recent years, the less it has been understood.
>
> (O'Connell 2001, p. 471)

Is the term simply a way of 'repackaging' philanthropy and making it more acceptable? Unless the current stagnation in public giving is reversed, it is quite possible that government funding in all its forms will become, as indeed it already has in Scotland, the principal source of finance to the UK voluntary sector. Does this matter?

We think it does. Our approach has been throughout this book that financial management in the voluntary sector cannot be divorced from the external environment. The accounting standard process is not some scientific neutral free activity and the charity SORP is part of a bigger picture of the role of the voluntary sector in our society and its relationship with the State (Palmer and Vinten 1998).

We believe that increased government funding will increase the focus on the accountability and ability to deliver by voluntary organizations. At a micro-organizational level, for those voluntary organizations engaging with local government, the 'best value initiative' will be the basis which will be used by local government for assessing that relationship over the next few years. Despite the bold themes of the Compact we do not believe that local government or most statutory agency funding will pay more than 'lip-service' to its themes. As Graig and Manthorpe (1999) note, the local government sector is not homogeneous and practices and attitudes to the voluntary sector vary widely. At the grass-roots level the Community Accounting Projects report that they are constantly being confronted by a lack of understanding by local government of the smaller voluntary sector and the arbitrary nature of funding conditions; for example, the insistence on full audits for grants of £10,000 (Community Accounting Network 2001).

What would be the impact of the government becoming the largest funder to the sector? Would it really matter? The very genesis of the voluntary sector is one of being outside the State and as we have seen recently with action against the G7 summit, World Bank and 'reclaim the city', voluntary action will occur and voluntary organizations will come into and out of existence. Many voluntary organizations are too small to consider funding from government; others do not wish to receive government funding. To these voluntary organizations and charitable trusts such debates would seem immaterial. From another perspective it matters considerably. Would it impact detrimentally on giving if the public believed that the State was now a 'charities funder'? This is an important question and one we do not have the answer to. However, we feel confident that the charity sector will be able to understand and develop the appropriate strategies. In part, our confidence is based upon some of the developments in the sector in the 1990s, notably:

- the work for the Almanac which provides a solid foundation for understanding the finance of the sector and has led to the third sector foresight programme;
- the work of the respective Deakin and Kemp commissions which provided a policy framework from which the sector has begun to openly debate its relationship with government and has spurned a series of initiatives on charity governance, law accountability, etc.;
- the infrastructure of the sector, particularly organizations such as the Charity Finance Directors' Group which have done much to improve the quality of the sector's workforce and act as a forum for debate;
- the renewed interest in the sector within the universities which will bring a critical robustness to understanding the voluntary sector; and most importantly
- the sector itself, which is about individual and collective expression which will always find an outlet.

We ended the first chapter by suggesting that we believed the voluntary sector had entered into a fifth phase – which we referred to as the period of exchange – in its relationship to the State. Our definition encompassed both the physical transfer of assets and also the transfer of ideas. The exchange of ideas is the more important of the two and we hope the voluntary sector will rise to the challenge and like all good partners be constructive and critical. In meeting the challenges of the next few years the voluntary sector has to learn to think strategically and participate actively in discussions about future directions. Too often the voluntary sector acts reactively. The sector must speak up without fear, when appropriate, and campaign when policies are having an adverse effect. Shelter, the homeless charity, was quite right to be publicly critical of the rough sleepers' initiative before Christmas 2000 when many other voluntary organizations funded by the government kept quiet. Shelter is the campaign for the homeless. If it does not speak up then who will? As Thomas Moore observed on the King's reform of the monasteries and what would happen to the poor:

> But now to the poor beggars: what remedy findeth their proctor for them . . . Is not this a royal feast, to leave these beggars meatless.
>
> (Tigar 1977, p. 207)

We hope that Chris Holmes the Director of Shelter will not meet Moore's fate, but how loud were the finance professionals of the sector when the government abolished ACT with a guaranteed £350 million lost to the sector and replaced at the moment by a promise?

The foundations for strategic thinking have been created with the third sector foresight programme. According to Passey (2001) the sector should be participating in the following debates:

- Legislation
- Funding
- Public perception
- Political party agendas
- Planning – particularly emanating from the Census findings.

The voluntary sector will be subject to a number of external drivers of change including.

- Demographic and family structures – for example the impact on legacies
- Technology – flows of information – role of the voluntary sector as 'trust brokers'
- Environment – climate change, sustainability and civil society
- Global, national and local – multinational and global economic power, the influence of the European Union, the devolution of the UK State, for example, Scotland, and how viable is a continuing nation structure?
- Attitudes and values – fragmentation, quality of life, trust accountability.

The foresight programme enables us to project what the future voluntary sector could look like. Will it be a sector that is dominated by a few 'super-brands'? – organizations who do not talk of partnership but instead see statutory authorities as competitors for central government and other funding sources. A map of the voluntary sector in 2010 may look like the following.

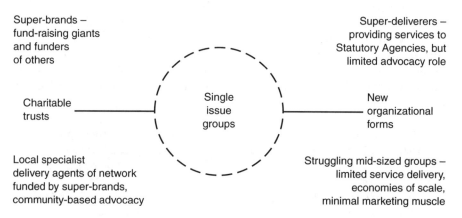

Super-brands – fund-raising giants and funders of others

Super-deliverers – providing services to Statutory Agencies, but limited advocacy role

Charitable trusts

Single issue groups

New organizational forms

Local specialist delivery agents of network funded by super-brands, community-based advocacy

Struggling mid-sized groups – limited service delivery, economies of scale, minimal marketing muscle

This is but one scenario. In an age of exchange it is up to us to participate.

Appendix

The ABC Charity

The ABC Charity

This is a charitable company with one non-charitable subsidiary and producing consolidated accounts. It carries out a variety of different types of work. It has a substantial investment in tangible fixed assets. The accounts have to comply with SORP 2000, accounting standards and the Companies Act 1985.

A separate Income and Expenditure account is not presented, although technically it is required by the Companies Act, because the "net movement in funds" includes both realised and unrealised gains. However, the difference between any surplus on this basis is not materially different from that presented and hence it is considered sufficient to note this difference on the bottom of the SOFA.

Trustees' report

One of the main features of the trustees' report in this example is that it includes considerable detail on Corporate Governance and disclosures on internal financial controls in addition to the required statement regarding risk (SORP 2000 paragraph 31(g)). It also contains descriptions of:

- the relationship with connected charities;
- fund-raising activities and future developments;
- voluntary help and gifts in kind;
- its reserves policy;
- policies on employee involvement.

Financial statements

Materiality

As explained above, the concept of materiality (SORP paragraph 13) has been used and a separate income and expenditure account has not been prepared. Instead, a note on the face of the SOFA explains the amount of the net income under Companies Act reporting requirements.

Tangible fixed assets

There has been considerable investment in tangible fixed assets and a note on changes in resources applied for fixed assets (SORP 2000 paragraph 180) is given (page G.10) to show the movement in funds available for future activities.

Cashflow statement

Cashflow from investment income is considered to be part of the "operational activities" rather than a return on investments as this charity considers its investments to be an integral part of its operations.

Related party disclosures

There are related party transactions (note 7) and these are disclosed in accordance with SORP paragraph 163.

Trading activities

In order to give an indication of the breadth of the activities carried out a segmental analysis is given of trades carried out by the trading subsidiary (note 19). This is particularly important where the fact that one distinct trading activity is loss making and could be masked by other activities. This matter is highlighted in the trustees' report.

Corporate income falls to be treated as donations on consolidation as it falls within the definition of donations in SORP paragraph 87.

Legacies

Certain legacies may be receivable but have not met the tests for inclusion as income (SORP paragraphs 89 to 93). This fact is disclosed with an estimate of the values (based on probate value) in accordance with SORP paragraph 94.

Statement of funds

The statement of funds in note 17 shows the movement in all the group's funds in the year (SORP paragraph 49). An explanation of the nature and purpose of each fund is given except where this is explained by the title to the fund.

Accounting policies

The significant accounting policies are:

* Recognition of income particularly grants and legacies.
* Group financial statements are prepared taking advantage of various exemptions so a separate SOFA or income and expenditure account is not presented for the charity.
* Intangible income and gifts in kind.

Example

The ABC Charity
(A company limited by guarantee)

Report and Financial Statements

Year ended: 31 March 2001

Charity no: 87654321
Company no: 12345678

Legal and administrative information

Trustees
H Singh*, Chairman
J J Meade*, Treasurer
J Lloyd (resigned 10 July 2000)
M Ross‡ (appointed 1 December 2000)
F Needham
W Williams, Secretary
E Corbett
N Kington
M Russell*
T Bird‡ (appointed 1 March 2001)
N Pascoe (resigned 1 December 2000)
J Morrison (resigned 10 July 2000)

* Member of Finance & General Purposes Committee
‡ Member of Fund-raising Committee

Chief Executive
A Brown

Registered Office
Charity House, Main Street, London, XX1 1AA

Auditors
An Auditor, 1 High Street, London, ZZ1 1BB

Bankers
National Bank Plc, 2 High Street, London, ZZ1 1BB

Solicitors
Wight and Wright, 4 High Street, London, ZZ1 1DD

Investment Managers
Asset Investment Managers Ltd, 3 High Street, London, ZZ1 1CC

Report of the trustees for the year ended 31 March 2001

The trustees, who are also directors of the charity for the purposes of the Companies Act, submit their annual report and the audited financial statements for the year ended 31 March 2001. The trustees have adopted the provisions of the Statement of Recommended Practice (SORP) "Accounting and Reporting by Charities" issued in October 2000 in preparing the annual report and financial statements of the charity.

The charity is a charitable company limited by guarantee and was set up on 2 October 1955. It is governed by a memorandum and articles of association which were last amended on 17 July 1991. Its objects are to carry out activities that relieve distress and suffering worldwide. The Strategic Plan adopted in 1999 identified four key delivery mechanisms where the charity has developed core competencies:

- Residential care in UK;

- Childcare overseas;

- Emergency services world-wide;

- Informing and educating governments, the public and the corporate sector about sustainable development to relieve poverty and other causes the charity supports.

Review of activities and future developments

The Statement of Financial Activities for the year is set out in the financial statements. A summary of the financial results and the work of the charity is set out below.

Income Generation

The charity's income increased from £11,035,000 to £13,340,000. This increase, amounting to over 20%, is a significant achievement and the charity thanks all its supporters for their work and generosity.

Donations and gifts increased by over £1.3 million. In our report for the years ended 31 March 1998 and 1999 we set out our plans for increased expenditure on fund-raising and developing our branches. The significant increase in voluntary income is a direct result of the increased emphasis on fund-raising in the past years. The key components of donations and gifts are highlighted in note 2 to the financial statements. The emphasis on broadening the income base continues and the charity will be expanding its corporate donors' plan which has grown by over 37% in the year.

Legacies continue to be a core but volatile source of income to the charity and this year has seen record levels of legacy income. The charity's budgets and spending plans include legacy income of £1.9 million for the year ended 31 March 2002 and on the basis of notifications received since the year end the trustees believe that this is achievable.

The Building Appeal for the new Residential Care facility at Rednib House raised £1.3 million in the last two years and during the year over £1.5 million has been applied on the redevelopment. The trustees are particularly grateful to the Friends of Rednib for their splendid efforts.

Merchandising through the charity's eighty shops and mail order operations have benefited from the most generous support of the Darlaston Retail Group which has donated its remainder stock to the charity for resale. This has contributed £250,000 to the merchandising surplus.

Investment policy and returns

The charity has adopted a total return policy for its investment income. The investment managers work towards a target return agreed with the trustees. During the year the return on the stock market investments was 8%. Although this was below the target return of 9%, the charity's investment managers have exceeded the target over the last three years. As permitted by the charity's memorandum and articles of association, the trustees have given the investment managers discretion to manage the portfolio within an agreed risk profile. It is the charity's policy to specifically exclude investments in the armaments sector.

Fund-raising

The trustees have reviewed the fund-raising strategy and return on fund-raising costs. Fund-raising costs were £690,000 (2000 – £550,000). The increased investment in fund-raising over the past few years is reflected in increases from donations, gifts and legacies which have increased in total from £7,330,000 in 2000 to £9,480,000 in the year ended 31 March 2001. However, since there is often a timing mismatch between costs and related income, the fund-raising strategy adopts a rolling three year profile. The charity has estimated that approximately £200,000 was expended during the year on activities that have yielded little or no return yet. These activities include new donor acquisition costs and a new legacy campaign. The building appeal is now being wound down.

Resources expended and services

The last financial year has seen the charity develop and consolidate its services. More information on the services and the achievements of the charity are included in the Annual Review that is sent to all our supporters. Further copies are available from the charity's offices.

Residential Care at a cost of £2,430,000 (2000: £2,545,000) continues to be a significant part of the charity's activities. However, in line with the strategic review carried out in 1999 the charity has refocused the nature of its care provision. This has come about through the strategic alliance with the DEF Trust that has taken on the acute care provision previously provided by the charity. As a consequence the number of individuals being provided with residential care has decreased by 6% with a decrease of 11% in cost. In addition to the expenditure charged to the Statement of Financial activities the charity has spent over £ 1.5 million on a new facility at Rednib House. This will provide excellent residential care, day care and respite care when it becomes fully operational later this year.

The charity is presently reviewing its fee and service levels to ensure that it meets the Charity Commission's guidance that charities should not subsidise with charitable funds services that the State is legally required to provide at public expense.

During the year three Inspection visits were conducted by funders and the trustees are pleased to report that the charity was commended on its innovative and caring service. The charity also surveys users and their visitors and once again the service achieved high customer satisfaction ratings.

The charity has continued to develop its childcare programmes following the principle that this is best achieved by improving the conditions for the communities within which the children live. Childcare expenditure has increased from £3,150,000 in 2000 to £3,400,000 in 2001. Of this amount £1,650,000 (2000: £1,400,000) has been spent in Africa. The Africa programme included the building of 14 new schools, and the immunisation of 7,000 infants against polio, cholera and hepatitis.

The Sudan Famine relief project accounted for £1,900,000 of the £3,100,000 incurred on Emergency services. Four refugee and displaced persons camps have provided food and shelter to 2,000 people.

Expenditure on information and education reduced from £300,000 to £100,000 as there were fewer publications produced this year. The charity is carrying out a joint research project with three other major charities and will be publishing, in 2002, a major report on sustainable development.

The trustees have implemented a performance measurement system that focuses on the cost, quality and time criteria of activities and, as part of this exercise, the charity is benchmarking its key processes against similar charities. The results of this exercise will be reported annually in the future.

ABC Enterprises Ltd

The charity's wholly-owned trading subsidiary carries out non-charitable trading activities for the charity. During the year the company made a gift aid payment of £250,000 transferring all its taxable profits to the charity. The results from the mail order operation continue to be disappointing with a loss of £20,000 in the year. This is somewhat mitigated by the donations of £3,300 that were received with mail order payments. The trustees have agreed with the Charity Commissioners that mail order trading will not be continued after 2003 if it continues to make losses. The charity has made an interest bearing loan to the subsidiary, secured on the assets of the subsidiary. This amounted to £100,000 at the year end. The directors of the subsidiary include two directors who are independent of the charity.

Reserves

The Trustees have reviewed the reserves of the charity. This review encompassed the nature of the income and expenditure streams, the need to match variable income with fixed commitments and the nature of the reserves. The review concluded that to allow the charity to be managed efficiently and to provide a buffer for uninterrupted services, a general reserve equivalent to £3,500,000 should be maintained. This equates to approximately seven months of unrestricted fund expenditure. During the year the charity's general reserve increased from £2,900,000 to £4,785,000 (see note 17). The budget for the next two years has forecast deficits to reduce the general fund to the level agreed by the trustees.

Restricted funds have decreased from £3,900,000 to £3,090,000. The Emergency services fund was in deficit by £145,000 at the year end and was temporarily funded from the general reserve. This was as a result of the need to incur expenditure in advance of anticipated income which has subsequently been received.

The charity has a number of other designated and restricted funds which are represented by investments and fixed assets. The purpose of these funds is detailed in note 17 in the financial statements.

Changes in fixed assets

The movements in fixed assets during the year are set out in note 10 to the financial statements.

Governance and internal control

A panel comprising existing trustees selects members of the trustee board. Applications for trusteeship are sought by advertisement. Trustees serve for a three year period and may be re-elected for a further three year period. The trustees meet six times a year; this includes a weekend meeting to review the strategy and performance and to set the operating plans and budgets. The Finance and General Purposes Committee and the Fund-raising Committee are made up of trustees and other individuals. Both committees operate under specific terms of reference which delegate certain functions from the trustee board. Each committee has its decisions ratified by the full board.

During the year the trustees carried out an exercise to review their composition and effectiveness. This identified the need for a trustee with marketing and public relations experience. The trustees are actively seeking candidates who will meet the requirements.

Company and charity law requires the trustees to prepare financial statements for each financial year which give a true and fair view of the state of affairs of the charity and of the surplus or deficit of the charity for that period. In preparing those financial statements, the trustees have:

- selected suitable accounting policies and then applied them consistently;

- made judgements and estimates that are reasonable and prudent;

- stated whether applicable accounting standards have been followed, subject to any material departures disclosed and explained in the financial statements; and

- prepared the financial statements on the going concern basis.

The trustees have overall responsibility for ensuring that the charity has appropriate system of controls, financial and otherwise. They are also responsible for keeping proper accounting records which disclose with reasonable accuracy at any time the financial position of the charity and enable them to ensure that the financial statements comply with the Companies Act 1985. They are also responsible for safeguarding the assets of the charity and hence for taking reasonable steps for the prevention and detection of fraud and other irregularities and to provide reasonable assurance that:

- the charity is operating efficiently and effectively;

- its assets are safeguarded against unauthorised use or disposition;

- proper records are maintained and financial information used within the charity or for publication is reliable;

- the charity complies with relevant laws and regulations.

The systems of internal control are designed to provide reasonable, but not absolute, assurance against material misstatement or loss. They include:

- A strategic plan and an annual budget approved by the trustees.

- Regular consideration by the trustees of financial results, variance from budgets, non-financial performance indicators and benchmarking reviews.

- Delegation of authority and segregation of duties.

- Identification and management of risks.

The trustees have, with advice from their auditors, introduced a formal risk management process to assess business risks and implement risk management strategies. This involved identifying the types of risks the charity faces, prioritising them in terms of potential impact and likelihood of occurrence, and identifying means of mitigating the risks. As part of this process the trustees have reviewed the adequacy of the charity's current internal controls. The trustees are pleased to report that the charity's internal financial controls, in particular, conform with guidelines issued by the Charity Commission.

In addition, the trustees have considered the guidance for directors of public listed companies contained within the Turnbull Report. They believe that although this is not mandatory for the charity it should, as a public interest body, adopt these guidelines as best practice. Accordingly they have:

- Set policies on internal controls which cover the following:

    - consideration of the type of risks the charity faces;
    - the level of risks which they regard as acceptable;
    - the likelihood of the risks concerned materialising;
    - the charity's ability to reduce the incidence and impact on the business of risks that do materialise; and
    - the costs of operating particular controls relative to the benefit obtained.

- Clarified the responsibility of management to implement the trustees' policies and identify and to evaluate risks for their consideration.

- Communicated that employees have responsibility for internal control as part of their accountability for achieving objectives.

- Embedded the control system in the charity's operations so that it becomes part of the culture of the charity.

- Developed systems to respond quickly to evolving risks arising from factors within the charity and to changes in the external environment.

- Included procedures for reporting failings immediately to appropriate levels of management and the trustees together with details of corrective action being undertaken.

The trustees have considered the need for a specific internal audit function and have decided not to appoint an internal auditor. However, head office staff visiting projects carry out internal audit reviews to a programme agreed with the finance committee and with the external auditors.

Volunteers

The charity is grateful for the unstinting efforts of its volunteers who are involved in service provision, charity shops and fund-raising. It is estimated that over 120,000 volunteer hours were provided during the year. If this is conservatively valued at £6 an hour the volunteer effort amounts to over £720,000. The charity has recently appointed a volunteer coordinator to ensure that best value is derived from the sterling efforts of our volunteers.

Employee involvement and employment of the disabled

Employees have been consulted on issues of concern to them by means of regular consultative committee and staff meetings and have been kept informed on specific matters directly by management. The charity carries out exit interviews for all staff leaving the organisation and has adopted a procedure of upward feedback for senior management and trustees.

The charity has implemented a number of detailed policies in relation to all aspects of personnel matters including:

- Equal Opportunities policy
- Volunteers' policy
- Health & Safety policy

In accordance with the charity's equal opportunities policy, the charity has long established fair employment practices in the recruitment, selection, retention and training of disabled staff.

Full details of these policies are available from the charity's offices.

Auditors

A resolution proposing that An Auditor be re-appointed as auditors of the charity will be put to the Annual General Meeting.

This report was approved by the Board on 16 June 2001:

H Singh (Chairman)

Report of the auditors

To the members of The ABC Charity

We have audited the financial statements on the following pages, and which have been prepared on the basis of the accounting policies set out later in the example.

Respective responsibilities of trustees and auditors

As described on the preceding pages, the trustees are responsible for the preparation of the financial statements in accordance with United Kingdom law and accounting standards. Our responsibilities, as independent auditors, are established in the United Kingdom by statute, the Auditing Practices Board and by our profession's ethical guidance.

Basis of opinion

We conducted our audit in accordance with Auditing Standards issued by the Auditing Practices Board. An audit includes examination, on a test basis, of evidence relevant to the amounts and disclosures in the financial statements. It also includes an assessment of the significant estimates and judgements made by the trustees in the preparation of the financial statements and of whether the accounting policies are appropriate to the group's circumstances consistently applied and adequately disclosed.

We planned and performed our audit so as to obtain all the information and explanations which we considered necessary in order to provide us with sufficient evidence to give reasonable assurance that the financial statements are free from material misstatement, whether caused by fraud or other irregularity or error. In forming our opinion we also evaluated the overall adequacy of the presentation of information in the financial statements.

Opinion

In our opinion the financial statements give a true and fair view of the state of affairs of the charity and group at 31 March 2001 and of the group's incoming resources and resources expended, including its income and expenditure, for the year then ended and have been properly prepared in accordance with the Companies Act 1985.

An Auditor

Registered Auditors
London

16 June 2001

Consolidated Statement of Financial Activities (incorporating an Income and Expenditure Account) for the year ended 31 March 2001

	Notes	Unrestricted Funds £'000	Restricted Funds £'000	Totals 2001 £'000	Totals 2000 £'000
Incoming resources					
Donations and gifts	2	4,130	3,200	**7,330**	6,000
Legacies	3	2,150	–	**2,150**	1,330
Building appeal	17	–	400	**400**	900
Activities in furtherance of the charity's objects:					
Government grants for residential care	17	–	700	**700**	400
Fees for residential car		1,200	–	**1,200**	1,000
Activities for generating funds:					
Merchandising income	4	1,140	–	**1,140**	900
Investment income	5	350	50	**400**	475
Net gain on disposal of fixed assets		20	–	**20**	30
Total incoming resources		8,990	4,350	**13,340**	11,035
Resources expended					
Cost of generating funds:					
Fund-raising costs		480	210	**690**	550
Building appeal costs	17	–	45	**45**	110
Merchandising costs	4	870	–	**870**	710
Investment management fees		80	10	**90**	110
		1,430	265	**1,695**	1,480
Charitable expenditure:					
Costs of activities in furtherance of the charity's objects:					
Residential care costs		1,400	1,030	**2,430**	2,545
Childcare		1,000	2,400	**3,400**	3,150
Emergency services		1,800	1,300	**3,100**	2,800
Information and Education		90	10	**100**	300
Support costs		110	80	**190**	180
Management and administration		210	60	**270**	230
		4,610	4,880	**9,490**	9,405
Total resources expended	6	6,040	5,145	**11,185**	10,885
Net incoming resources/(resources expended) before transfers		2,950	(795)	**2,155**	150
Transfers between funds	17	15	(15)	**–**	–
Net incoming resources/(resources expended)		2,965	(810)	**2,155**	150
Net gains on investment assets	11	100	–	**100**	250
Net movement in funds		3,065	(810)	**2,255**	400
Fund balances brought forward at 1 April	17	6,300	3,900	**10,200**	9,800
Fund balances carried forward at 31 March	17	9,365	3,090	**12,455**	10,200

All of the above results are derived from continuing activities. All gains and losses recognized in the year are included above. The surplus for the year for

Companies Act purposes comprises the net incoming resources for the year plus realized gains on investments and was £2,225,000 (2000: £230,000). Page 10 gives details of changes in resources applied for fixed assets for charity use.

Consolidated and Charity Balance Sheets as at 31 March 2001

	Notes	Group 2001 £'000	Group 2000 £'000	Charity 2001 £'000	Charity 2000 £'000
Fixed assets					
Tangible assets	10	5,500	4,000	5,500	4,000
Investments	11	2,000	3,000	2,001	3,001
		7,500	7,000	7,501	7,001
Current assets					
Stocks		300	400	100	150
Debtors	12	1,765	1,000	1,465	800
Short term deposits		3,400	3,000	3,400	3,000
Cash at bank and in hand		1,090	200	1,000	180
		6,555	4,600	5,965	4,130
Creditors: amounts falling due within one year	13	(1,500)	(1,260)	(911)	(791)
Net current assets		5,055	3,340	5,054	3,339
Total assets less current liabilities		12,555	10,340	12,555	10,340
Creditors: amounts falling due after more than one year	14	(100)	(140)	(100)	(140)
Net assets		12,455	10,200	12,455	10,200
Funds:					
Unrestricted funds					
General funds – includes revaluation reserve of £140,000 (2000: £110,000)	17	4,785	2,900	4,785	2,900
Designated funds	17	4,580	3,400	4,580	3,400
		9,365	6,300	9,365	6,300
Restricted funds	17	3,090	3,900	3,090	3,900
Total funds	17	12,455	10,200	12,455	10,200

The financial statements on pages 9 to 20 were approved by the trustees on 16 June 2001 and signed on their behalf by:

H Singh (Chairman)

Consolidated Cashflow Statement for the year ended 31 March 2001

	Notes	2001 £'000	2000 £'000
Net cash inflow from operating activities	20	2,090	595
Capital expenditure and financial investment			
Payments to acquire tangible fixed assets		(1,990)	(1,000)
Proceeds from sale of tangible fixed assets		130	170
Purchase of investments		(1,200)	(865)
Proceeds from sales of investments		2,300	915
		(760)	(780)
Cash inflow/(outflow) before increase in liquid resources and financing	20	1,330	(185)
Financing			
Finance lease payments		(40)	(40)
Management of liquid resources			
Increase in short term deposits		(400)	(200)
Increase/(decrease) in cash in the year	20	890	(425)

Statement of changes in resources applied for fixed assets for charity use for the year ended 31 March 2000

	Unrestricted Funds £'000	Restricted Funds £'000	Totals 2001 £'000	Totals 2000 £'000
Net movement in funds for the year	3,065	(810)	2,255	400
Resources used for net acquisitions of tangible fixed assets	(1,100)	(400)	(1,500)	(590)
Net movement in funds available for future activities	1,965	(1,210)	755	(190)

Notes forming part of the financial statements
for the year ended 31 March 2001

1 Accounting policies

(a) **Basis of preparation**
The financial statements have been prepared under the historical cost convention, with the exception of investments which are included at market value. The financial statements have been prepared in accordance with the Statement of Recommended Practice (SORP), "Accounting and Reporting by Charities" published in October 2000 and applicable accounting standards.

The statement of financial activities (SOFA) and balance sheet consolidate the financial statements of the charity and its subsidiary undertaking. The results of the subsidiary are consolidated on a line by line basis.

The charity has availed itself of Paragraph 3 (3) of Schedule 4 of the Companies Act and adapted the Companies Act formats to reflect the special nature of the charity's activities. No separate SOFA has been presented for the charity alone as permitted by Section 230 of the Companies Act 1985 and paragraph 304 of the SORP.

(b) **Company status**
The charity is a company limited by guarantee. The members of the company are the trustees named on page 1. In the event of the charity being wound up, the liability in respect of the guarantee is limited to £1 per member of the charity.

(c) **Fund accounting**
General funds are unrestricted funds which are available for use at the discretion of the trustees in furtherance of the general objectives of the charity and which have not been designated for other purposes.

Designated funds comprise unrestricted funds that have been set aside by the trustees for particular purposes. The aim and use of each designated fund is set out in the notes to the financial statements. Restricted funds are funds which are to be used in accordance with specific restrictions imposed by donors or which have been raised by the charity for particular purposes. The cost of raising and administering such funds are charged against the specific fund. The aim and use of each restricted fund is set out in the notes to the financial statements.

Investment income and gains are allocated to the appropriate fund.

(d) **Incoming resources**

All incoming resources are included in the SOFA when the charity is legally entitled to the income and the amount can be quantified with reasonable accuracy. For legacies, entitlement is the earlier of the charity being notified of an impending distribution or the legacy being received.

Gifts in kind donated for distribution are included at valuation and recognised as income when they are distributed to the projects. Gifts donated for resale are included as income when they are sold. Donated facilities are included at the value to the charity where this can be quantified and a third party is bearing the cost. No amounts are included in the financial statements for services donated by volunteers.

(e) **Resources expended**

All expenditure is accounted for on an accruals basis and has been classified under headings that aggregate all costs related to the category. Where costs cannot be directly attributed to particular headings they have been allocated to activities on a basis consistent with use of the resources. Premises overheads have been allocated on a floor area basis and other overheads have been allocated on the basis of the head count.

Fund-raising costs are those incurred in seeking voluntary contributions and do not include the costs of disseminating information in support of the charitable activities. Support costs are those costs incurred directly in support of expenditure on the objects of the charity and include project management carried out at Headquarters. Management and administration costs are those incurred in connection with administration of the charity and compliance with constitutional and statutory requirements.

(f) **Tangible fixed assets and depreciation**

Tangible fixed assets costing more than £1,000 are capitalised and included at cost including any incidental expenses of acquisition.

Depreciation is provided on all tangible fixed assets at rates calculated to write off the cost on a straight line basis over their expected useful economic lives as follows:

Freehold land	nil
Freehold buildings	over 50 years
Project and office equipment	over 5 years
Computer equipment	over 3 years
Motor vehicles	over 4 years
Equipment held under finance leases	over the life of the lease

(g) **Investments**

Investments are stated at market value at the balance sheet date. The SOFA includes the net gains and losses arising on revaluations and disposals throughout the year.

(h) **Stock**

Stock consists of purchased goods for resale. Stocks are valued at the lower of cost and net realisable value. Items donated for resale or distribution are not included in the financial statements until they are sold or distributed.

(i) **Pension costs**

The cost of providing pension and related benefits is charged to the SOFA over the employees' service lives on the basis of a constant percentage of earnings which is an estimate of the regular cost. Variations from regular cost, arising from periodic actuarial valuations are allocated over the expected remaining service lives of current employees on the basis of a constant percentage of current and estimated future earnings. Any difference between the charge to the statement of financial activities and the contributions payable to the scheme is shown as an asset or a liability in the balance sheet.

(j) **Finance and operating leases**

Rentals applicable to operating leases are charged to the SOFA over the period in which the cost is incurred. Assets purchased under finance lease are capitalised as fixed assets. Obligations under such agreements are included in creditors. The difference between the capitalised cost and the total obligation under the lease represents the finance charges. Finance charges are written-off to the SOFA over the period of the lease so as to produce a constant periodic rate of charge.

(k) **Foreign currencies**

Transactions in foreign currencies are recorded at the rate ruling at the date of the transaction. Monetary assets and liabilities are retranslated at the rate of exchange ruling at the balance sheet date. All differences are taken to the SOFA.

2 Donations and gifts

	2001 £'000	2000 £'000
Individuals	2,106	1,678
Charitable foundations	4,100	3,500
Corporate donors	1,100	800
Gifts in kind	24	22
	7,330	6,000

Gifts in kind comprise free accommodation for the charity's Childcare team in Wimbledon kindly provided by the Packwood Foundation. A corresponding amount is included within Childcare expenditure.

3 Legacies

The charity is the residuary beneficiary of a farm in Kent. This is occupied by a life tenant and has not been included in the financial statements. The existing unencumbered value of the farm is estimated at £400,000.

In addition, legacies with a probate value of £1,600,000 have not been included in the financial statements as no notification of impending distribution has been received.

4 Merchandising income and costs

	Donated goods £'000	Sale of purchased goods through ABC Enterprises Limited (see note 19) £'000	Total 2001 £'000	Total 2000 £'000
Merchandising income	280	860	1,140	900
Cost of sales	–	700	700	620
Administrative expenses	100	70	170	90
Merchandising expenses	100	770	870	710
Surplus	180	90	270	190

5 Investment income

	2001 £'000	2000 £'000
Interest receivable	260	300
Dividends receivable from equity shares	90	105
Dividends receivable from investments and unit trusts	50	70
	400	475

The transitional tax credit included above was £14,000 (2000 – £5,000).

6 Total resources expended

	Staff Costs £'000	Other Direct Costs £'000	Other Allocated Costs £'000	Total 2001 £'000	Total 2000 £'000
Fund-raising costs	210	360	120	690	550
Building appeal costs	25	5	15	45	110
Merchandising costs	80	560	230	870	1,040
Investment management fees	–	90	–	90	110
Residential care costs	2,000	330	100	2,430	2,545
Childcare	2,800	345	255	3,400	3,150
Emergency services	1,980	870	250	3,100	2,800
Information and education	25	65	10	100	300
Support costs	45	110	35	190	50
Management and administration	85	145	40	270	230
Total resources expended	7,250	2,880	1,055	11,185	10,885

Other direct costs include:	2001 £'000	2000 £'000
Auditors' remuneration:		
Audit fee	14	13
Accountancy, taxation and other services	6	9
Operating lease rentals – Land and buildings	110	110
– Plant and equipment	70	70
Depreciation	380	270
Finance lease interest	12	14

7 Trustees' remuneration

The trustees neither received nor waived any emoluments during the year (2000: £Nil).

Out of pocket expenses were reimbursed to trustees as follows.

	2001 Number	2000 Number	2001 £'000	2000 £'000
Travel	2	3	640	530
Visit to Sudan Project	1	–	1,200	–
Other	1	1	40	65
	4	4	1,880	595

During the year payments of £2,500 were made to the Harvey Print Company for the printing of the Annual Report. Mrs W Williams, a trustee of this charity, is a director of that company. Mr H. Singh a trustee is also a trustee of the Packwood Foundation that provided free accommodation to the charity during the year valued at £24,000.

8 Staff costs

	2001 £'000	2000 £'000
Wages and salaries	6,050	5,820
Social security costs	700	650
Pension costs	500	480
	7,250	6,950

The number of employees whose emoluments as defined for taxation purposes amounted to over £50,000 in the year was as follows:

	2001 Number	2000 Number
£50,001–£60,000	1	1
£60,001–£70,000	1	2

All employees earning more than £50,000 participated in the pension scheme.

The average number of employees, calculated on a full-time equivalent basis, analysed by function was:

	2001 Number	2000 Number
Charitable activities	264	260
Cost of generating funds	12	10
Management and administration of the charity	3	3

9 Pension costs

The charity operates a defined benefit pension scheme for the benefit of the employees. The assets of the Scheme are administered by Pension Scheme Trustees in a fund independent from that of the charity.

Pension costs are assessed in accordance with the advice of a qualified actuary using the Projected Unit Method. The assumptions which have the most significant effect on the results of the valuation are:

Rate of investment	–	10% per annum compound
Rate of pensionable salary increases including promotions	–	8.5% per annum compound
Rate of increase to pensions in payment	–	5.5% per annum compound
Rate of increase in dividends	–	5.0% per annum compound

The most recent actuarial valuation of the Scheme was at 1 October 1999 and showed the market value of the Scheme's assets was £9,100,000 and that the actuarial value of the assets was 110% of the liabilities accrued to 1 October 1999 allowing for future increases to salaries.

The pension cost for the year was £500,000 (2000: £480,000). The surplus is being recognised over 12 years being the average remaining service life of employees. The balance sheet includes £40,000 (2000: £37,000) in respect of accrued pension costs.

10 Tangible fixed assets

	Freehold land and buildings £'000	Project and office equipment £'000	Computer equipment £'000	Motor vehicles £'000	Total £'000
Cost					
At 1 April 2000	4,350	400	250	200	**5,200**
Additions	1,700	180	100	10	**1,990**
Disposals	(300)	–	–	–	**(300)**
At 31 March 2001	5,750	580	350	210	**6,890**
Depreciation					
At 1 April 2000	800	200	150	50	**1,200**
Charge for year	90	150	88	52	**380**
Disposals	(190)	–	–	–	**(190)**
At 31 March 2001	700	350	238	102	**1,390**
Net book value					
At 31 March 2001	5,050	230	112	108	**5,500**
At 31 March 2000	3,550	200	100	150	**4,000**

Project and office equipment includes assets with a net book value of £140,000 (2000: £180,000) held under finance leases. Freehold land and buildings includes freehold land of £1.2 million that is not depreciated.

Capital expenditure contracted for, but not provided in the financial statements, was £250,000 (2000: £190,000).

11 Fixed asset investments

	2001 £'000	2000 £'000
Group:		
Market value as at 1 April 2000	3,000	2,800
Additions	1,200	865
Disposal proceeds	(2,300)	(915)
Net investment gains	100	250
Market value at 31 March 2001	2,000	3,000
Historical cost at 31 March 2001	1,860	2,890
UK listed investments are represented by:		
Fixed interest securities	900	1,600
Equity shares	620	580
Investment trusts and unit trusts	480	820
Total	2,000	3,000

Investments held by the charity also include an additional £1,000 (2000: £1,000) investment in the subsidiary company at cost (see note 19).

12 Debtors

	Group 2001 £'000	Group 2000 £'000	Charity 2001 £'000	Charity 2000 £'000
Trade debtors	560	505	290	325
Legacies	755	170	755	170
Other debtors	225	205	125	125
Amount owed by subsidiary undertaking	–	–	100	80
Prepayments and other accrued income	225	120	195	100
	1,765	1,000	1,465	800

The amount owed by the subsidiary undertaking is secured by a charge over the assets of the subsidiary.

13 Creditors: amounts falling due within one year

	Group 2001 £'000	Group 2000 £'000	Charity 2001 £'000	Charity 2000 £'000
Trade creditors	525	580	325	400
Taxation and social security costs	355	315	46	66
Other creditors	190	125	160	105
Obligations under finance leases	40	40	4	40
Accruals and deferred income	390	200	340	180
	1,500	1,260	911	791

14 Creditors: amounts falling due after more than one year

Group and charity	2001 £'000	2000 £'000
Obligations under finance leases	100	140

15 Obligations under finance leases

Group and charity	2001 £'000	2000 £'000
The amounts fall due as follows:		
Within one year	40	40
In the second to fifth year inclusive	100	140
	140	180

16 Financial commitments

At 31 March 2001 the group has annual commitments under non-cancellable leases as follows:

Expiry date:	2001 Land and buildings £'000	2001 Other £'000	2000 Land and buildings £'000	2000 Other £'000
Two to five years	40	70	–	70
Over five years	70	–	110	–
	110	70	110	70

17 Statement of funds

	At 1 April 2000 £'000	Income £'000	Expenditure £'000	Investment gains £'000	Transfers £'000	At 31 March 2001 £'000
General reserve	2,900	8,990	5,995	100	(1,210)	**4,785**
Designated funds						
Cyclical repair fund	300	–	45	–	95	**350**
Fixed asset fund	3,100	–	–	–	1,130	**4,230**
Total unrestricted funds	6,300	8,990	6,040	100	15	**9,365**
Restricted funds:						
Building appeal	900	400	30	–	–	**1,270**
Anita House	100	75	125	–	–	**50**
Other residential care	375	700	1,010	–	–	**65**
Childcare	2,400	1,775	2,535	–	(15)	**1,625**
Emergency services	105	1,100	1,350	–	–	**(145)**
Information and education	20	100	95	–	–	**25**
The E J Marf fund	–	200	–	–	–	**200**
Total restricted funds	3,900	4,350	5,145	–	(15)	**3,090**
Total funds	10,200	13,340	11,185	100	–	**12,455**

The General reserve represents the free funds of the charity which are not designated for particular purposes.

The Cyclical repair fund has been designated by the trustees for the major refurbishment and repairs to Bailey House. It is expected that the repairs will be carried out in 2002.

The Fixed asset fund has been set up to assist in identifying those funds that are not free funds and it represents the net book value of tangible fixed assets except for the residential care facility in Wimbledon, which has been funded from the capital appeal.

The Building appeal fund represents the net book value of the new residential care facility in Wimbledon. The fund balances are reduced by the depreciation charged on the facility.

The Anita House fund represents funds raised by the Friends of Anita House for use at Anita House.

The Childcare fund was established in 1994 by a gift from the Darlaston Foundation to be used solely for the Childcare projects. Since then sundry restricted gifts for child care have been added to the Fund. During the year an unexpended balance of £15,000 has been transferred to the general fund with the permission of the donor.

The negative balance on the Emergency services fund represents the excess amount that has been spent on emergency services in anticipation of an appeal that was launched after the year end. By June 2001 the appeal raised £180,000.

The E J Marf fund was received during the year to support a sustainable development programme around the Jim Corbett National Park in India. The fund is represented by short-term deposits and is expected to be applied during 2001.

18 Analysis of group net assets between funds

	Restricted Funds £'000	Designated Funds £'000	General Funds £'000	Total £'000
Fund balances at 31 March 2001 are represented by:				
Tangible fixed assets	1,270	4,230	–	**5,500**
Investments	–	–	2,000	**2,000**
Current assets	1,820	350	4,385	**6,555**
Current liabilities	–	–	(1,500)	**(1,500)**
Long term liabilities	–	–	(100)	**(100)**
Total net assets	3,090	4,580	4,785	**12,455**

19 Subsidiary company

The charity owns the whole of the issued ordinary share capital of ABC Enterprises Ltd, a company registered in England. The subsidiary is used for non-primary purpose trading activities, namely the mail order retail operation and the sale of bought in goods through the charity's shops. In addition corporate sponsorships and non-tax exempt events are also carried out by the subsidiary. All activities have been consolidated on a line by line basis in the SOFA. The total net profit is gifted to the charity. Corporate income is treated as donations. A summary of the results of the subsidiary is shown below:

ABC Enterprises Ltd	Mail Order 2001 £'000	Shops 2001 £'000	Corporate 2001 £'000	Total 2001 £'000	Total 2000 £'000
Turnover	400	460	350	**1,210**	1,300
Cost of sales	390	310	150	**850**	900
Gross profit	10	150	200	**360**	400
Administrative expenses	30	40	40	**110**	130
Net profit/(loss)	(20)	110	160	**250**	270

The aggregate of the assets, liabilities and funds was:

Assets	**590**	470
Liabilities	**(589)**	(469)
Funds (representing 1000 ordinary shares of £1 each)	**1**	1

20 Cash flow information for the group

(a) Reconciliation of changes in resources to net inflow from operating activities

	2001 £'000	2000 £'000
Net incoming resources before revaluations	**2,155**	150
Gain on sale of tangible fixed assets	**(20)**	(30)
Depreciation	**380**	270
Decrease in stocks	**100**	450
Increase in debtors	**(765)**	(225)
Increase/(decrease) in creditors	**240**	(20)
Net cash inflow from operating activities	**2,090**	595

(b) Reconciliation of net cash flow to movement in net funds/debt

Increase/(decrease) in cash in the period	**890**	(425)
Cash outflow from decrease in lease financing	**40**	40
Cash outflow from increase in liquid resources	**400**	200
Movement in net funds and debt in the year	**1,330**	(185)
Net funds and debt at 1 April 2000	**3,020**	3,205
Net funds and debt at 31 March 2001	**4,350**	3,020

(c) Analysis of net funds/debt

	1 April 2000 £'000	Cashflow £'000	31 March 2001 £'000
Cash at bank and in hand	200	**890**	1,090
Liquid resources	3,000	**400**	3,400
Finance leases	(180)	**40**	(140)
	3,020	**1,330**	4,350

Bibliography

Anheier, H. K. and Seibel, W. (eds) (1990) *The Third Sector: Comparative Studies of Non-profit Organisations*. Walter de Gruyter, New York.

ASC (1985) Exposure Draft ED38. Accounting Standards Committee, London.

ASC (1988) *SORP 2. Accounting by Charities*. Accounting Standards Committee, London.

Ashby, J. (1997) *Towards Voluntary Sector Codes of Practice*. Joseph Rowntree Foundation, York.

Ashford, J. K. (1991) *Chapter in Financial Reporting 1989/90*. Institute of Chartered Accountants in England and Wales (ICAEW), London.

Ashford, J. K. (2000) The SORP Compliance Record. In: *Charity Finance Yearbook 2000*, pp. 93–95, Plaza, London.

Atkinson, H. and Wilks-Heeg, S. (2000) *Local Government from Thatcher to Blair: The Politics of Creative Autonomy*. Polity Press, London.

Auditing Practices Board (1996) Practice Note 11. *The Audit of Charities*. Currently in revision. Auditing Practices Board, London.

Bashir, H. (1999) *The Good Financial Management Guide*. NCVO, London.

Beach, A. (1994) Saving the baby from the dirty bathwater: voluntarism and the Labour Party c1940–1950. Paper presented to Voluntary Action History Society, 24 November.

Belkaoui, A. (1992) *Accounting Theory*. Dryden Press, London.

Bennett, N. (1999) Diana's fund lawyers in the dock. *Sunday Telegraph*, 30 May. Business B3.

Beveridge, Lord (1948) *Voluntary Action*. George Allen & Unwin, London.

Billis, D. (1993) Sector blurring and non-profit centres: the case of the United Kingdom. *Nonprofit and Voluntary Sector Quarterly*, 22 (3), 241–257.

Billis, D. and Harris, M. (1987) Internal auditing in charities. *Internal Auditing*, 10 (7), 195–198; 10 (8), 231–236.

Billis, D. and Harris, M. (1992) Taking the strain of change: UK local voluntary agencies enter the post-Thatcher period. *Nonprofit and Voluntary Sector Quarterly*, 21 (3), 211–225.

Bird, P. (1986) Chapter in *Financial Reporting 1984/85*. Institute of Chartered Accountants in England and Wales (ICAEW), London.

Bird, P. and Morgan-Jones, P. (1981) *Financial Reporting by Charities*. Institute of Chartered Accountants in England and Wales (ICAEW), London.

Blair, T. (1998) Message from the Prime Minister in *Compact: Getting it Right Together*. Home Office.

Bonds, J. (1997) A talk given to the Charity Accounts Conference, Manchester, September.

Bottomley, V. (1996) *Raising the Voltage: The Government Responses to the Deakin Commission Report*. Department of National Heritage.

Bourdillon, A. F. C. (1945) *Voluntary Sector Services*. Methuen.

Breckell, P. (2001) Developing a predictive model for the fund-raising cost income ratios of registered charities in England and Wales. MSc thesis, South Bank University, London.

Brenton, M. (1985) *The Voluntary Sector in British Social Services*. Longman, London.

Brindle, D. (1998) Figure skating. *The Guardian*, 23 September, p. 21.

Brown, G. (2001) Let the people look after themselves. *The Times*, 11 January, p. 22.

Brown, M. (1977) *Introduction to Social Administration in Britain*. Hutchinson, London.

Brown, R. (2001) The New Trustee Act 2000. In: *Investment Matters* – a newsletter for charities. January, p. 8. Chiswell Associates.

Bruce, I. (1994) *Meeting Need*. ICSA Publishing, Hertfordshire.

Brudney, J. L. (1990) *Fostering Volunteer Programs in the Public Sector*. Jossey-Bass Inc., San Francisco.

Bubb, S. (2000) Winning plaudits for social audits. *Third Sector*, Issue 197, 30 November, pp. 19–23.

Burt, E. (1992) An examination of changing organisational capabilities in third sector organisations with responsibility for the delivery of aspects of social policy. Paper presented to the British Academy of Management Conference Doctoral Workshop. University of Bradford, September.

Butler, R. A. (1960) Second reading of the 1960 Charity Bill. *Hansard* 622, No. 102.27.4, pp. 409–410. HMSO, London.

Byrne, T. (1981) *Local Government in Britain*. Penguin, Middlesex.

Cadbury, A. (1992) *Report of the Committee on the Financial Aspects of Corporate Governance*. Gee and Co., London.

CAF (1989) *Charity Trends*. Charities Aid Foundation (CAF), Tonbridge.

Cancer Research Campaign (CRC) (1991) *Annual Accounts and Report for 1991*. Cancer Research Campaign.

Charity Commission (Various years) *Annual Report*. Charity Commission.

Charity Commission (1988) *Charity Accounts – Consultation Paper*. Charity Commission.

Charity Commission (1995a) *Accounting by Charities. Statement of Recommended Practice* (Charity SORP).

Charity Commission (1995b) CC51 – *Charity Accounts: The New Framework*.

Charity Commission (1996) CC3 – *Responsibilities of Charity Trustees*.

Charity Commission (1997) CC19 – *Charities' Reserves*.

Charity Commission (1999a) CC48 – *Charities and Meetings*.

Charity Commission (1999b) Facts & Figures – Charity Commission website, 18 March.

Charity Commission (2000) CC62 – *Charities SORP 2000: What Has Changed?*

Chesterman, M. (1979) *Charities, Trusts and Social Welfare*. Weidenfeld & Nicolson, London.

Cole, G. D. H. (1945) A retrospect of the history of voluntary social services. In: A. F. C. Bourdillon (ed.), *Voluntary Sector Services*, pp. 11–31. Methuen, London.

Committee of Public Accounts (1988) *Monitoring and Control of Charities in England and Wales*. HMSO, London.

Community Accountants Conference (2000). Funding Issues debate. Retford.

Community Accounting Network (2001) Focus group held at Community Accountants Conference. Retford.

Connolly, C. and Hyndman, N. (2000) Charity accounting: an empirical analysis of the impact of recent changes. *British Accounting Review*, 32, 77–100.

Courtney, R. (1996) *Managing Voluntary Organisations: New Approaches*. ICSA Publishing, Hertfordshire.

Davies, M. (2001) Interview with Unity Trust Bank Charity Banking Relationship Officer, 18 January.

Deakin, N. (1993) Contracting in the UK – the policy context. Paper presented to conference – Contracting Selling or Shrinking. South Bank University, July.

Deakin, N. (1994) Evolving relations between government and third sector in Britain: the case of community care. Conference paper at the International Society for Third Sector Research, PECS, Hungary.

Deakin, N. (1995) Report of The Commission on the future of the voluntary sector. NCVO, London.

Demos (1994) Rethinking charity finance. Working paper 2. Demos, London.

Directory of Social Change (1999) *Fundraising Costs*. Directory of Social Change, London.

Ellis, S. J. (1996) *From the Top Down*. Energize Inc.

Fairbairn, P. (1998) *Financial Monitoring of Funded Organisations*. City Parochial Foundation, London.

Falush, S. (2000) Are charities premier league? *NGO Finance*, December, p. 5.

Family Planning Association (1988) *Annual Report*. Family Planning Association.

Fenton, L. S. (1980) *The Honorary Treasurer: Charities and Voluntary Organisations*. Institute of Chartered Accountants in England and Wales (ICAEW), London.

Finlow, A. (1998) How do charities measure the efficiency and effectiveness of their volunteers? A case study based on four Christian Evangelical Missions. MSc thesis, South Bank University.

Flynn, N. (1993) *Public Sector Management*. Harvester Wheatsheaf, Hertfordshire.

Foot, M. (1972) *Aneurin Bevan: A Biography*. Davis Poynter, London.

Forest, R. and Murie, A. (1988) *Selling the Welfare State: The Privatisation of Public Housing*, p. 91. Routledge, London.

Gambling, T., Jones, R., Kunz, C. and Pendlebury, M. (1990) *Accounting by Charities: the Application of SORP2*. Chartered Association of Certified Accountants, London.

Graig, G. and Manthorpe, J. (1999) Unequal partners? Local government reorganisation and the voluntary sector. *Social Policy and Administration*, 33 (1), 55–72.

Gutch, R. (1992) *Contracting Lessons from the US*. NCVO, London.

Handy, C. B. (1988) *Understanding Voluntary Organisations*. Penguin, London.

Hansmann, H. B. (1980) The role of non-profit enterprise. *Yale Law Journal*, 89, 835–898; reproduced in Rose-Ackerman, S. (1986) *The Economics of Non-profit Institutions*. Oxford University Press.

Harries (1993) Harries and Others v Church Commissioners for England and another. *All England Law Reports*, 300–310.

Harris, M. (1993) The changing role of the voluntary sector in welfare. Paper presented, Contracting Selling or Shrinking Conference, South Bank University, London, May.

Harrison, J. (1994) *Managing Charitable Investments*. ICSA Publishing, Hertfordshire.

Harrow, J. and Palmer, P. (1998) Reassessing charity trusteeship in Britain? Towards conservatism not change. *Journal of Voluntary and Nonprofit Organisations*, 9 (2), 171–186.

Harrow, J., Palmer, P. and Vincent, J. (1999) Management information needs and perceptions in smaller charities: an exploratory study. *Financial Accountability and Management*, 12 (2), 155–172.

Hassell T. (1999) *Charities Internal Audit Checklist*. Plaza, London.

Hatch, S. and Mocroft, I. (1983) *Components of Welfare – Voluntary Organisations, Social Services and Politics in Two Local Authorities*. Bedford Square Press, London

Headley, R. and Davis Smith, J. (1994) Volunteers and the contact culture. *Voluntary Action Research*, Paper 1 Series 3, Volunteer Centre UK.

Hind, A. (1995) *The Governance and Management of Charities*. Voluntary Sector Press, London.

Hines, A. and Jones, M. J. (1992) The impact of SORP2 on the UK charitable sector: an empirical study. *Financial Accountability and Management*, 8 (1), 49–67.

HM Treasury (1992) Proposed EC statutes for: a European co-operative society, a European mutual society and a European association and accompanying directives regarding the involvement of employees. Banking Group 1, HM Treasury, London.

Hobsbawm, E. J. (1969) *Industry and Empire*. Penguin, London.

Home Office. (1988) *The Regulation of Charitable Appeals in England and Wales*. HMSO, London.

Home Office (1989) White Paper: *Charities: A Framework for the Future*. HMSO, London.

Home Office (1990) *Efficiency Scrutiny of Government Funding of the Voluntary Sector*. HMSO, London.

Home Office (1995) *Charities (Accounts and Reports) Regulations*. HMSO.

Home Office (1998) *Compact on Relations between Government and the Voluntary and Community Sector in England*. Home Office, London.

Houghton, Lord (1992) Revised marshalled list of amendments to be moved on report HL Bill 24-1, p. 371. HMSO, London.

Hudson, M. (1999) *Managing Without Profit*. Penguin, London.

Hyndman, N. and McKillop, D. (1999) Conversion ratios in charities in England and Wales: an investigation of economies of scale. *Financial Accountability and Management*, 15 (2), 135–153.

ICTA (1988) Various sections.

IIA. UK (1999) Control and risk self-assessment. Professional briefing Note Fourteen. Institute of Internal Auditors (IIA).

Inland Revenue IR75. *Tax Relief for Charities*.

Inland Revenue (1995) Charities Series CS2 – *Trading by Charities*.

Inland Revenue (2000) *Getting Britain Giving*. Inland Revenue Guidance Note for Charities.

Isaacs, M. (2000) Costs and compliance. MSc Thesis, South Bank University.

Jack, A. (1993) Accountancy: spectres linger at war on want battleground. *Financial Times*, 16 December, p. 14.

Jackson, P. W. (1999) How can branches of learned societies add value to the charity? MSc Thesis, South Bank University.

Jones, L. (1998) Ethical investment policies. In: *Charity Finance Yearbook 1998*, pp. 60–64. Plaza, London

Jordan, W. K. (1958) *Philanthropy in England 1480–1660*. George Allen & Unwin, London.

Kam, V. (1990) *Accounting Theory*. Wiley, New York.

Karn, G. N. (1982) Money talks: a guide to establishing the true dollar of volunteer time (part 1). *The Journal of Volunteer Administration*, 1–17.

Kazi, U., Paton, R. and Thomas, A. (1992) Feasibility study for a national observatory of voluntary and non-profit organisations. Four working papers. Open University, Milton Keynes.

Kendall, M. (2000) The mainstreaming of the third sector into public policy in England: whys and wherefores. Centre for Civil Society Working Paper 2. London School of Economics.

Knapp, J. (1990) *The Voluntary Sector in the United Kingdom*. Manchester University Press, Manchester.

Knapp, J., Robertson, M. E. and Thomason, C. (1990) Public money, voluntary action: whose welfare? In: H. Anheier and W. Seibel (eds). *The Third Sector: Comparative Studies of Non-profit Organisations*. Walter de Gruyter, New York.

Knight, B. (1993) *Centris: Voluntary Action in the 1990s*. Home Office, London.

Lamont, H. (1997) Charity audit survey. *NGO Finance*, 7 (6), 16–28.

Lamont, H. (1998a) Accounting for the myth, auditing the reality. *NGO Finance*, 8 (4), 16–20.

Lamont, H. (1998b) Charity audit survey. *NGO Finance*, 8 (8), 18–30.

Leat, D. (1988) *Voluntary Organisations and Accountability*. NCVO, London.

Leat, D. (1993) *Managing Across Sectors: Similarities and Differences Between For-profit and Voluntary Non-profit Organisations*. City University Business School/ VOLPROF.

Lee, S. (2001) Is Labour working? *Professional Fundraising*, February, 12–14.

Lehman, C. R. (1992) *Accounting's Changing Roles in Social Conflict*. Paul Chapman, London.

Lloyd, T. O. (1986) *Empire to Welfare State. English History 1906–1985*. Oxford University Press, Oxford.

Local Government Association (2000) *Local Compact Guidelines*.

Manley, K. (1977) A Corporate report – 1877 style. *The Accountant*, 177 (5371), 787–9.

Manley, K. (1979) Accounting for charities. *The Accountant*, 181 (5473), 391–5.

Mattocks, A. (1992) Financial reporting by charities. BA (Hons) degree project, Plymouth Business School.

Mayo, E. (1999) In: *Fundraising Costs*. Directory of Social Change, London.

Milton, J. (1999) Evaluate whether it is possible for charities to increase the return on their short term investments without increasing risk. And, if so, what are the barriers to them doing so? MSc Thesis, South Bank University.

Morris, D. (2001) *Legal Issues in Charity Mergers*. Charity Law Unit, University of Liverpool.

Morton, A. L. (1969) *The English Utopia*. Lawrence & Wishart Ltd, London.

Mullin, R. (1995) *Foundations for Fundraising*. ICSA Publishing, Hertfordshire.

Murray, G. J. (1969) Voluntary organisations and social welfare. University of Glasgow social and economic studies research paper no.3. Oliver & Boyd, Edinburgh.

Nathan, Lord (1952) Report of the committee on the law and practice relating to charitable trusts. HSMO, London.

NAO (1987) Monitoring and control of charities in England and Wales. HMSO, London.

NCVO (1992a) *On Trust: Increasing the Effectiveness of Charity Trustees and Management Committees*. NCVO, London.

NCVO (1992b) European White Paper: Policy considerations. NCVO Draft Submission. NCVO, London.

NCVO (1995) *Building on Trust*. NCVO, London.

NCVO (1996) *UK Statistical Almanac*. NCVO, London.

NCVO (1998) *The UK Voluntary Sector Almanac 1998–99*. NCVO, London.

NCVO (1999) Foundations of charity. A report on a Conference held 14/15 September. NCVO, London.

NCVO (2000) *The UK Voluntary Sector Almanac 2000*. NCVO, London.

NCVO (2001) Discussion on charity law reform at NCVO National Conference, 7 February.

Nightingale, B. (1973) *Charities*. Allen Lane, London.

Norrington, H. (1999) Monitoring investment performance. In: *Charity Finance Yearbook*, 1999, pp. 56–61. Plaza, London.

O'Connell, B. (2001) Civil society: definitions and descriptions. *Nonprofit and Voluntary Sector Quarterly*, 29 (3), 471–478.

Orloff, A. S. and Skocpol, T. (1984) In: Mclennan, G. *Marxism, Pluralism and Beyond*. Polity Press, Cambridge.

Osbourne, S. P. (1996) *Managing in the Voluntary Sector*. International Thomson Business Press, London.

Owen, D. (1965) *English Philanthropy 1660–1960*. Oxford University Press, Oxford.

Palmer, P. (1992) *Internal Audit and Control in Charities*. Moores Rowland.

Palmer, P. (1995) External regulation and internal control in the charity sector. PhD thesis, City University, London.

Palmer, P. (1996) Internal auditing in charities – a revolution still awaited. *Managerial Auditing Journal*, 11 (6), 11–18.

Palmer, P. (1999) A history of charity regulation. Paper presented to University of Wales History Conference, Bangor.

Palmer, P. and Harrow, J. (1994) *Rethinking Charity Trusteeship*. ICSA Publishing, Hertfordshire.

Palmer, P, and Vinten, G. (1998) Accounting auditing and regulating charities – towards a theoretical underpinning. *Managerial Auditing Journal*, 13 (6–7), 346–355.

Palmer, P., Wise, D., Hoe, E. and Penney, D. (1998) Sales of goods and services by charities. Report of a survey conducted on behalf of the NCVO. Centre for Charity and Trust Research, South Bank University, London.

Palmer, P., Wise, D. and Penney, D. (1999) Selling goods and services by charities: a clearer view of an emerging picture. *Nonprofit and Voluntary Sector Marketing*, 4 (2), 121–134.

Palmer, P., Issacs, M. and D'Silva, K. (2001) Charity SORP compliance – findings of a research study. *Managerial Auditing Journal*, 16 (5), 255–262.

Park, K. (1997) Activity based costing. *Charity Finance Yearbook*, pp. 102–105. Plaza, London.

Passey, A. (2001) Lecture to South Bank University Charity students on the future of the voluntary sector. 11 January.

Passey, A., Hems, L. and Jas, P. (2000) *In the UK Voluntary Sector Almanac*. NCVO.

Paton, R. (1993) Organisation and management studies on voluntary and non-profit organisations in the UK: achievements and prospects. Paper for symposium researching voluntary and non-profit organisations in the UK: state of the art. May 1993, South Bank University.

Paton, R. (1999) Performance comparisons in fundraising – the case of fundratios. *International Journal of Nonprofit and Voluntary Sector Marketing*, 4 (4), 287–299.

Perri 6, (1991) *What is a Voluntary Organisation?* NCVO, London.

Pharoah, C. (1997) *Managing Finance in the Voluntary Sector – A Delicate Balance*. Charities Aid Foundation, Tonbridge.

Phelan, D. (2000) Hard labour for charity shops, In: *Charity Finance Yearbook 2000*, pp. 252–255. Plaza, London.

Phillips, A. (2000) Playgroup perils. *The Guardian*, 29 March, p. 22.

Pirie, M. and Butler, E. (1989) *Extending Care*. Adam Smith Institute, London.

Pollack, H. (1994) Review of '*protecting soldiers and mothers: the political origins of social policy in the United States*' by Theda Skocpol. *Nonprofit and Voluntary Sector*, 23 (1).

Quint, F. (1994) *Running a Charity*. Jordans, London.

Ramanathan, K. V. (1976) Toward a theory of social accounting. In: R. Bloom and P. T. Elgers (eds), *Accounting Theory and Policy: a Reader*. Harcourt Brace Jovanovich, New York.

Randall, A. (2001) The ICSA Guide to Charity Accounting. ICSA Publications, London.

Randall, A. and Williams, S. (1996) *Charities and Taxation*. ICSA Publishing, Hertfordshire.

Randall, A. and William, S. (2001) Charity Taxation. Jordan Publishing, Bristol.

Randall, A., Young, F. and Epton, A. (2000) Preparing Charity Accounts. Accountancy Books, London.

Redfern, A. (1998) Social auditing for charities. In: *Charity Finance Yearbook 1998*, pp. 140–143. Plaza, London.

Rooff, M. (1957) *Voluntary Societies and Social Policy*. Routledge & Kegan Paul, London.

Salamon, L. and Anheier, H. (1993) A comparative study of the non-profit sector: purposes, methodology, definitions and classifications. In: *Researching the Voluntary Sector*, 1st edn, pp. 179–195. Charities Aid Foundation, Tonbridge.

Salamon, L. and Anheier, H. (1994) The non-profit sector cross nationally: patterns and types. In: *Researching the Voluntary Sector*, 2nd edn, pp. 147–163. Charities Aid Foundation, Tonbridge.

Sams, M. (1978) *Charities and Voluntary Organisations. Guidance Notes on Financial Planning and Control*. Institute of Chartered Accountants in England and Wales (ICAEW), London.

Steinberg, R. and Gray, B. H. (1993) The role of non-profit enterprise in 1993: Hansmann revisited. *Nonprofit and Voluntary Sector Quarterly*, 22 (4), 297–316.

Stoker, J. (2001a) Keeping the focus. *NGO Finance*, February, pp. 26–27.

Stoker, J. (2001b) Sharing the windfall. *Charity Times*, January/February, p. 13.

Taylor, M. (1988) *Into the 1990s: Voluntary Organisations and the Public Sector*. NCVO and RIPA, London.

Taylor, D. (1999) The Charities Consortium. In: *Charity Finance Yearbook 1999*, pp. 121–124. Plaza, London.

Tigar, M. E. (1977) *Law and the Rise of Capitalism*. Monthly Review Press, New York.

Turnbull. (1999) *Internal Control – Guidance for Directors on the Combined Code*. Institute of Chartered Accountants in England and Wales (ICAEW), London.

Underdown, B. and Taylor, P. J. (1985) *Accounting Theory and Policy Making*. Heinemann, London.

Vatter, N. J. (1947) *The Fund Theory of Accounting and its Implications for Financial Reports*. University of Chicago Press. (Reprint edition 1978, Arno Press.)

Vincent, J., Harrow. J. and Palmer, P. (1998) Trustee decision making in small UK charities. *Nonprofit and Voluntary Sector Marketing*, 3 (4), 337–352.

Vinten, G. (1989) Charities: regulation, accountability and audit. City University Business School, Working paper series. Working paper No. 95.

Vinten, G. (1993) Reviewing the current managerial ethos. In: L. Wilcocks and J. Harrow (eds), *Rediscovering Public Sector Management*. McGraw Hill, London.

Warburton, J. (1993) Legal studies on voluntary and non-profit organisations in the UK: achievements and prospects. Paper for symposium – Researching voluntary and non-profit organisations in the UK: the state of the art. May, South Bank University.

Ware, A. (1989) Religious charities and the State. In: A. Ware (ed.), *Charities and Government*. Manchester University Press, Manchester.

Webb, A. and Wistow, G. (1987) *Social Work, Social Care and Social Planning: The Personal Social Services since Seebohm*. Longman, London.

Weisbrod, B. A. (1988) *The Non-profit Economy*. Harvard University Press, London.

Weston, J. F. and Copeland, T. E. (1988) *Managerial Finance*. 2nd UK edition adapted by A. F. Fox and R. J. Limmack. Cassell, London.

Whelan, R. (1999) *Involuntary Action: How Voluntary is the 'Voluntary' Sector?* IEA Health & Welfare Unit.

Williams, S. and Palmer, P. (1998) The state of charity accounting – developments, improvements and accounting problems. *Financial Accountability and Management*, 14 (4), 265–279.

Wilson, M. and Gatward, M. (1998) Social accounting and audit: what it is and how to do it. *Accountancy*, 121 (1253), 110–111.

Wise, D. (1995) *Performance Management for Charities*. ICSA Publishing, Hertfordshire.

Wise, D. (1997) Size and administration costs in the voluntary sector: a note. *Financial Accountability and Management*, 13 (1), 82–88.

Wise, D. (1998) *Accounting and Finance for Charities*. ICSA Publishing, Hertfordshire.

Wolfenden, Lord (1978) *The Future of Voluntary Organisations*. Report of the Wolfenden Committee. Croom Helm, London.

Woodfield, P. (1987) *Efficiency Scrutiny of the Supervision of Charities*. HMSO, London.

Wrong, R. M. (1945) Some voluntary organisations for the welfare of children. In: A. F. C. Bourdillon (ed.), *Voluntary Social Services*, pp. 31–56. Metheun, London.

Young, D. R. (1983) *If not for profit for what? A behavioural theory of the non-profit sector based on Entrepreneurship*. Lexington Books, Massachusetts.

Young, F. (2001) Management and administration costs in charities. MSc thesis, South Bank University, London.

Index